SO-AEG-951

University of St. Francis
GEN 810.9 M112
McCaffery, Larry,
Alive and writing :

3 0301 00086456 7

1992

Alive and Writing

Can you hear me, wake up
Where's the voice of America?
　　　　　—Steve Van Zandt

What really knocks me out is a book that, when you're
all done reading it, you wish the author that wrote it
was a terrific friend of yours and you could call him
up on the phone whenever you felt like it.
　　　　　—Holden Caulfield in *The Catcher in the Rye*

Interviews with
American Authors of the 1980s

Alive and Writing

Conducted and edited by
Larry McCaffery and Sinda Gregory

LIBRARY
College of St. Francis
JOLIET, ILLINOIS

UNIVERSITY OF ILLINOIS PRESS
Urbana and Chicago

For Robert Coover

© 1987 by the Board of Trustees of the University of Illinois
Manufactured in the United States of America
1 2 3 4 5 C P 5 4 3 2 1

This book is printed on acid-free paper.

Library of Congress Cataloging-in-Publication Data

McCaffery, Larry, 1946-
  Alive and writing.

  Includes index.
  1. American literature—20th century—History and
criticism. 2. Authors, American—20th century—Interviews.
2. Authorship. I. Gregory, Sinda, 1947- . II. Title.
PS225.M34 1987 810'.9'0054 86-25075
ISBN 0-252-01385-9 (cloth)
ISBN 0-252-06011-3 (paper)

810.9
M112

Acknowledgments

Our thanks, first of all, to all the writers, for their willingness to talk seriously with us about their lives and their writing. Our editor, Ann Weir, encouraged us and made useful suggestions at virtually every stage of our work on the manuscript. We are also grateful to San Diego State's University Foundation, College of Arts and Letters, and Department of English and Comparative Literature for supplying mini-grants, travel money, and released time to work on the project. Special thanks of a more personal nature go to Munmun and Asoke Chanda, Robert Coover, Tom Held, Edie Jarolim, Bob and Laura McCreery, Kathy Sagan, Neil Barron, Marilyn Scheer—and especially to our son, Mark Urton.

We thank, too, the editors of the journals where some of these interviews or parts thereof first appeared: *Conjunctions, Fiction International, The Literary Review, The Mississippi Review, The Missouri Review*, and *The Paris Review.*

145,574

Contents

Introduction

When Walter Abish observes that contemporary American writers "have no actual scene to speak of, no real center," he is referring to a lack of literary community—the absence of a physical place, like Paris or Rome, that American writers can flock to, or even of a major literary magazine that could provide them with a rallying point (or point of attack) the way *Tel Quel* and *The Evergreen Review* did a generation ago. Abish's remarks also suggest a more abstract "absence" shaping the nature of the best contemporary fiction. The absence to which we refer is precisely the lack of a shared aesthetic orientation of the sort that provided a loose sense of unity to the works of such diverse authors as Pynchon, Coover, Gass, Barth, Barthelme, Sontag, Federman, Vonnegut, Reed, DeLillo, and other writers who became important during the 1960s and early '70s. This orientation grew out of a common sense that a crisis was at hand, for literature and for society at large—and that extreme measures were needed to rescue the novel and the community from the grips of outmoded assumptions.

One of the conclusions that can be drawn from the conversations we conducted with the following thirteen authors, all of whose careers have been established in the aftermath of those mid-'60s disruptions, is that the struggle for greater diversification in fictional forms has been won. Writers no longer feel obliged to develop their work in response to a prior, dominant set of conventions. The theoretical concerns of the previous generation—the impassioned skirmishes over such issues as realism versus experimentalism, moral versus "immoral" fiction, self-reflexive versus mimetic forms—have lost their energy. Most of the writers included in this volume simply take it for granted that many of the features of postmodernism that once seemed extreme (the casual mixture of the fantastic and the mundane, authorial intrusion, the flaunting of artificial design and texture, the use of collage and other discontinuous formal methods) are perfectly valid ways of approaching the creation of fiction. They've made judgments about which nontraditional strategies have exhausted their potential and which ones remain viable and can be further explored. They share the attitude that attacking the notion of realism as if it were a monolithic structure is fundamentally misguided; hence they're more willing to admit that "realism" encompasses many stylistic approaches. With our culture saturated with mass-produced images and slogans selling everything from jeans and lite beer to detoxification centers, famine relief, invasion, and salvation, and with our daily reality transformed by television and computers, the postmodernist debate over the "artificiality" of the fiction-making process seems less relevant than discovering a means by which to depict the increasing artificiality of the mundane.

Just as Gabriel García Márquez has insisted that the events of his works are not "magical" at all, but simply realistic presentations of the fabulous world he grew up in and was shaped by, so are similarly flexible notions of "realism" evident in the works of the authors we talked to. Consider the way Max Apple and William Kennedy approach the handling of public mythological figures—Kennedy's use of "Legs" Diamond in *Legs*; Apple's use of Walt Disney, Howard Johnson, Fidel Castro, and J. Edgar Hoover in various works. At first the differences in approach are sure to strike the reader: Kennedy's portrayal, with its vivid specificity of names, dates, and physical details of setting and character (all painstakingly researched, he tells us), seems traditional in its realism; Apple's method is more overtly fabulous in that he freely invents his details ("I have never researched these characters," he says, "I never *want* to know") and concentrates on presenting his public figures as two-dimensional icons whose "essences" are the values and meanings they embody for most Americans. But a crucial similarity is evident when one compares how Kennedy and Apple describe their intentions. Kennedy says, "What I was really interested in . . . was a way of focusing on Legs as a mythic hero, who was made into a movie hero. . . . That notion of myths remained with me and became central to the final version of the book: the idea of how myth is created: an act which becomes a public fascination, and then is blown out of all proportion, so that the doer is given legendary status; then the legend is passed on, and becomes one of the defining myths of the age." Apple, likewise, is much less concerned with the "reality" surrounding familiar figures than with their mythic dimensions, and with what that mythic content suggests about our culture. "These myths are out there, and writers may as well make use of them. . . . But I never research these characters. In fact, it's just the opposite: I want the freedom to change things because, finally, what difference does it make if I'm inventing rather than transcribing?. . . . I'm interested in the central thing about my characters, not in details . . . what these figures represent, what arises from these institutions, the characters that evolve from them." Despite their differences in style and form, Kennedy and Apple both are responding to the recognition that the significant "realities" today are often mythic projections whose imaginative qualities are more compelling than the "real." The contemporary Germany to be found in Walter Abish's *How German Is It*, with its profusion of sharply etched details about people and place, is a purely abstract Germany projected into existence on the basis of Abish's sense of the way Americans imagine Germany to be. Beneath its deceptive surface realism (especially deceptive in that Abish, who had never visited Germany before writing the novel, imposes a number of specific details from his own environment onto his invented landscape), Abish's Germany becomes an impenetrable mask of ambiguities, misleading signals, and contradictory impressions; ultimately the mask tells us as much about ourselves and our complex, conflicting attitudes toward the Germany of our minds as it does about the Germany of actuality. The San Francisco that emerges from Ron Silliman's plotless, characterless *Ketjak* is a palpable "place" despite the fact that it is derived purely from the words, sentences, and images that Silliman encountered during the period of the text's composition.

Such diversity of realities and realisms might be frustrating to writers seeking the comforts of a secure literary home and to critics anxious to label and categorize these unruly tendencies, but it suggests that the aesthetic disruptions of the '60s indeed opened up new options for fiction. When we set out to talk with as many of the creators of these new options as circumstances would allow, we knew in advance that we didn't want to limit our selection process by talking only with writers who would fit into a specific literary slot. The thirteen writers interviewed in this volume are fundamentally different from each other in their approaches to form, voice, and sense of the world around them. None of them are traditional realists, and several—Abish, Silliman, Delany, Le Guin, Hoban, White, Robbins—have developed forms every bit as extreme as those produced by the experimentalists of the '60s. Even the works of Raymond Carver, who is often regarded as the central figure of the so-called New Realist movement, are much less ordinary than they might at first appear. His prose, stripped of all ornamentation, his focus on the small mysteries of daily life (mysteries "articulated" only by nuances and by poetically charged symbols), his stories' lack of resolution or progression—these, too, are features of a nontraditional vision.

Idiosyncratic and often excessive, the "voice of America" today is really a cacophony of sounds that have somehow resisted the homogenizing effects of our mass-market mentality. It can be heard in the music and poetry of Kennedy's Albany gangsters and street bums, in Barry Hannah's crazed Southerners, in the interaction of found languages of Silliman's San Francisco. It shows up in the playful exuberance of Robbins's mind-expanding metaphors, and in the self-revealing chatter of Ann Beattie's modish East Coast commuter crowd. It is embodied in Delany's futuristic lingoes, in McGuane's quirky dialogues, in the baroque lyricism of Edmund White, and in the beautiful expressiveness of the debased language spoken by Russell Hoban's Riddley Walker.

What seemed important to us in conducting these interviews was to encourage each author to articulate the sources of his or her voice and perspective—to seek some explanation of the writing process, the inspiration, the choices involving *craft*. For every interview there was a specific issue, a central kernel, that we felt was fundamental to our sense of what made the writer unique. What was it about Albany that had sustained Kennedy's imagination? What would Hannah say about his fiction's deeply ambiguous attitude toward the relationship of violence and death to beauty and sexuality? Why had Carver's *Cathedral* exhibited such differences in texture and tone from his earlier work? What sources, aesthetic or otherwise, accounted for the roughly equal doses of odd, self-deprecating humor and machismo in McGuane's work, and why was the father figure of such recurrent importance? How would White situate his own work relative to other gay art, and why was each of his novels so different in formal features? What connections did Hoban see between his career as an illustrator and creator of children's books and his recent adult fiction—and why had he waited until he was in his forties to begin writing adult works?

Of course, we went into each interview having read and reread all of the author's works, and having endlessly analyzed, discussed, and argued about what approach to use, what questions to open with. By the time we sat down for the actual interview (which we taped), we were armed with dozens of pages of neatly typed questions, all arranged to provide shape and direction. Once the discussion began, however, our predetermined program was far less important than rapport—developing a sense of what sort of person the writer was, revealing enough about ourselves to establish a mood conducive to genuine exchange. We were always aware that while writers are anxious to talk about some topics, they prefer not to deal with others. Our main task was to let the writers expand on what was important to them, while also looking for ways to probe those avoided issues that we felt needed exploring.

We have made every effort to be sure that the final form of these interviews (the results of much splicing and tinkering, by us and by the authors) is coherent, shaped and directed — as it should be, authors being, after all, people of letters who are concerned with the rightness of their public words. Yet what is often lost in the process of distillation is the personal element that gave texture to the discussion. A good interview is not only a sequence of questions and replies, but also a dynamic exchange with an undercurrent of understanding and response. Certainly there's something pleasing about the illusion of precision that the question/answer format creates, but this precision often seems to come at the expense of the sense that human beings have actually been talking — with all of their digressions and hesitations, gestures, smiles and frowns. Thus our conversation with Walter Abish sounds far more solemn than what actually took place over a convivial dinner with him and his wife, Cecile, and the final version of the Barry Hannah interview only partly suggests the wildness and intensity of an encounter in which tumblers of whiskey, pool tables, old Elvis records, and discussions of literature were all significant elements.

In a sense, we view the interview process as a response to the current critical emphasis on "the authorless text" and the notion of "the reader as writer" — the view that the text is less a specific structure than an open-ended process, the idea of the text as an endless play of signifiers without a center, essence, or meaning. But if we can accept the view that books neither refer to objects in the world nor are they expressions of an individual subject, this reduction of books to larger, impersonal structures still goes against our grain. Certainly literary constructs are never simply the result of individual expression; however, literary voices *do* emerge from the mouths of real people, and books *are* generated from a distinct consciousness that exists but once, and briefly.

In the end, though the focus of these interviews is primarily on style and on the creative process, there is more here than aesthetics. These writers may inhabit different realities, but they share a concern for issues common to us all. If they lack a "real center" (geographically, culturally, politically, aesthetically) they are united in the conviction that language and ideas can expand, rather than restrict, our options — and in the hope that talking and writing can make a difference. Even with most of the irrelevancies edited out — the talk about kids or rock-and-roll or baseball, the jokes about southern California, the commiseration over current events—what remains is what this book is really about: the excitement of meeting the writers, of finding the source, and the conscience, of the voices that ring in their fiction. As Raymond Carver points out, the 1980s are "a fine time to be alive, and writing"— and a fine time, too, to be alive and reading.

Cecile Abish

An Interview with
Walter Abish

Walter and Cecile Abish live in a loft in Manhattan's East Village. The area above Houston Street and below 14th Street, between the Bowery and Avenue C, now has more than fifty galleries, dozens of theaters, close to one hundred restaurants, and is bursting with vitality, having in recent years emerged as a center for artists, writers, and performing artists. Even in the gentrified areas there are, of course, the homeless on the street, but Walter had told us that they were not a threat; so, as we entered their tall loft building, we were less worried than curious. The elevator opens directly into the studio, with the living room, kitchen, and sleeping quarters partitioned off from a large area in which Cecile works on her projects. Several of her large photo-works mounted on metal sheets adorn the walls, as does the framed photo of a man astride a horse that appears on the cover of *How German Is It*. The following interview is based on the conversation we had that night in August 1983.

The Abishes have both been immersed in New York City's art scene since the 1960s, and during the evening it seemed obvious that they reinforce each other's creative energies. Not surprisingly, there is evidence of this in Abish's fiction. Several of his stories were launched, imaginatively, in response to specific artworks: "With Bill in the Desert" and "Non-Sites" were inspired by pieces by Terry Fox and Robert Smithson, respectively.

Abish's fascination involves the methodology of writing and the way characters and events can be shaped and manipulated for specific effects. Abish structures his fiction to deny readerly expectations with respect to character or plot. Typically plot and character development are impeded, creating a heightened sense of ambiguity and a resulting sense of discomfort for readers who seek clear-cut explanations or "meaning."

Abish is rarely interested in retelling events or describing the reality outside his doorstep, although the imaginative textures of that reality constantly intrude into his fiction. Rather, he seeks ways to disturb our sense of the familiar, to reenergize it, to explore the ambiguous elements that surround us, typically unexamined or unnoticed. Abish actively inhibits readerly identification by "flattening" his creations, by creating contexts for irony, play, and ambiguity. Even in his most apparently realistic work, the P.E.N.-Faulkner Award–winning *How German Is It* (1980), the reader enters a world of signs, the world of Germany-as-perceived-by-America—in short, a world of encoded actions intended to provoke a "German" response. Though it is not the actual Germany, it is a validated view of Germany that is as much accepted by Germans as by anyone else. It is the universal response to German signs, not the "real" Germany that Abish, traveling on a Guggenheim fellowship, visited for the first time only after the publication of his novel.

We knew in advance that we would be talking about different issues with Abish than with most other writers we interviewed. The conversation would inevitably turn to the art world—photography, sculpture, film, painting—and its relationship to his work. We knew we wanted to keep circling formal issues, since Abish's restless, imaginative exploration of those issues is the most striking aspect of his work. We wanted to probe Abish's responses to questions about form: What about the arbitrary structuring devices used in *Alphabetical Africa* (1975), in which the first chapter uses words beginning only with "a," the second also with "b," the third adding "c," and so forth; or in "99: The New Meaning," which consists of page 99 of 99 texts taken from 99 authors? What strategies does he employ to create the sense of ambiguity that animates so many of his texts? What does he gain by refusing to supply the usual psychological background for his works? What specific interaction does he see between his work and that of other New York artists? Lurking behind these questions was the fundamental issue of what relationship (if any) Abish wishes to establish between the territory of his imagination—the intertextual construct with its disturbing, ambiguous surfaces—and the world outside the page.

Larry McCaffery: Perhaps we could begin somewhat obliquely by talking about how you came to select the jacket photograph for *How*

German Is It—the picture of the man astride the horse at the seaside. It seems to suggest a sense of sexuality and menace appropriate to the novel; but of course it "represents" nothing in the novel directly, except those one or two references to the image. Did your wife take the photo after you had formulated the image?

Walter Abish: The photo was taken by Cecile before we had met. As I was nearing the completion of *How German Is It* I began to look around for a suitable photo for the book jacket. I actually visited a number of photographers. I saw some first-rate work, but nothing that to my mind meshed with the book. I really didn't know what I was looking for. Anything that I could relate to the book. Preferably a snapshot. Something that would also work together with the title without explaining it. I vaguely remembered Cecile's photo of the rider. She managed to find it, and also to unearth the negative. The moment I saw the photo I knew it was the right one. I then introduced into the text mention of the photo, perhaps to reinforce my decision to use it.

I like the photograph because it is so variously suggestive and yet somewhat mysterious. The question "How German is it?" might be asked of the rider. The incongruity of the barefoot, stiff-backed rider, almost military in appearance, the rope in his hand actually a noose around the horse's neck, appeals to me. A horse lover at New Directions, not concealing her disdain, remarked that the horse was ready for the glue factory. Interestingly enough, unlike most of the other foreign publishers, the Germans balked at using the photo. They kept looking for one that would sanitize the book—make it more commercially acceptable. I was told that they had first picked a photo of an elderly waiter inside a restaurant; then, to my dismay, they chose the one in which a high-fashion mannequin in high heels and fur coat is standing on a rustic wooden bridge beneath which an elderly man is placidly rowing a boat. The publisher and I exchanged a number of heated letters on the subject. I felt very indignant. I saw it as an attempt to impose a banal interpretation on the text and thereby to diminish what I had set out to do. I am happy to say that Suhrkamp used Cecile's photo for the paperback edition of *How German Is It*.

LM: Does the photograph reinforce the sense of ambiguity that is so much a part of your work?

WA: Ambiguity often necessitates a closer reading. I wanted the cover not so much to reinforce ambiguity as to announce a purpose. The cover is a sign as much as the title, which is missing a question mark. Clearly the American book designer felt unhappy with my signs, for he promptly altered the illustration beyond all recognition. The sky and landscape were eliminated, and a grainy texture transformed the

horseman into a somewhat archaic figure, statuesque and heavily symbolic. Something out of the remote German past. I am happy that my
choice prevailed.

Sinda Gregory: When you are proceeding in a text, are you conscious
of injecting mystery or ambiguity into a structure that is clear for you?
Or are you as puzzled as the reader?

WA: Surely not all readers are puzzled? Everything is spelled out—
though not in a customary fashion. I do not intentionally create mystery.
But why should the novel reveal what, under similar circumstances in
life, is not revealed? I simply do not extract explanations from my
characters. I would rather not know them too well. Quite frequently
I proceed in a state of not knowing, or a state of unknowing. I rewrite.
Frequently I discard material because it would expand the book beyond
what I consider to be its reasonable parameters. In *How German Is It*
I reluctantly discarded a chapter in which Paula, blindfolded, is being
interrogated by the police. For one thing, I did not wish to depart from
the essentially middle-/upper-middle-class panorama. In order to depict a radical left point of view I would have had to introduce a
politicized jargon. I should point out that the strategies involved in
writing a short text or a conspicuously structured work such as *Alphabetical Africa* differ greatly from those employed in the writing of
How German Is It. For one thing, the shorter fiction allows me to be
far more playful. In "How the Comb Gives a Fresh Meaning to the
Hair," I was able forcibly to unite two essentially antithetical texts, one
dealing with a young married couple in Albuquerque, the wife working
with a group of retarded children, the other relying in large part on
George Painter's remarkable biography of Proust. While writing it I
established a tenuous link between the two by now interwoven texts,
namely between the children I nicknamed the Rets and Proust's alleged
fascination with rats. From the beginning the conjoining of the stories
created something entirely unpredictable. In "With Bill in the Desert"
I used a similar idea. Part I, based on a gallery installation by the
sculptor Terry Fox, is a story of two men in a New York loft who
pretend to live in the Sahara. In Part II, I shifted them to the desert.
I don't intentionally create difficulties for myself; in the most implau-
sible situation I wish to convey a plausible response. While I do not
wish to fool the reader or to elicit a false response, I would like to
insure that a certain tension, even a discomfort, is always present.

LM: Yet you also seem intent on confronting the reader with details
of the reassuring world—in part, I take it, to eventually undermine
our faith in the familiar world, to break through that "deadly barrier"
(as you refer to it in "Access") that the "pleasant and overwhelmingly
familiar can often conceal."

WA: I do not so much confront the reader with it as feel the need to establish a reassuring world. The question of the familiar continues to fascinate me. What constitutes the familiar world? How do we respond to it? People tend to familiarize everything they encounter. How familiar is a ride on the train? I think an individual might focus on something in the train that is reassuring, and thereby block out everything else. If the familiar is the means by which the "self" establishes a tenuous link to "otherness," then Kafka, and Dostoyevsky in his "Notes from Underground," show the "self" with no access to the otherness that it may, in fact, wish to embrace. For a conference I once wrote a paper on aspects of the familiar world as perceived in everyday life and literature, trying to determine the function and place of the familiar and of defamiliarization of topography in fiction. In my own work I have tended to seek out foreign topography—Africa, Germany, places I did not know well. After all, the Germany in one's head is frequently more valuable as a source than the Germany one may visit. Germany, even to the Germans, is pretty confusing. Is it all right to once again use the word *Vaterland*? As for our vision of America— for that one may have to turn to the mail-order catalogs, *National Geographic*, movies, novels, the *New York Times*. I am not suggesting that these sources will encapsulate the vision of America—but they will yield an alert writer material that is uncluttered. I think it is necessary to begin with a simple, uncomplicated picture that will then allow for all kinds of changes.

SG: Is there any consistent way in which your works begin for you?

WA: In *Alphabetical Africa* it was the idea of writing the first chapter with words that all began with the letter "a," the second using "a" or "b," until in the twenty-sixth chapter I reached the letter "z" and then reversed the process. In the fifty-second and final chapter I again had to use words that began only with "a." There was also the excitement of having to relinquish a certain control. I could not write in the first person until I reached the ninth chapter, in which the letter "i" could be introduced.

In "Ardor/Awe/Atrocity" I wanted to describe a young woman traveling to California by herself; then, halfway through the story, after she had settled in Los Angeles, I switched the point of view, seeing her only through the eyes of an old friend who had run into her at the airport. Actually, I recently came across a first draft of the story and discovered to my astonishment that I began the story with a young man. What I had in mind as I started was simply a picture of a car on the road. A color: yellow? And something that I would describe as a tone. The key thing was to determine how I might enrich this tone, as well as sustain it. I suppose the tone might influence the growth of the story. It is important for me not only to read the text, but also to hear it. I have to keep the text at a high pitch, to retain a tension. As soon as the tension diminishes, I have to reenergize it, perhaps by returning to something that took place in an earlier section. A kind of reorientation, you might say. How do most writers respond to the question of how they begin their work?

SG: Many of them say they begin with a character, for whom they then need to invent a plot; or with a plot, whose outlines they know and which must be "fleshed out."

WA: I guess I would like to treat the story in a pictorial way—I would like all of the components to share equally in the presentation of the text's reality. I want language to focus with the same intensity on what is central and what may be less central, thereby unifying the book. In a sense, my innate resistance to development of character places a greater burden on language. The entire text—not just the characters—must convey meaning. Writing is manipulation; by now the reader must be fully aware of this. In fact, I would say that the reader is fully aware of this complicity between himself and the writer. A secret understanding. The writer likes to please . . . and the reader who has a specific preference, a taste for one kind of book or another, would like his pleasure. If character development is important to a reader, it is basically because that reader is a voyeur who has developed a fondness for case histories.

LM: You've referred elsewhere, in a *Semiotext(e)* interview, to your "awareness of the limitation of writing" and to "a certain ambivalence" with respect to the role of the writer. *How German Is It* seems directly concerned with these issues. Can creating a work of fiction ever lead the writer to discoveries that lie outside the text?

WA: Well, I believe in accidents and incorporate them into my writing. One of my favorite songs is Blondie's "Accidents Never Happen in a Perfect World." I believe that a discovery, as you put it, incurred or revealed by a text may eventually lead the writer back to yet another text. It happens not infrequently. In life one is forever coming face to face with something about which one has written, or is intending to write. It makes the writer increasingly sensitive to what, for lack of a better word, I would call a "literary context." Just as a reader might exclaim: "Why, this is straight out of fiction!," the writer is in a position to recognize that something he encounters is straight out of his text. I had an experience in Frankfurt last year that strongly reminded me of *How German Is It*, which had not yet appeared in Germany. The guests (all Germans) at a party given in my honor appeared to do their utmost—I doubt that it was conscious—to play out certain roles, as if to engage or at least challenge my interest. Did they wish to have me raise the question: How German is it? Similarly, a few weeks ago I received a curious reminder of my book in the form of a clipping. A critic in Hanover who had recently written a full-page article on my work for the *Frankfurter Rundschau* thought it might interest me. The newspaper story dealt with a visit of a journalist to the quiet and beautiful town of Flossenbürg in Bavaria. The journalist had come to interview the mayor; among the questions he raised was why the town had decided to erect a small housing project of a hundred units on the site of a former concentration camp where over 25,000 inmates, not counting Russian prisoners, were murdered. I was astonished that my new city of Brumholdstein, which consisted of 2,500 units, was not as farfetched as it may have appeared at first. Now what I have written seems, within a fictional context, perfectly reasonable. The mayor of Flossenbürg was put out by the journalist's question, replying that housing was needed for Germans who were fleeing from the east. So much for the moral issue. Have I really been able to *enter* Germany so successfully? As a writer I am somewhat superstitious. A writer performs the role of seer—unintentionally, perhaps. As a result, I take all kinds of precautions not to kill the *symbolic* father whenever he may appear in my stories. I prefer, if you've read "Crossing the Great Void," to simply lose track of him. It's all right not to locate him, even though he may be standing for all to see, in the middle of the story. To kill the father is something I cannot bring myself to do. I am extremely aware of this as I write. In other words, the inhibitions I feel while writing are formed by things outside the text. I make use of this uneasiness. It becomes an inducement for me to investigate these hesitations, these misgivings. I do so, but only circuitously.

LM: You mentioned earlier that the reality outside your doorstep doesn't usually interest you as a fiction writer. But at least two of your stories—"With Bill in the Desert" and "Non-Sites"—were apparently inspired by works of art. Could you talk about what started those two stories?

WA: Both the piece by Robert Smithson and the one by Terry Fox conveyed a view of an eerie and rarefied landscape in which man's participation, though indicated, was not definable. I don't recall which of the several Non-Sites by Smithson I may have had in mind. Certainly the title itself activated my imagination. The very idea of a non-site seemed to evoke a kind of non-participation—a withdrawal? On the other hand I remember quite vividly Fox's piece, which was exhibited at the Reese Pailey Gallery in New York. At the far end of a large, empty loft Fox had placed a large (at least eight-foot by eight-foot) tarp on the floor, and then suspended another tarp of the same size five feet above it. The only illumination came from a very bright naked lightbulb dangling above the suspended tarp. It sounds very simple, but the effect, especially when seen from a distance, was astonishing. Fox not only managed to evoke the desert, but he was also able to present a vision of the desert that is lodged in the mind. It was the desert we might carry around with us after a brief visit to a desert. I returned later in the day to have another look at the installation; this time I found five or six men and women, in jeans and overalls, casually lounging beneath the stretched tarp, drinking beer, behaving as if they were not—or so it seemed to me—inside a gallery, but outdoors. The slightly wrinkled tarp looked like sand. The shadows on the ground appeared to be shadows made by the sun. It was an amazing tableau. It gave me the idea for the story. A well-known literary magazine was willing to publish Part I, but not Part II. They couldn't accept the indoor desert juxtaposed with the actual outdoor desert—I suppose because the outdoor, too, wasn't real enough. Also, it is possible to explain the men's fantasy of being in a desert, but the track through the quasi-real desert nullifies that explanation.

SG: The image of the desert recurs in your fiction, especially in the stories. It seems to have a particularly expressive power for you, perhaps as a symbol of emptiness, perhaps suggesting the landscape that all your characters move through ("vast empty stretches of space, separating unseen obstacles"—in "Crossing Friends"). Did your years in the tank corps have something to do with your interest in the desert, providing you with stories or images, that you have since mined in your fiction?

WA: While I was in the Israeli army I spent three weeks in Ein Husub, a godforsaken spot in the Negev, right on the Jordanian border, a border that was then not as peaceful as it is today. There were two dozen of us in the small fortlike enclosure on top of a hill. I've attempted to write about the three weeks, but evidently the truth of the event, like the reality or truth of other events, so dominates the text that writing about it is merely a means of retelling a story. I don't have the freedom I need. There's no room for the unexpected, no room for invention. My stay in the desert makes a good after-dinner story.

The desert I've created is more closely linked to the idea of a desert as in Terry Fox's sculpture. A number of artists have built large outdoor works in a desertlike setting (Robert Morris, Smithson), or indoor installations (Fox, Bruce Nauman, whose work I like a great deal). Cecile has built both indoor and outdoor installations that have fed my imagination—her marble works, installations that cover the interior of an entire gallery space, evoke the emptiness of the desert. That sense of desert that these artworks leave in my mind is more real than my turbulent three weeks in the Negev. I am reminded of Freud, who, despite his dreams of Rome which he kept analyzing, avoided Rome on his first few visits to Italy. Rome represented a threat, something with which he could not come to grips. I wonder what Freud's first trip to Rome must have been like, especially given Freud's attachment to antiquity. On second thought, it is not inconceivable that somewhere in that action-filled three-week stay in the Negev lies buried an event or incident that might elucidate my frequent use of the desert in my stories.

LM: With the exception, perhaps, of the characters in *How German Is It*, the "people" in your works don't "develop" the way most literary figures do. This is intentional on your part, of course, but I am wondering what process is involved in creating them.

WA: My characters tend to emerge at first as two-dimensional figures. They are quite ghostly to me. They present an ideal point of view and point of departure. In the rewriting they acquire another dimension and, as a result, much more readily recognizable psychological traits. I can immediately recognize in what direction each is heading. At this point, I must hold the characters in a firm grip, not of understanding but of necessity. I know the characters as well and as little as I know myself. Sooner or later we are all flooded with a self-awareness and a self-understanding. It seems almost inevitable. In "The Alphabet of Revelations" the three blue-collar workers, employees of New Jersey Bell Telephone, break up with their wives; they become interesting only because I treat the breakup as a ritual. What interests me is how the couples divide their possessions, or fail to. I allow the men and the women a certain individuality, but at the same time I wish them to hold onto the sweet vulnerability of New Jersey and to retain a New Jersey working-class identity. The characters permit a double journey, one inward, to their TV longings, the other into a state that, among other things, contains one huge swamp, which is also a bird sanctuary, and a million supermarkets. It is my love story for the self-conscious and sometimes detested neighbor of New York.

SG: Do you have a predetermined end in mind while working?

WA: Uwe Johnson, the German writer, once somewhat solemnly explained that he spent a year mapping out his novel and a year writing it. Similarly, Michel Butor methodically plans or used to plan his books before writing them. I don't know to what extent writers who have specific endings in mind thereby exclude the possibility of chance. At any rate, endings present a great problem. I can think of a number of books that would be greatly improved if one could only rip out the ending. I don't know my precise endings, but I have a pretty good idea of what will take place. One arrives at endings by a process of elimination. This is ruled out, so is that . . . I am fond of Robbe-Grillet's

endings in his early books and in his film *L'Immortelle;* the ending in
the film replicates a violent act that had already taken place, thereby
thrusting the viewer back into the film. Examples of great endings are
in Pynchon's *The Crying of Lot 49,* and in Thomas Bernhard's as yet
untranslated novels, *Ja* and *Beton.* Only the final paragraph of *Ja* explains the title. Bernhard writes books that, in a sense, are all endings.
Endings are the subject matter. But doesn't Dostoyevsky in his "Notes
from Underground" announce with his first line—"I am a sick man . . . I
am a spiteful man"—what is to be the ending?

SG: That gesture that ends *How German Is It*—Ulrich raising his
hand to pacify the hypnotist—is highly charged, but hardly a "wrapup" in the traditional sense.

WA: There is no wrapup to *How German Is It.* That's why I wrote
the book. That's why I picked Germany. Because, to this day, hardly
anyone can mention Germany, or write about Germany, without feeling
the necessity to, as you say, "wrap up Germany." Everything German
necessitates an explanation and, of course, it is invariably the same
familiar explanation. I suspect that one brings up the subject of Germany only in order to arrive at the explanation. To me the literary
challenge was to see to what degree it would be possible to write about
Germany without fulfilling those obligations. The ending is highly
charged because it is denied the explanation that will defuse it.

The last scene was based on my visit in New York to a hypnotist,
whom I had gone to see in order to learn how to hypnotize myself.
The visit had not been entirely successful. I had instantly established
a rapport with him, which proved an impediment when he finally got
down to hypnotizing me. I was no longer relaxed. A standard test in
evaluating a person's response to hypnosis is to induce the subject
being hypnotized to raise his right arm. For a second I experienced this
quandary when I, with my eyes shut, heard the agreeable voice of the
hypnotist inform me that my right hand, then resting on the arm of
my chair, was actually beginning to rise up in the air. I could feel the
weight of my arm resting on the chair. I felt that I, not the hypnotist,
would be instrumental in making it rise. Yet, wishing to benefit from
this encounter, I didn't want to impede him. Slowly I raised my arm,
convinced that he was able to see through me. I suspect he knew,
though when I opened my eyes nothing on his face indicated this.
Subsequently, when I mentioned this to a psychiatrist friend, he remarked that quite possibly I had been hypnotized but felt the need to
rationalize my compliant behavior.

As for the ending of the book: by raising his hand in a Hitler salute
in the office of the hypnotherapist who was trying to regress Ulrich
to his childhood, Ulrich, indeed, was thrust back into a period when

the outstretched arm signified a unanimity—it was the icon that lay at the heart of Nazism. In time, even for believers, the salute must have become a perfunctory greeting; nevertheless, at first, with Hitler in power, if one is to trust photographic evidence, the salute embodied a tremendous ecstatic affirmation, a belief, a sense of unity, a sense of being one with the Volk.

SG: Were you implying that fascism still exists in Germany?

WA: The salute, in itself, is an anachronism. Now it belongs as much to Hollywood as to Germany. To give the Hitler salute in Germany would be to violate what is essentially an enormous taboo. The few who do it do it, I suspect, in response to the taboo. An Englishman not long ago told me that in a working-class bar somewhere in Bavaria he had seen young men, as they entered the bar, give the Hitler salute, but it was done quite casually. It may be true. Certainly there are fascists in Germany. Not long ago the SS had a reunion just outside Frankfurt. I see this as aberrational. These characters tend, like Franz in my novel, to be in search of an identity. To outrage others is to acquire an identity. The fascism they represent is dead, but a right-wing resurgence, which is entirely possible, can occur without the, to us, familiar signs.

LM: Since you don't invite the reader to identify with the action from a psychological standpoint, is there a single thing you could identify that you are aiming to create for the reader?

WA: The marvelous experience. But am I creating it for the reader? The reader is too remote. I think the book's production—the reality principle of publishing, book merchandising—actually comes between the reader and myself. If I am to be aware of one, why not be equally aware of the other? One is as important as the other. The readers are there, as are the reviews, the critics, the interviews, the bookstores, the shelf life. How can one keep all of this in mind? Almost everything is an impediment to further work. What do I give the reader? I give him years at the typewriter, I suppose. I permit him, if he is so inclined, to enter a world I have created. I give him no more or less than what other writers have given me. I think the question suggests a vision of the writer as creator that is, in essence, romantic. I believe that my readymade stories—"What Else," "Inside Out," and "99: The New Meaning"—represent a deliberate though playful diminution of the creative. Literature is used as a vast dictionary from which what is extracted, according to a system, is assembled to create a so-called story. The three works are things I did for my amusement, yet they are readable. What does the reader get out of them? Foremost, the conflicting ideas.

LM: Why choose an arbitrary device—like the 99-page idea, or the

alphabetical structure in *Alphabetical Africa*—that would seem to limit
your imagination? Or do such structures *free* you, in a sense, since you
don't have to concern yourself with certain aspects of form?

WA: For me there is little freedom once I have selected a system.
One might say that I am imprisoned by it. Indeed, I choose systems
because from the start they present a journey past and over obstacles.
Can this be equated to everyday existence? Each obstacle creates a kind
of anxiety, presents a problem that must be surmounted. If the obstacle
is an intrinsic element of the system, it cannot be avoided; one is boxed
in. But I frequently encounter the same quandary in works that are
not predicated on a rigid system. For instance, I kept banging my head
against a wall trying to extricate Ulrich from Switzerland, at the end
of "The Idea of Switzerland." I simply did not know how to get him
out. Writing never provides a sense of relief. It can be exhilarating
when it goes smoothly. A year before I began *Alphabetical Africa* I
happened to see, listed in an Abercrombie & Fitch advertisement for
their annual sale, an African diary that had been reduced from $90 to
$5. What is an African diary, especially one that costs $90? My mind
was racing. It occurred to me that I might be able to use it to write a
novel set in Africa. I envisioned the diary as the kind of useless object
that someone with a great deal of money who was about to go on a
safari might acquire. I took the bus to Manhattan from New Jersey,
where we were living at the time, to purchase the diary. By the time
I arrived at the now defunct Abercrombie & Fitch, at quarter to nine,
there was a long line of people waiting in front of the store. I reasoned
that not everyone would be interested in an African diary, but by the
time I finally reached the counter where the diary was being sold, it
was too late, the last copy was being sold just as I arrived. I saw the
man handing the saleswoman five dollars and receiving a bulky wrapped
package. To this day I have not seen the diary. I felt as if my novel
had just gone down the drain. So the unseen diary was the precursor
for the structured novel that I wrote a year later.

I really owe *Alphabetical Africa* to James Laughlin. He had liked
"Minds Meet," which I had published in *TriQuarterly*, and asked me
if I had anything similar for the New Directions anthology. When I
started I had no idea it would develop into a novel; it was just going
to be a fifteen- or twenty-page piece. But as I wrote I became more
and more involved in the work. I was concentrating on writing a
straightforward linear text, which, in light of the obstacles, was impossible. I found that I could sustain the energy within any given
chapter only for so long. The lengths of the chapters are a measure of
an energy level. I tried to avoid going past that point where the energy
dropped off. Having completed the first half, I sent it to J. with the

explanation that I had discovered that I now had a novel on my hands. In a prompt reply, he said that if the second part was as strong, he would publish the book. Just before it came out, he told me not to feel downcast if only a hundred copies of it were sold.

LM: Why Africa at all? Obviously America or even Austria would have fit into the alphabetical pattern equally well.

WA: Because it is the continent to which our childhood as well as adult fantasies of glory, adventure, riches, and sexual rewards are inextricably linked. Africa is a continent of taboos that seem to have little bearing on the taboos we encounter in the West. It is a playground for the wealthy on safaris, and a testing ground for the hunter and the mercenary. Its history is the distorted, unreliable history of colonialism. When writing was introduced in Africa, it was done in order to impose law and order—to dominate, not to elucidate. Africa's boundaries are still in dispute—they are unclear, for the actual boundaries are tribal ones. Linguistically the continent has not been properly charted. The pygmies of the Ituri forest, for instance, are much too cautious to reveal themselves; hence, what they say about themselves is unreliable. The whites who predominate in my book see only their own world, regarding everything black as alien, remote, not worth investigating. Of course, there are exceptions. The struggle to overcome the structural barriers I had devised for the text was my way of "controlling" and "dominating" a difficult text. Clearly, there's a parallel to be drawn between my struggle to depict and, as a white writer, come to terms with the "mysterious" world of Africa and the intrinsic challenges of the text. Although as a child I briefly set foot in South and West Africa, my Africa is colored by the writings of Conrad, Gide, Hemingway, Burton, and Turnbull, as well as by Edgar Rice Burroughs and Hollywood.

LM: Was Roussel an influence?

WA: Not at all. I hadn't come across *Impressions of Africa* when I wrote *Alphabetical Africa*. I continue to remain fascinated by Roussel, and I regret that so little is available on Roussel in English. As for his novels, I find them rather inaccessible. Roussel expends most of his energy demonstrating the ingenuity and lifelikeness of his rather remarkable mechanical devices—really toys—that serve to animate but actually stifle his text. I found the two books available in English translations unbelievably tedious. The prose—the main function of which is give shape to his mechanical monsters—seems equally mechanical. Yet I am drawn to the books on account of Roussel, his dreams of success, his pronounced eccentricities, his hermetic existence. Once in a while I pick up the books, out of a deep fondness and respect for the author. I must admit that I am disturbed that I'm not able to make any headway with them.

SG: Your books don't seek to present actual places as much as to focus on what these places (Africa, Germany) are in our imaginations. What is required in writing about such places?

WA: As far as I'm concerned, the places I write about *can* all be located on a map, even if I have to draw it myself. In writing *How German Is It*, I kept looking at the maps of towns and small cities in old Baedekers and Michelin guides of Germany, trying to piece together a map of Brumholdstein and all the other places I had invented. To my mind the fictitious towns became quite real. I think of Michel Butor, who, in his excellent novel, *Passing Time*, created the city of Blessington, a counterpart to Manchester. Why didn't he simply settle for Manchester? I think it was because he would have been greatly hampered by the reality and historicity of Manchester. Manchester would have impeded what he had set out to do, namely to describe, in diary form, the way in which a sensitive and overly imaginative young French clerk confronts and challenges the sometimes hostile environment during his year's stay in the labyrinthine city. Everything—the people as well as the architecture, new and old—is drawn into this conflict between what is essentially the self and otherness. I can understand what Butor set out to do. For my part, I want the cities, the medieval towns in Germany, even the oasis in the desert of my shorter fiction, to help shape the text and not to serve as a romantic or lyrical backdrop. The cities, the towns, the architecture, and the parks, as well as the interiors I describe, are not merely convenient locations for the characters. Their purpose is not to authenticate the characters—to make them more German, or North African. When I started "The English Garden" and subsequently *How German Is It*, one of my problems was to find a way to slip into Germany. I kept looking for an opening. From what point of view was I to describe the country I had never seen? I kept my research for the novel to a minimum. Otherwise I would have drowned in superfluous information. Of course, I was bound to make mistakes. It didn't really matter to me if German school buses were painted yellow or not; I made them yellow. If they're not yellow today, nothing really rules out the possibility that Germany, in order to oblige me, will paint its school buses yellow tomorrow. And I'm only half-joking. In my mind I kept strolling through the towns and cities I had created. They were my cities. To my astonishment they were not at all different from the towns and villages I saw when, for the first time, I visited Germany last year. It seemed appropriate that my first guide should have been a Dutch journalist who spoke fluent German and was quite obsessed by the Germans. Later I learned that his family had been pro-Nazi and toward the end of the war had to flee Holland to find refuge in Germany. He drove us from Amsterdam to Köln and then followed the Rhein to Koblenz, where we picked up the Mosel, which we followed for an hour. In all a seventeen-hour trip, most of it at high speed. He was eager to get my response to the Germany I had never seen. He was writing an article on my work and he wanted my reactions to the medieval villages, the castles and the people. I don't know what he expected; I only know he was disappointed. In the end I learned more about him than he was able to learn about me for his article. He kept asking: Are you sure you've never been here before? I had been apprehensive that the Germany I would encounter might invalidate much of what I had written—but it didn't.

LM: Despite your insistence that you are mainly interested in society's imaginative constructions (their sign systems and surfaces, for instance), your fiction has often presented preferences and situations that seem highly political—from the references to revolution and Mao in *Minds Meet*, to the more highly charged situations that you created in *How German Is It*. Although you disavow political intentions, don't you feel that you illuminate the reality behind the sign systems of which your texts are comprised? Or do you feel that, in writing about our imaginative systems (the set responses to Germany, say), you are engaged in a form of political comment?

WA: It depends on how one would define this "political consciousness" of the artist. An artist who is politically aware can rightly claim that every relationship in a book possesses political overtones. Given a political context or awareness, everything—even inertia—evokes political vibrations. I am certain that in Latin America, or in Eastern Europe, or for that matter in Italy, the writings of Updike, or Vonnegut, or Heller, or Pynchon are scanned with a seismographic political awareness and a judgment that simply is not an aspect of our own reading of the same material. To read a book in Poland or in Latin America, I am convinced, is to interpret politically, just as we, when we read Drieu la Rochelle or Céline, are made aware of a political position, albeit an unstable one that we no longer need to take seriously. My work is indeed political, but I very much doubt that any American political entity, left or right, would recognize this. I am interested in describing how people function and adjust to the hierarchical in everyday life. Of course, the hierarchical values and divisions are much more conspicuous in certain societies—England, for instance. On a certain level, I suppose hierarchy contributes to a loss of freedom. To what extent we function as well as depend on hierarchies is to me a political question. Compared to us, the Germans and to a lesser degree the

Austrians, but certainly the Swiss, are extremely law-abiding people. The law is obeyed—no one ever seems to question whether it makes sense. One could say that to despise and persecute the Jews in the '30s and early '40s was, in essence, an extension of the law. Of course, an intense hatred of Jews had preceded many of the Nazi racial laws, but these laws legitimized the persecution. That was important, for a law-abiding people, despite their innate hatred, would find it extremely difficult to yield to their baser instincts if it meant transgressing the law. Everything the Germans and Austrians did was within the framework of the law. In certain societies anyone who breaks a law, no matter how petty the law, is regarded as a threat to the public good. When a friend of mine, while parking his car just outside Zurich, dented the fender of a parked car, at least a dozen people who happened to be passing stopped to watch us. I counted at least three who, quite openly, jotted down the license number of my friend's car. Another two walked over to the other car to read the note my friend had pinned to the windshield, evidently to see if the information he had given was correct. Not a word was said. No jokes were made to alleviate the tension. The people who observed us were quite expressionless. I give this as an example of how people seem to function in a law-abiding society where one law is as significant as the next. Our society is anarchical by comparison. At any rate, in my writing I like to call attention to as well as seek to undermine the so-called political stability of everyday life that is, in essence, implied in most fiction. For example, even the novelists who were most critical of the American involvement in Southeast Asia tend, in their books, to affirm the intrinsic stability of our society. To me, this stability is open to exploration. My interest in Germany is not to explain it, but to highlight the German "signs" that elicit a set response—a German truth—which in my book is either subtly questioned or negated or defamiliarized.

LM: This sounds a bit like what Coover does in many of his fictions; you introduce the familiar archetype, the clichéd pattern, in order to undermine it.

WA: Formula truths in fiction, be it about Germany or the United States, deplete the text, though on the surface they may provide a reasonable explanation for the text. I retain a measure of ambiguity, partly to energize the text.

SG: So you would agree with William Gass when he asserts that the real value of a text is the truth it produces, not its ability to reproduce an external truth?

WA: I agree with Gass, though I would maintain that this does not rule out an external truth. But, as far as I'm concerned, "external truths" are to be regarded as material to be tested, undermined, defamiliarized.

A strong work produces its own truth. Whatever else emerges from the text—even one written by a writer with the most deplorable political or moral convictions—a certain "internal truth" is pivotal to the work of art, the center of its tension. This internal truth is so secure that it remains a measure for the significance of everything else. Artistry transcends historicity. But remember: I am referring to a text, not to life situations.

SG: Are there any contemporary writers whose work you especially admire?

WA: I should preface this by explaining that I am an eclectic reader. I am, furthermore, an impatient reader. I like to acquire books, and I buy and receive far more books than I can possibly read. Most recently I have been reading Fernand Braudel's *The Structure of Everyday Life*, George Steiner's *Heidegger*, a book that has made Heidegger much more accessible to me, and Thomas Bernhard's most recent book, *Der Untergeher*, and Victor Segalen's fascinating *Le Fils du ciel* in a German translation, since my French is deplorably weak. I mention Segalen because I greatly admire him. I have referred to his novel *Rene Leys* in *How German Is It*. He is for me vital and contemporary, though in fact he died in 1916. A list of contemporary writers I admire, for one reason or another, would be rather lengthy. I will name some: Beckett, Pynchon, Gass, Gaddis, Coover, Hawkes, Barth, Barthelme (Donald and Frederick), McElroy, Paul West.

SG: Your wife, Cecile, is well known in the New York art scene. Have your careers affected each other in any way?

WA: We not only share a large loft, we also share an approach to work—a sensibility. Cecile is my first reader and, in turn, I'm generally the first person to comment on her large indoor installations, or outdoor work, or photo-related works. I've written an introductory essay for *Firsthand*, a book of her photo-works. We have an ongoing dialogue and provide a kind of measure for each other. By and large, in the art world one is more exposed to a methodology of work. Work is always being tested on an audience. I don't mean to imply that work presented is participatory. The literary critic Marthe Robert implies that to understand Kafka it is more important to raise the question "how" about his work rather than to ask "what." In general, this applies to the art world. The central question is always "how," not "what." The "what," be it with respect to minimalism or post-expressionism, invariably leads to a deciphering of content in order to arrive at an explanation that may satisfy the viewer or reader. It may mean investing the work with a psychological or humanistic intent that is not part of the work. Frequently the question "what" is not pertinent. For instance, *what* does Walter de Maria's one-kilometer-by-one-mile "Lightning Field" *mean*? I suppose the question might elicit an answer, but the work is under no constraint to explain itself. In the art world, I think, the distinction between "what" and "how" are clearer. I believe artists, in general, appear to be more open to and curious about what is going on around them, without demanding or supplying an explanation. I think there's a greater excitement and more tension in the art world, as well as a more conspicuous hierarchy, due in part to the investment of large sums of money, the obsession with fads. This, in turn, tends to make the art world somewhat constrictively fashion conscious. The literary world, by comparison, is much more sheltered and comfy. Fiction writers, unlike poets, tend to be loners. We have no actual scene to speak of, no real center. But little is to be gained from a comparison of these disparate worlds. What matters is that a good deal of work produced in the art world has been of importance to me. Certainly it has affected the way I see things.

LM: The critic Jerome Klinkowitz has written several essays in which he draws analogies between your work and that of certain contemporary painters, especially the photorealists (or superrealists)—and he suggested that your work can be seen as extending the concerns of "experimental realism" in painting. Has the work of any painters indeed been a conscious influence on your work?

WA: I happen to like Chuck Close, who is considered a photorealist. I like his work because of the way he is able to deconstruct it. The photorealists as a group produce a sort of "out of the corner of one's eye" view of America that I find intriguing. We rummage in the same junkyards. But for that exhilarating trip from the Port Authority on the way to the Newark airport, past the great wasteland of New Jersey, I would much prefer to turn to Robert Smithson. I admit that the deliberately commonplace pictures the photorealists produce are part of a stream of information I also ingest, but I prefer photographs and movies. Frequently I buy stills, although the ones I want from the films of Pasolini (*Salo*), Godard, Tanner, Fassbinder, Rohmer, and Kubrick, to name some of the directors I find interesting, are not easily available. I am stimulated by films and photographs. A number of characters in my books are based on photographs that have appealed to me for one reason or another. As for the painters, the title of my story "The Alphabet of Revelations" is taken from a painting by Magritte. I am drawn to Twombley, Agnes Martin, Artschweiger, Sol Levitt, Robert Ryman, as well as to early pop art. But influence? I can only think of Godard's early films. That uneasy relationship between his revolutionary fervor and his aesthetic concern. Godard always tried to merge the two but never quite succeeded. This uneasy product, in which the gratuitous act of violence was perfectly framed, affected me more than anything else. But that was the beginning.

LM: Have your fictional interests changed over the years? Do you find yourself approaching your works differently, looking for different things, becoming energized by different aspects of writing?

WA: Everything changes and yet, oddly enough, very little seems to change. One grows older. One develops new strategies with which to approach one's work. I suppose one text leads to the next. In Part I of a recent essay, "The Fall of Summer," I write about the *thinking of death* in the work of Thomas Bernhard. For Bernhard this thinking of death is paradoxically a method of measuring life. It is the only way he chooses to view life. Everything about which he writes ineluctably leads to death; yet, in thinking of death, he clings to life. In Part II I describe two recent visits I made to Vienna while using Bernhard's books *Ja* and *Beton* as a kind of Baedeker. In other words, I found it a challenge to allow Bernhard's measure of life, his thinking of death, to become my guide to a city that has consistently embraced death and yet, with great dexterity, drained history—I should say, its history—of all terror. My next book, a novel, begins in St. Petersburg, Florida. It's a city that's trying to change its image. It doesn't like to be considered a city to which retired people come to live out their remaining years. I am trying to find a happy ending for the book. It's the least I can do.

College of St. Francis Library
Joliet, Illinois

/ 45, 514/

Marion Ettinger

An Interview with

Max Apple

Born and raised in the center of America's Midwest, Max Apple is, at heart and in his fiction, an emigré. With an outsider's eye for the incongruous, for irreconcilable peculiarities, he manages to penetrate the mythological world that shimmers just beyond the golden arches, the orange roofs, the magic kingdoms that line our main streets and freeways. No writer is better at examining the middle ground between the ideal and the reality of the American Dream, because few others have such a real appreciation for the ambition and the magnitude of the Dream, or such a basic understanding of the impossibility of its fulfillment. In his two collections of stories, *The Oranging of America* (1976) and *Free Agents* (1984), and in his novel, *The Propheteers* (1987), he deals with the ambiguous qualities inherent in American enterprise, which Apple (like Stanley Elkin) rightly perceives as partly a con man's pitch and partly a visionary response to genuine human needs and desires. Apple peoples his stories (and his novel, *Zip* [1978]) with real made-up men behind the real made-up myths: Howard Johnson becomes (in Apple's best-known story, "The Oranging of America") not just a brand name, but a man with a mission who follows the trails of Lewis and Clark, of Johnny Appleseed—chauffeured, of course, in his black Lincoln as he crisscrosses the United States to feel its body through his own, to feel when it needs a rest, an iced tea, ice cream, magic fingers. Similarly, when Apple takes other figures whose presences have become predominantly mythical—Walt Disney, Fidel Castro, Norman Mailer, J. Edgar Hoover—and places them into his fiction, he is in fact dealing with what is more real about them: not their flesh-and-blood reality (why should a fiction writer care about *that*?) but their status in our collective imagination.

In the hands of most contemporary writers, the mythic monuments of American culture fare poorly. The focus is on the *results* of these mythic impulses—the ugly, monotonous architecture; the useless, tasteless junk; the whole disposable, non-biodegradable tackiness of it all; the ideologies that began as liberation and ended as dogma. But Apple is primarily interested in the impulse itself, in that initial and very American urge to enlarge, to grow, to keep moving. Why stop at five restaurants, or even thirty-five, when you can sell your special sauce to the entire world? If ice cream can be preserved by American know-how, why not preserve the human body? His fiction explores the energy, the restlessness, the intensity with which Americans pursue the new, the improved, the never-before-on-the-market, and it traces how our zeal for better products connects to a primal need for security, safety, and immortality.

Part of Apple's fascination with American culture lies in the fact that he grew up under circumstances that tended to set him outside that culture. Like Ira, the main character in *Zip*, Apple comes from a strongly traditional Jewish home that was dominated by grandparents whose values, outlook, and language (Yiddish) remained resolutely those of the old country. Growing up in the middle of a working-class Polish neighborhood in Grand Rapids, Michigan, and being smart, Jewish, and short, at an early age he had to learn to accommodate the aliens around him, to make sense of impulses foreign to him (like wolfing down a cheeseburger). Our interview circles the circumstances of his youth—the indelible mark his grandmother left on him, with her magical stories, her vital spirit trapped in a decaying body; the key role that sports and sports talk played in his household; the effect of his father's death; his involvement with politics during the 1960s—because we sensed that Apple's distinctive perspective on America had deep roots.

"When I get off the plane," Max Apple had said on the phone, "you'll recognize me because I'll be the only guy who's not carrying a *Wall Street Journal*—I'll be the little Jewish-looking guy in jogging shoes." Sure enough, the next night (March 16, 1983) as we watched people filtering through the entrance gate at the San Diego airport, Max was easy to spot: sporting jeans and running shoes, he was a slightly built man with a prominent graying beard and astonishingly bright eyes. It was pouring rain, and as we wove our way through San Diego's flooded freeways we talked about the horrible weather, the Houston Cougars' chances for an NCAA basketball championship, the latest about some of our favorite writers, such as Robert Coover, Barry Hannah, Cynthia Ozick. By the time we reached the motel where Max was to stay, we had passed through the polite exchanges of strangers and were ready for what the evening had to offer, which turned out to be an extended Mexican dinner. The experience was like catching up with an old friend from graduate school—and in fact we *had* all gone to graduate school in the Midwest during the turbulent '60s. When we sat down together the next morning to begin the interview that follows, it was hard to remember that we'd just met.

Larry McCaffery: Your fiction has a realistic element in it, but finally its impulses seem to me to lie elsewhere—in fantasy, parody, even myth. Why haven't you been attracted to more conventional forms?

Max Apple: Mainly because I'm *bored* by that kind of fiction. We just took a ride from La Jolla to your house. I can do the kind of writing that would describe that ride in shimmering detail: the cascading waves, the sun-drenched beach, the look of people in the street. Anyone could do that, and most of the writing around us is that kind. Some of it is probably good, but I don't see it as being good; I'm just not interested. In my own writing I want to get to everything right away. One of the few things I'm conscious of is that I want *speed*—I like to get two or three things going, like a juggler. The line that comes to mind is one I tell my students: "Description is revelation." I'm not interested in description that's not that. I don't want to see what everybody's eating or hear weather reports. To me that's *not* realism but a convention that we've been following for too long now. I don't mind reading it in George Eliot, but I'm often very bored with it in my contemporaries, unless it leads to something. That's part of my objection to conventional realism, but I'd also argue that things don't behave the way that so-called realistic fiction depicts them. Let me give you an example. In my freshman English class I taught *One Hundred Years of Solitude*; I think it's a wonderful book. Many freshmen did not understand it— they thought it was weird and claimed that nothing like that could ever happen. One student finally got up and said that he much preferred *The Red and the Black*, and he had all these historical examples about Napoleon that he used to demonstrate that Stendhal was a more realistic writer than Márquez. So I said, Look, if you take a course in the history of World War I, you're used to reading paragraphs that give you the four reasons for the war; in a kind of intellectual way, you're told about the end of feudalism or the assassination of the archduke, the pitting of one empire against another, and so on. We're used to all these kinds of political and economic ways of talking about what's happened. But,

I said, Márquez is telling you about these things in another way. Suppose you start a story like this: Once upon a time there was a vegetarian with one testicle who decided he wanted to kill all the Jews in the world, and one of the most sophisticated nations in the history of the world went along with him. I said, Look what history *is*! Look at what you're living in the midst of! Everyone was worried about the oil crisis then, so I said, What is Saudi Arabia? They had no water in 1922 (or whenever). There was a bedouin chieftain who wanted to pray in Jerusalem before he died, but he never made it. One of his cousins killed him because he had allowed television in his country. I said, Don't you see that the world, that history itself, is even more incredible than anything García Márquez could ever make up? What's so incredible about a guy having seventeen sons fighting in thirty-two civil wars? The student said, What about Pilar, who is one hundred years old and still taking lovers? And I said, What about Zsa Zsa Gabor, who's probably seventy and still enthralling you on Johnny Carson every night? Most people don't see that the world around them is just as mysterious as Macondo. I can't get interested in the kind of fiction that most people think of as realism—detective novels or political thrillers. To me, that fiction is not realistic at all.

Sinda Gregory: What is your definition of realism, then?

MA: The way Márquez is writing is realistic. There is some hyperbole, some exaggeration, but it's close to my sense of the way the world is. One of his characters, Remedios the Beautiful, disappears while shaking crumbs off a tablecloth. When she vanishes, everyone misses the tablecloth. To me, that's what happens in the world: people die, disappear, and what do we do? We miss tablecloths, we worry about property. The tablecloth is a shortcut, and even though *One Hundred Years of Solitude* is a long novel, it's still full of similar shortcuts. He gets everybody's lives going at once, gives you the texture of life—not in single lives, but the whole thing. That's what I'm interested in, though I don't have the terms for it—magical realism or postmodernism or whatever. I have some patience with that old-fashioned, description-centered realism with slow building of details, but never for my own work. Nathanael West, a writer I like, said he wanted his sentences to explode. I want those explosions, sentence by sentence, which is hard to achieve. Leonard Michaels writes like that, trying to get everything more and more dense, more compact. Of course, there's the danger of losing readers when you get so dense, and I don't want my writing to be so dense that it's only personal; that's what's happened to a lot of poetry. But you can learn to pace things to make the work accessible to other people. Still, the writing process is only interesting to me if that density is there, if I'm developing those shortcuts I was talking about. So although I can admire something like Thomas Mann's *Magic Mountain*, with all those wonderful discussions about the meaning of life, I want to say all that in one image, one sentence, one tablecloth.

LM: It sounds like you're aiming at the compression we usually associate with poetry.

MA: Yes, it's probably the same thing. I'm not close to contemporary poetry, but in prose I see this compression in Coover and Michaels. Actually the people I see doing the most with language aren't poets at all but the fiction writers called postmodernists — people like Cynthia Ozick, who I think is one of our very best writers, or Ray Carver. At the same time I can still appreciate Saul Bellow and Philip Roth — or George Eliot or Tolstoy or Stendhal, for that matter. Basically my tastes are very catholic. I went to a university and studied English literature. I have not wholly escaped that background, though my tastes now tend to run to less conventional types — Coover, Barthelme, Grace Paley, Barry Hannah, Michaels. I like writers who get two or three things going and who do so quickly. I also like John Barth, even though he gets things going in long works.

LM: Thomas Pynchon seems a conspicuous omission.

MA: I'm not a Pynchon fan. I haven't read *Gravity's Rainbow*, partly out of fear. Everyone has told me it's so good that I'm afraid it may really *be* that good; if it is, it may make me not write. And I'm afraid it may disappoint me because the Pynchon that I have read I haven't liked. I don't really know why. He plays games of the most incredible and imaginative sort, but for some reason I don't respond. Maybe it's a failure of my sensibility.

SG: How do you answer the charge that most of the writers you've mentioned as admiring are mainly technicians — that they're cute or overly abstract, that they're playing with forms and words but not addressing the "big issues" of our day?

MA: I don't like mere cuteness, but the writers we're talking about do their best work with absolute seriousness. I want abstract people in my fiction, not the characters you find in the so-called realists, but the issues involved in these abstract people are the absolute central issues of human affairs. I'm not just playing with them; I certainly don't take them lightly. I very much dislike writers who don't respect their characters, who don't love them. So when I say I don't make "whole characters," it's not because I don't love them; it's just that I've decided to leave out certain things because I don't have the time or the interest or the patience. To me, one of the best lines I've ever written was in "Inside Norman Mailer," where I was describing all that prize-fighting stuff and then I said, "You've all seen it — imagine it yourself!" That was a wonderful shortcut because I didn't want to write five pages describing prize fighting. I was interested in the metaphysical aspects of the situation, the metaphor for that.

SG: You say that you don't "just play" with your fiction, but it's almost always playful in tone. How do you keep a balance between your serious intentions and your sense of play?

MA: Playing is the most serious thing I do. Always.

SG: But aren't you tempted to try your hand at forms that aren't playful?

MA: The tragic never changes. Oedipus will always be Oedipus, and that tragic world or tragic vision that he's a part of is unchanging. In a way, the tragic vision deals with a cosmic dimension, while the world of comedy deals with the human dimension—which pretty well sums up its appeal. I mean, the pattern of everyone's life is about the same: we're all born and then certain things happen to us. Insurance actuaries are very good at predicting these things—they can predict when we will reach our physical peak, our sexual peak, our emotional peak, then when we'll get old and wither away and die. These things happen to everybody, it's absolutely unchangeable, and no amount of cunning or wit, no amount of prayer and hope, can change the pattern. That's what tragedy deals with. But comedy looks at things from a much smaller view—for instance, it examines our petty discomforts. I was reading *The Life of Johnson* the other night, and at one point Boswell asks Johnson about some trivial discomfort he has and says, "I hate to bother you with this." And Johnson says, "Sire, there is nothing too trivial for so small a creature as man." From the large perspective, Johnson is always right. Human beings can't always have that cosmic view, though we can try. The world is *only* small in the sense of this cosmic view. That small world is the comic world, and that small world is a correctable world, which is why I think I'm instinctively drawn to it. Comedy helps us correct our world, make it a better place; it has achievable goals. Making fun of things, of oneself, has a lot to do with the comic vision but it has nothing to do with jokes. This is crucial to understand. The people who tell jokes are usually *not* funny. So the comic spirit is a corrective to the way things are in the world, but it is not joke-writing and it often is not even funny. Comedy is as removed from the world of jokes and laughter as the tragic spirit is. It's that spirit of correctability that makes the comic world more interesting to me than the tragic. Comedy is not a vision carved in stone, so there's room for play.

LM: "Play" here seems to imply a freedom of movement, a lack of restriction. In working within the comic mode, do you ever feel the conscious need to place limits on what you do? Does your freedom create problems for you?

MA: In my world, as opposed to the realists' world, I can get away with anything, but this doesn't seem to be a problem. On the contrary, I *want* to get away with as much as possible. For example, I enjoyed being able to end "Gas Stations" with imitation Arabs riding away on camels. Originally that wasn't even supposed to be a story—it was to be a straight essay that Nora Ephron assigned on the subject of gas stations for a special bicentennial issue of *Esquire.* I started to write that straight story but it wasn't any good, it was boring as hell. I kept remembering a gas station from my childhood and I started merging this with other, fantastic materials. That was a crucial story for me, because it was the first time I consciously trusted my fantastic impulses completely. On this issue of artistic freedom let me again quote Dr. Johnson. He was once talking about *Antony and Cleopatra,* and of course this was back in the eighteenth century, when you were supposed to conform to the unities of time and place, so there was a lot of controversy about Shakespeare's Fourth Act, where there are seventeen or eighteen scene changes (Dryden had even rewritten the play to clear up Shakespeare's "errors"). Anyway, Boswell asks Johnson about the defensibility of all these fantastic things, and Johnson says, "Sire, anyone who goes into a theater and thinks he is walking into ancient Egypt is crazy to begin with!" So when you enter *my* stage, my stories, you are entering the fabric of my reality. The delight for me is to take you into this world as far as I can. I fail as a writer if I can't get you into the artifice, if I can't exercise the full range of my comic imagination.

LM: You were speaking a minute ago about your interest in compression—is this why you've tended to write short fiction instead of novels?

MA: No, it's more a matter of not having had the time for novels. The one period when I had an extra three months to work, I wrote *Zip.* If I had more time, more grants, I'd write more novels. Some stories, of course, can't ever be more than stories, but with other stories you can add a few characters, let things go further, and pretty soon a novel is forming. Usually by the time I get to page ten I'm already looking for an ending. Still, if I could give myself months rather than weeks, I might be looking in different directions. That's the situation with Ray Carver, by the way—he says he's never had time to write a novel, so he's settled for short fiction. For most of us, that's the difference between being a story writer and being a novelist.

SG: How have you arrived at page ten? Do your stories have any consistency in the way they begin?

MA: No, not that I'm aware of. Sometimes they start with a name or just a line, it's never much. A few years ago, I found the note in which I wrote out the whole first part of "The Oranging of America." My wife had worked as the dean of a beauty academy that was located on the top floor of an old motel. On the bottom floor was a guy who sold pots and pans to engaged women: The Cadillac of Cookery, he called it. I was unemployed and writing four or five pages of the kind of stuff I've just been complaining about—realistic stuff about a beauty academy, this odd place with mannequin heads in the windows. But something about that place struck me. It was *not* a Howard Johnson's motel. Then suddenly—and I have no idea where this came from—I turned a page of the notebook and the first half of "The Oranging of America," with Howard Johnson and Millie and all of that, emerged right in the middle of that other story. What triggered it was, I guess, the motel. So, on the one hand, I had consciously been working with all this realistic, really dull material, and then suddenly something else took over, the material came to life and was transformed in "The Oranging of America." It's that "something else," and not my conscious mind, that gets my stories going when I'm working well.

SG: This sounds like a very intuitive process.

MA: It certainly is *not* an intellectual process. I don't start with an idea, nor do I ever know what's going to happen next or use any outlines. That's why writing is exciting for me. I get interested in the characters and I want to see what's going to happen next. I have to feel my way toward the end, intuit what will work. Since I like the stories and the people in them, I usually want to give my work a happy ending. That's the child's wish for good behavior that I have carried wholly with me into adult life.

LM: Your writing has a distinct sound or cadence to it, despite all the voices you project. Do you write for a listener as well as for a reader?

MA: I don't read my stuff aloud while I'm writing, but I know how it sounds. So I'm not writing for the listener precisely, but I am writing rhythmically. Since I literally don't know what my stories "mean," in a conscious way, my touchstone is actually the rhythm, the cadence. As long as it sounds right, I don't mind much whether it's true or not.

SG: Do you have a set writing routine?

MA: No, I have children with whom I'm busy most of the day. I try to write early in the day, rather than later on, so I won't be too tired. But I don't have much in the way of organized habits. Everywhere I go these days writers are all talking about computers and word processors, and I'm embarrassed to admit that I don't even know how to type. I could probably stand a computer more than a typewriter, since at least they're quiet. And I love the idea of being able to have a clean copy right away because I rewrite things so many times that a lot of times I can't decipher my own scribblings. I don't write with a quill pen, but I am old fashioned.

LM: One of your distinctive features has been your tendency to freely insert "real people" into your works. What's your interest in these figures?

MA: They're shortcuts. If I use J. Edgar Hoover in a work, it seems to me that everyone in our culture who has done his job has already created Hoover in their minds. Why should I have to use an anonymous figure to represent this type of man? I'd have to do all this kind of thing: the gray fedora, the mustache—you know, the G-man image— the steel blue suit, glinting eyes, black revolver, the shoes shined every day. Then I'd have to show him with a shoeshine boy, show him with his trusty lieutenants, show him moving around in the bureaucracy. Why should I bother with all that? It's already been created for me. Everyone who's ever read a newspaper already knows all that. This is what's wonderful about using someone like Howard Johnson or the man who made Kleenex or Coca-Cola: I can give you all that with just a name. Yet I can make these figures into something that's my own. Of course, this sort of reliance can become silly, but in a way that's what famous people are for. That's why we watch television and sports. *Myths* is probably a better word than *shortcuts*, but these myths are out there and writers may as well make use of them. Why do people put their names on things if they don't want us to use them? J. C. Penney, F. W. Woolworth, Sears. If you look back far enough, they're people. When you go through public buildings you can see that everything is named after some person. What's this town? San Diego must have been named after somebody, some saint. We forget that the origins of all these things are people, that Howard Johnson was once a human being. And of course most fictional characters are based on real people anyway. Not wholly, but writers often take a fragment of a real person and then invent and change things.

LM: Obviously, though, when you choose a specific person for your stories—like Howard Johnson in "The Oranging of America" or Walt Disney in "Disneyad" or Hoover in *Zip*—you have something specific in mind. You could have used other franchise names in "The Oranging of America," McDonald's or Colonel Sanders or whatever. You must have selected Howard Johnson because his name has a certain specific resonance.

MA: Sure, because I was interested in the specifics of what Howard Johnson represented to me. I was interested in that image of the little dots he had in the car that made up his image of America, and what he was doing to that image. That's why I use specifically biblical language to describe what he does. I was interested in comfort and safety, all those things that motels *are*. Last night, on that cold, rainy evening when I flew in here to San Diego, I was *glad* to have that La Jolla motel to check into.

LM: Reviewers certainly seem to misunderstand the way in which you're using the materials of popular culture—they seem bewildered that you're not being purely ironic.

MA: Right. Some people fail to see that I'm not interested in that *economic entity* at all, with either Howard Johnson or Walt Disney. My interests aren't in the literal stuff but in what these figures represent, what arises from these institutions, the characters who evolve from them. Who provides that kind of refuge and human safety? I didn't care so much that they make money from these situations (though they do, of course); I wanted to present that image of understanding human limits and needs.

SG: I was struck with some of the little details you provide for some of your mythic figures: J. Edgar Hoover never sending any inter-office memos, that sort of quirky information. Do you make any effort to research the lives of these people, or is all this fabricated?

MA: I never research these characters. In fact, it's just the opposite: I never *want* to know. This seems a bit odd, but with a historical figure I wouldn't ever want to know more than I already do about what people wore, say; I want to be perfectly free to make all that up. If I were writing about seventeenth-century Russia or England and I wanted the people to wear Levi's, I would have them wear Levi's. I want the freedom to change things because, finally, what difference does it make if I'm inventing rather than transcribing these details? I'm interested in the central things about my characters, not in the details.

SG: Disney appears in several of your works. What did he represent for you?

MA: Disney was a shortcut that let me get right at all the craziness of America. It's a wonderful image: Disney*land*, Disney*world*. These are glorifications of childhood that make sense to me, yet they're such trivializations. So in "Small Island Republics" I had Taiwan being safe, not as a political state, but under the protection of Disneyland. That's an enormous trivialization. That story is an example of the way in which I think I am being a social critic: I was suggesting that letting everything be trivialized into this cute mouse is where all the safety is today. I was very interested in politics with that story, and the political situation is very complicated in Taiwan. That kind of political complexity demands complex treatment, which is why I want all the doubleness suggested in that story. There is no single answer to the situation. As a leftist, I can't support the regime in Taiwan; on the other hand, we have a continuing relationship with Taiwan involving several gener-

ations of people and huge, well-functioning economic ties. So what
are you going to do?

SG: There appear to be a lot of similarities between you and your
character Ira in *Zip*.

MA: To an extent, sure. I changed Ira's grandmother into a pretty
harsh character—she was actually based on my grandfather, who just
died last October at the age of 106. Like Ira, I lived with my grandmother; we all lived in the same house in Grand Rapids. It was a
Protestant town, not only Protestant but Calvinist, so there I was,
observing all those strange cultural things that I am still amazed at.
My family was always fascinated by what the *goyim* did. *Goyim* were
marvelous creatures to me—we'd go to the supermarket and watch
goyim shop, watch them eat, all sorts of things. The analogy that comes
to mind is the way Isaac Babel describes the Cossacks. In one of his
stories there's a wonderful description of Babel in his Odessa ghetto,
looking up at a Cossack dressed in leather boots up to his hips, his
legs like a beautiful girl's, and there's this sickly sweet smell of soap
all over him. In some ways that may be what I'm getting at in all the
sports stuff I write—I look up at Moses Malone like that, although of
course there's not anything political or anti-Semitic about Malone. But
for me they're all absolutely marvelous creatures, not just seven-foot
basketball players but all *goyim*. In some ways, all people. My grandmother was a child in Odessa during World War I and then she came
right after the war to a town in Michigan and lived there fifty or sixty
years. She never spoke English and was continually amazed by the
life around her, as if she were living on the moon. Partly because of
her, I've never taken the other, *goyim* side of life for granted. I'm
constantly amazed by the things I see around me: the motels, the
supermarkets, the daily behavior of regular people, who are wondrous
creatures to me.

LM: Maybe that helps explain why you adopt the perspective of the
perpetual outsider. Is that a conscious strategy?

MA: Not at all. I'm just surprised that other people aren't as amazed
as I am by daily life.

LM: The figure of the orphan, or the person whose father dies,
appears in a lot of your fiction, in ways that make me suspect your
own father's death had a big impact on you.

MA: It changed my life. My father died when I was twenty-two,
and by that time I had already started thinking of myself as a writer.
I was at Stanford in the graduate writing program when he died, and
I came back to Michigan and was out of school for a year working,
driving a truck. After his death I seemed to lose that intense ambition

to be a writer. His death affected me in all sorts of ways that must filter into my fiction, though not consciously.

SG: Was a writing career something you'd been interested in even as a kid?

MA: No, what I really wanted to be was a basketball player. I still do. My father had been a club fighter, so boxing was always on my mind, too. One of the earliest sports events I remember was going to the Golden Gloves. I was four years old and I remember it very clearly. I thought *I* was going to fight. I came home in tears; here I had gone to the Golden Gloves at the Grand Rapids Civic Auditorium with my father and his best friend, and I took my boxing gloves. I really wanted to get in the ring and knock 'em dead. I caused such a ruckus that my father finally had to take me home. But I always knew I could write. My grandmother was a great storyteller, so I grew up as close to stories as people do to the daily weather reports. My grandmother was always telling stories about her village in Lithuania, so I was also living in this town she described, totally immersed in everything she talked about: the names of the people, the odd Russian and Lithuanian characters, all this told without any historical perspective. She didn't know she had lived through the Russian Revolution or World War I; she only knew these things as they had affected her village. So I had both things at once: mainstream white Protestant America, and always that distant oral European world. I knew I wasn't part of that world of my grandmother's memory, yet I was.

LM: Were you raised mainly in a home where Yiddish was being spoken?

MA: Yes. Choosing English as my language was very important to me. I knew Yiddish before I knew English, which puts me in Isaac Singer's generation, linguistically, though I am two generations removed from most people who grew up with Yiddish. I was comfortable with Yiddish. When I finally chose to start writing in English, to start writing on one side of the page rather than the other—this was a conscious choice, made while I was in grade school—I saw that I belonged in the real world of Michigan in 1950 rather than in the world of my grandmother's imagination, the Lithuania of 1910.

SG: The spectre of death and the issue of people's relationship to death haunts a lot of your fiction. Your characters almost try to figure out ways of outwitting death.

MA: You've hit on another thing that, in retrospect, I can see is very central to my work and to my life as well. These jogging shoes I'm wearing aren't just for decoration! But this business about trying to figure out ways of outwitting death—isn't that what all our life *is*?

LM: Let's talk about the political and social values in your work.

Despite what a lot of reviewers have claimed, your fiction is almost all highly politicized. Growing up a Jew in a Protestant neighborhood must have made you aware of ideological issues early on.

MA: My political awareness evolved in a highly complicated fashion. My grandfather, who was an exploited laborer all his life (he was a baker), was totally anti-union. He was the right-wing faction of the family. According to my grandmother, the only time he made any money at all was after he retired; he got some job in a major bakery where there was a union. So he probably was seventy-five before he earned anything like a decent wage. I used to go to the voting booth with him. In '52 I was a ten-year-old Stevenson liberal, and we had a big argument in the voting booth because he wanted to vote for Eisenhower, along with everyone else. We were in there for half an hour arguing loudly in Yiddish, and finally a poll worker came in and said, "There's not even supposed to be two of you in here!"

We were working-class people and even though we were not a political family I guess I automatically understood that my sympathies were with the workers. We lived in a poor neighborhood, where most of the houses had tin cans and broken glass lying around, so I felt guilty because we had a car and a house with grass and a hedge around it. It was an interesting kind of slum, a Polish neighborhood where the people carried an Eastern European anti-Semitism with them. I grew up with Polish spoken in the streets, and most of the swearing in Polish, but it was a strange situation: the Polish Gentiles knew we were Jews, so they helped us build a *succah*. They would institutionally hate us since we were Jews, yet we were perfectly friendly with them. They thought *we* were crazy because we built this hut in September and didn't turn on the lights on Saturday. We thought *they* were crazy because we could watch them kill chickens in their backyards and get drunk. So we would marvel at all the things they did, and they would marvel at us, and there was a sort of safe anti-Semitism. In a way it was like living in Isaac Babel's world, and in a way it was like living in Dwight Eisenhower's world.

SG: With that kind of background, going away to college—especially during the social and political upheavals of the '60s—must have been a strange experience. You must have had to break away from the provincial Jewish world you've just described and confront a lot of larger political issues.

MA: Yes, it was both things at once. I was strongly politicized in college in the SDS days, and at the same time I was being exposed to the white bourgeois Jewish world for the first time. I belonged to a Jewish fraternity—in fact, I was president of it—yet I became very involved in the political activities of the '60s, too. When I went to

Stanford, it was a perfectly conventional, right-wing place; the student newspaper even supported Barry Goldwater. I didn't stay there long enough for that atmosphere to affect me much. So while my leftist orientation didn't specifically come from my family, it did come from understanding the nature of the lives of the poor all around me.

LM: Your stories frequently return to mind-body dualism. This is at the center of "Free Agents," for example.

MA: Again, I can't explain this emphasis any more than you can. But look at me: I'm 5'4" and weigh maybe 115 pounds. But part of me still thinks that I'm a basketball player, this enormous being in the world. All my life I've literally lived by my wits, my cunning, my mind. At the same time, even though my family were all short, in-bred, Eastern European Jews, my grandmother told me I was one of the truly big people in the world. So I think I have a different sense of myself than what I objectively am, the way other people see me. What *you* see is a short, thin man. But I see myself as Dr. J! That's part of this obsession, though there is probably more to it that I don't understand.

LM: The ideal in your work seems to be developing some sort of harmony between mind and body—isn't that what Ira says the meaning of "zip" is, "The mind and body together"? This idea is evident in the yogurt story and "Vegetable Love," and in a way that's Millie's problem in "The Oranging of America"—that inability to separate her mind from her body.

MA: Well, it all comes down to this: the most interesting things about all of us are, of course, our minds. We know this not only from all the twentieth-century interest in inwardness in literature, but from what we see about one another. I'm interested in your physical presence here, but your spiritual presence is the most important thing. This presence is wonderful and seems to me to touch on all the things that are transcendent, eternal; but on the other hand we have these bodies failing us all the time. That's what death is, and sickness, and disease. I've understood frailty right from the start. My grandmother had an extraordinary mind and seemed to understand everything, even though she was not educated and didn't even speak the language around her. But she had a stiff leg and it was difficult for her to walk, ever since she fell off a freight train somewhere in Russia. She spent most of her time in the kitchen but would come into the living room to watch "I Love Lucy" and "The $64,000 Question." And she understood what was going on right off. She watched "The $64,000 Question" and I'd translate for her into English and right off she told me it was a fake. We had big arguments about that. She didn't think anyone could know all that stuff and she didn't believe they even gave them the money. Only dummies like me were taken in by the whole thing. While I was growing up, these other processes were going on around me—I'd see my grandmother as frail and old, yet she was an incredibly powerful person because of her mind. So I always understood that the mind was everything. I was constantly angry—and I still am—that the body holds us up. Yet I also love the body. The love is one reason I wrote that book about fighting and have written so many stories about sports heroes. The body is also a marvelous thing.

LM: Several of your most interesting characters are entrepeneurs. A contrast typically develops between the faceless, mass-market, big-business types (the big boss in "Gas Stations" or the Colonel in "My Real Estate") versus the small-time businessman. What is there about this business aspect of the American Dream that you find so compelling?

MA: I'm interested in business in very direct ways. I had a small health food store for a while. It was a porch in an old building, not as big as your living room, but I thought I was going to become a millionaire. We paid a hundred dollars a month in rent, and if we made three dollars a day we'd figure we had made enough for the rent and we'd close down. So I obviously wasn't very good at it. We were the first people in Houston to sell Celestial Seasonings teas. I should have stayed with that—if I had become the distributor then and given up teaching, I probably would have been much better off financially. But I had all those dreams about selling dried beans and franchises all over the world, and there we were barely making three dollars a day to stay in business. My grandmother's vision was that I'd become a merchant and have two stores (I guess with two I could have made six dollars a day!). So I've always been interested in business. Even as a writer I think of myself as a merchant. Among other things, I like to make money by my work, to get paid for what I'm doing. I'm not interested in art for art's sake.

SG: Your thinking of yourself as a merchant is interesting, since your work so often criticizes the whole capitalist system. But in *Zip*, where you seem to be openly attacking capitalist exploitation, you don't present figures like Castro sympathetically, either.

MA: I am not altogether full of admiration for Castro. These situations are mixed bags. Now I understand my own political feelings. I know I wouldn't vote for Reagan and I pretty much identify with the leftists in all causes, but not universally. For instance, I split with SDS very early over the issue of Israel. I'm an ardent Zionist, and although I'm critical of many Israeli policies right now, back in the '60s many of my colleagues on the left saw a one-to-one connection between Israel and South Vietnam that just wasn't there. Ironically, many of these young people were militant Jews with much different backgrounds from mine. I saw very clearly that they were reacting against their mothers and fathers on this issue, whereas I continued to understand Israel mainly as a refuge. So there are no simple divisions on any political situation.

LM: In "Understanding Alvarado," you have that baseball player being caught between two guys who only want to use him to preach their own ideologies, while the poor middleman just gets screwed.

MA: That's exactly what I was intending. With all ideologies, it's always the guy in the middle—that's all of us—who's getting screwed.

LM: Was that player based on Minnie Minoso?

MA: Yes, although I had to change his name. It was the sound of that name that got me started with that story, so it was a great problem for me when I discovered I would have to change it. Somehow real names often trigger my imagination. I don't know why I use them— I make up everything except the names. But the Bantam Books lawyer told me that Minnie Minoso was a private person in a way that, say, Howard Johnson or Richard Nixon was not, so I couldn't use his name. But I couldn't change the story completely—I needed those o's for the rhythm. And I needed a heroic name like Minoso's: Orestes "Minnie" Minoso. So I finally came up with Achilles Alvarado, which still isn't as good, but I wanted that Greek heroic suggestion.

SG: Since you've brought up heroic parallels, maybe you could discuss the ending of *Zip*, where you have Jesus ascend into the heavens. Was that purely ironic? After all, Jesus doesn't seem to do much in the way of redeeming anybody in *Zip*, which made me wonder if we should view him sympathetically.

MA: I guess I was criticizing the Christian worldview. Jesus just ascends and, as you've put it, nobody's redeemed. Unconsciously that's probably what I was implying there, but mainly I was just being playful. Jesus in *Zip* is another of those middlemen we were talking about a minute ago. Not that Ira was trying to exploit him—Ira was all tied up in the tangle of his own life and wasn't trying to use Jesus in a conscious way—but if you look at the situation in another way you can see Ira as being a kind of ideologue who *is* exploiting him. Both views could be true at once.

LM: And Jesus is obviously being exploited by the communists as well.

MA: Yes, he's the man in the middle, in his own way, the way Alvarado is the dupe in "Understanding Alvarado." I've always been interested in that ability to understand that there's more than one way of seeing the same thing. That's the texture I'm after: given all the same events, there are always many possible interpretations. I don't want to create those single, simple interpretations in my works because you can't do that with the world. So I like the story to be simple in a certain way, I like the narrative to be simple and straightforward but created with all these other textures. I want my readers to be able to understand what I'm doing. I don't like to mystify readers. I want to be clear and then, through reverberations, pass along in a straightforward narrative that fertile unclarity that's in my mind.

SG: Why do you use sports and sports figures so much in your writing?

MA: Sports were very much part of the background of my childhood. Boxing was one of the few things in America that my grandpa liked; we watched the Friday night fights after we had a very traditional Shabbat dinner. My father was a great sports fan, too, so I grew up literally listening to 154 baseball games a year. For the big games my father would come home and we'd listen to the game together. Then with early television the Cubs games used to come in, so often I'd be watching the Cubs and listening to the Tigers, and sometimes to the White Sox, too, since we could get that station. So there was all that *sports talk* in the air, which is really what interested me more than any of those other things in a story like "Alvarado." Literally, those voices.

SG: Was it this involvement with boxing that determined the central focus of *Zip*?

MA: In the original version there was no fighter at all. Ira wasn't the manager of a fighter; he was a truck driver, just as I had been when I returned to Michigan after my father died. In fact, the original book was much closer to being a direct description of things that I had really experienced than the version that eventually appeared. After I had worked on the novel for three or four years, I realized that the version was *too* autobiographical and that I needed the metaphor of boxing to create distance. I seem to need that realistic background work before I can take the imaginative jump to *not* telling it the way it was. I have a version of a novel I'm working on now for which I've done the background stuff. This background won't necessarily be the specific material I'll use in the novel, but it lets me get to know the characters so that I can later make them up. I need to first see things straight and then I can let my imagination go off to see what happens. It's like introducing myself to my characters first.

SG: Were there any books you read as a young man, or in graduate school, that helped shape your literary sensibility?

MA: The literary experiences that mattered were much earlier than graduate school. I read all those boys' books, and one that had a great influence on me was by a guy named John R. Tunis.

LM: *The Kid from Tompkinsville*? That book had a big impact on me, too, when I was planning on a major-league pitching career.

MA: That was it—I'd forgotten the title. Those books formed me, probably taught me morality; they were very powerful works in their own way. The first "real" book I remember was *Les Miserables*, which I didn't know was French; and I read Dostoyevsky. I just picked these books up at the library and started reading them, and to me they were all English books—it took me a while to figure out why they all had these funny names. I was only dimly aware of other languages, which is odd because I was so aware of Yiddish and Polish. My two older sisters were both English majors and they brought home books all the time. When I was in the seventh grade my oldest sister was already in college, so I remember her bringing back *Catcher in the Rye*, which I knew was a terrific book even though I didn't know anything about literature. It was the first book about sexual things that I'd read, so it was an important book for me. Basically I read the equivalent of whatever courses my sisters were taking at the time. I tried to read *Ulysses* in the ninth grade; I was totally mystified, but I worked at it and understood some of the funny stuff. I'm against giving kids too much direction in their reading—they should be free to read everything. I know I was. So at the same time I was reading *Catcher in the Rye* I was also still probably reading one of those kids' biographies of George Washington Carver. Those early readings form you in many ways. Certainly as soon as I found *Les Miserables* I could never again go back to the boys' books and science fiction. That book also taught me something about circumstantiality (though I didn't learn that word until much later)—that sense that you'd never see a certain character again and then, 150 pages later, there he'd be. That seemed to be the way it would be in the real world. That's why I expect Nixon to be back, emerging from the sewers of San Clemente one of these days.

LM: Did you try your hand at writing as a kid?

MA: No, I was just reading everything I could when I wasn't out playing ball. I read Flaubert, Dostoyevsky, a lot of the classics when I was in high school but I wasn't thinking that I was going to be a writer. I wasn't even thinking about going to college very much at that stage. Everyone had told me how hard college was going to be, especially since I had come from a very bad high school, but fortunately my grandmother had told me I was smart, and I chose to believe her. When I got to college, pre-orientation week was the worst time. You had all those mixers and parties every night, and I was awful at that since I was so shy and embarrassed. But once school started it was wonderful. I just ate up reading. I had come from a macho world of people stealing cars, my grandparents' serious Jewish life, and my father's middle-class life of sports-watching, so I never thought that I'd be reading Shakespeare and liking it. It was actually a great relief.

SG: So where did this impetus to be a writer come from?

MA: I was always interested in storytelling (as opposed to just *writing*), mainly because of my grandmother. When I was in kindergarten and the only Jew in school, I heard all this stuff about Santa Claus and the Baby Jesus and the stars in the sky and the wise men and the crucifixion, and all this seemed very wonderful to me. So I came home and told this to my grandmother in Yiddish, and she said, "That's news to me." The way she'd heard it was that Jesus was a kind of magician who was killed by Jewish women—he was on a flying carpet and they threw stones and cabbages at him, and knocked him down and killed him, and thereafter there had been all this emnity against the Jews by all the Gentiles. And she told me that all the Santa Claus stuff was made up. When I went back to school and told all the kids that Jesus was a magician and that Santa Claus was a fake, I was instructed not to come to school around Christmas time. Anyway, I knew as early as five or six how much I loved stories because of how much I loved my grandmother's stories. Her stories weren't self-conscious—she wasn't a writer—but she was telling about the adventures of her life; she knew what storytelling was and she got right to the central matters of human understanding. She was also a great satirist about what little she saw of the American world around her.

I knew very early on that *that* was what I loved—storytelling—but for a long time I didn't know what one *did* to become a writer. So I went to writers' school at Stanford. The stuff I did later on, after my father died, like getting my Ph.D. in English literature, was just something I did that would maybe get me a job. I never lost that desire to read, but I also never could take writing academic papers very seriously. I wanted to tell stories.

SG: As I was reading "Inside Norman Mailer," it was tempting to see that story as an expression of your own ambitions.

MA: Yes, that's me there, and that's my favorite early story. It was a piece that came all at once. I was driving from Michigan back to Texas—a lot of writers have told me they do their best work while they're driving—and on one of those desolate stretches of road between Texarkana and Houston the whole story, the whole metaphor of fighting Norman Mailer, just came to me. When I arrived in Houston I had to shut myself away because I wanted to finish it, to see what happened. I had no idea who was going to win that fight. I was gearing myself up to teach Homer at the time, and that's why the story is filled with classical allusions (it even ends with a Homeric simile, you'll notice). I enjoyed mingling that literary criticism with the boxing talk, but what was really happening was that I was thirty-two at the time and thought I was a pretty good writer. I wanted to be known, wanted to say, "Hey, why don't you people pay attention to *me*?" But by the end of the story, I also came to the understanding that some of this sense was a young man's bravado, that Mailer would eat me up in a real confrontation, that he possessed this enormous presence. So I was announcing (the way a young man does) my intentions, my power, but by the end of the story I realized that this wasn't enough. It's that enlightenment I achieve at the end that's important. Mailer had become a kind of Zen teacher. The story has often been misunderstood as an attack on Mailer, but I meant it to be full of praise for him; he's supposed to be seen as a glowing, soporific continent, a Buddha, someone who has taken all the risks, who has to be dealt with. At the end of the story I felt I had become a seer in relation to Mailer and also in relation to my own writing. That's why it's my favorite story. I came out of the experience with a lot of confidence, almost as if I really *had* done battle.

LM: What's your reaction to the kind of pigeonhole that reviewers seem to have placed you in—the "zany," "pop writer" kind of tags?

MA: I've been generally angry about that reaction. I was really pissed off when *The Nation* referred to me as being "zany" when they reviewed *Zip*. Part of the problem might have been the book's title—I hadn't been able to think of one, and "Zip" was the idea of Ted Solotaroff, my editor. It was a good title but it allowed book reviewers to go for the easy mark. *Zip* is not a zany book to me, nor was I interested in zany situations. If anything is zany, it's not my books but the world. It's Kissinger and Nixon and people who go around saying "At this point in time." That's where writers like Coover and I are on the same frequency. *I'm* perfectly lucid, it's Ronald Reagan who's zany! *I* know that catsup is not a vegetable.

Thomas Victor

An Interview with
Ann Beattie

We met Ann Beattie at the front desk of the Ambassador Hotel in Los Angeles in rainy twilight in January 1982. Her room was freezing, she said, so we all welcomed the excuse to troop across the lobby, buzzing with acupuncture conventioneers, to a dimly lit bar. She was dressed casually—Eastern casual, despite her cowboy boots—and with her long brown hair and open youthful face she might easily have been mistaken for the English graduate student she had been just a few years earlier.

It was a relaxed, enjoyable conversation, partly due to Beattie's easy humor and utter lack of pretension, and partly due to a background of shared experiences—we were the same age, had gone to college in the '60s, and had experienced similar cycles of graduate school, divorce, and arrivals at careers based on literature. She was visiting Los Angeles as a consultant for a Public Broadcasting System production of one of her stories, and she fell easily into a series of amusing anecdotes that touched on West Coast vs. East Coast sensibilities, the surreality of Los Angeles and television, and her own efforts at getting through it all. These stories and the ones that followed at The Beanery, where we went to dinner following the interview, were told with zest and delight—Ann Beattie clearly enjoys telling stories, enjoys festooning the absurdities and frustrations of experiences for the amusement of herself and others. Despite the frequency with which she pokes fun at her own supposed neuroses, these personal recollections, like her fiction, have an air of sane clarity.

Since her short stories first began appearing in the mid-1970s, mainly in the *New Yorker*, Ann Beattie has emerged as one of the most distinctive voices in contemporary American fiction. Her first two book-length works appeared in 1976: *Chilly Scenes of Winter*, a novel, and *Distortions*, a collection of stories. Widely praised when they appeared, these two volumes also attached to her the label of "post-sixties chronicler"—a label that has, unfortunately, tended to deflect attention from Beattie's much broader concerns with the difficulties of making sense out of our past and of making ourselves understood in the present. These first works did, however, exhibit the chief aspects of her method and particular vision. Presented in strikingly dispassionate, unadorned prose, these books captured the mundane rhythms of the lives of people whose youthful dreams and ambitions are slowly fading amidst the offices, shopping malls, commuter trains, and suburban banality of middle-class America. *Chilly Scenes of Winter* (later made into the film *Head Over Heels*) can perhaps best be likened to *Catcher in the Rye*, for there, too, we are given a quirky protagonist—wonderfully brought to life through his habits of speech and behavior—who feels alienated from a society dominated by phoniness and crass materialism. Like Holden, Charles is a romantic innocent ill equipped to cope; his nostalgic dreams about the '60s really just obscure his inability to face the present, as he transforms the memory of a lost love's chocolate-orange soufflé into an emblem of all that he has lost.

These early works, which include her next story collection, *Secrets and Surprises* (1978), also exhibit other Beattie trademarks, in their focus on friendship (romantic or sexual relationships usually lead to disappointment and frustration), their fusion of background and foreground, and a tendency to leave conflicts unresolved. Like the art of the superrealists whose paintings she admires, her art is deceptively simple: her eye for telling details—the names of songs playing in the background, the nicknames emblazoned on café waitresses' uniforms, the myriad ticky-tack items that clutter our lives and define our personalities—allows her to present characters and situations in a vivid, remarkably economical manner. This emphasis on depicting the surface features of her characters' lives suggests that Beattie isn't interested in delving into the complex moral and psychological underpinnings of modern life; but if Beattie is more effective in showing us situations than in analyzing them, the accumulation of surface nevertheless literalizes the emptiness, triviality, and bewilderment of the people she presents.

Four more recent books, *Falling in Place* (1980), *The Burning House* (1982), *Love Always* (1985), and *"Where You'll Find Me" and Other Stories* (1986), show Beattie refining her methods, bringing in a wider range of narrative approaches and voices, thickening the textures of her material. This increasing complexity is certainly noticeable in *Falling in Place*, with its multiple perspectives and interweaving plot lines. Essentially comic in tone, the novel also develops a satiric, disturbing view of the loneliness, dissatisfactions, and repressed anxieties and fears of ordinary Americans, who are metaphorically likened to George Segal's eerie, lifeless dummies. Like Raymond Carver and Frederick Barthelme—the two contemporary authors most similar in terms of stylistic and thematic concerns—Beattie focuses on what Grace Paley calls "the little disturbances of man." This emphasis allows her to develop a wide-ranging critique of the perils and attractions of life in America today.

Larry McCaffery: Family relationships in your books are often pretty awful. Are you dredging up something out of some dark past?

Ann Beattie: I'd say that family relationships in my books tend to be made fun of more than being really nightmarish. The situation in *Falling in Place* is an exception in that John and Louise have a relationship that is pretty terrible. But my presentation of family in *Falling in Place* isn't autobiographical. For instance, the inspiration for my presentation of the kids, John Joel and Mary, didn't grow out of my childhood but from the kids I watched on the commuter train going from Westport to New York. Not only did I not have a brother or sister myself, but I didn't have a lot of close friends as a child, partly because I lived in a neighborhood where there were no other children and partly because I was very shy. As for my own parents, I get along really well with my family, and I always have. I don't think we have a world in common in terms of the way we look at life, but we have a lot of other things we can share. Both my mother and my father have a bizarre sense of humor, for example, and so do I (although all three of us have distinctly different *kinds* of bizarre senses of humor). So I don't have anything nightmarish to say about family life based on my own experiences (although notice I don't have a family of my own). Actually I've watched more families from a distance than I really know personally.

LM: Do you think that growing up without a brother or sister might have made you more receptive to the sense of friendship that seems to appear so often in your books?

AB: Probably. Right now I live alone (I'm divorced) and it means a lot to me to have close friends these days. Being close to your friends was more or less taken for granted in college—I mean, everyone could appear at everyone else's place, mainly because it was just across the hall, so you could just knock on anyone's door. Now I'm living in New

York City and I'm vulnerable to all kinds of things (I barely trust what I hear through the intercom). So a certain type of closeness just isn't possible anymore; the people that I could knock on the doors of ten years ago have a two-year-old kid whom I'd wake up now if I came knocking. But this is a digression. Yes, close friendships are very important to me, maybe now more than ever, and I believe in friendship as an ideal because that seems easier than being part of a family or being in love.

LM: Were you one of those people, like Charles in *Chilly Scenes of Winter* and like me and most of my friends, who *almost* went to Woodstock and were *almost* arrested for demonstrating?

AB: I almost went to Woodstock, totally inadvertently, not knowing what it was going to be and not even particularly liking that music at the time. A friend of mine had her brother's car that weekend and was thinking about going up there, but for some reason we didn't go and I don't regret having missed it. I watched the '60s on TV. I did go to a couple of the marches on Washington and I was on the right side of things, but I didn't march up and down on the streets to support these things. I probably should have, but I didn't. Frankly, I don't think the '60s have much to do with my work.

Sinda Gregory: Why do you think it is that every time you're interviewed you seem to have to field all those questions about the '60s and the counterculture?

AB: I seem to have gone on record saying a number of things that I would never have instigated, so that now I'm put in the position of having to vehemently deny that the '60s have anything to do with my work. Really, this position probably results from the overreaction by critics, initially, who felt that the '60s were so central to my work.

LM: Of course, some of your characters *do* lament the passing of the '60s, seeming to be involved with it at least in a nostalgic sense. *Was* there something special about the '60s that makes your characters feel that way?

AB: Personally speaking, yes—and for the obvious reasons that don't even need to be gone into anymore. There was some kind of feeling of closeness in the society during that period. People had a mutual anger, and people were moving toward—or feigned to be moving toward—some sort of mutual respect. Those things were different from what existed in the '50s, or from what exists now. But I don't think, if you go through my books and stories one by one, that you can find many characters who give voice to lamenting the '60s. I think this impression is largely the one created by Charles in *Chilly Scenes of Winter*. And what I meant to be doing with Charles there is similar to what Salinger was doing with Holden Caulfield. People misread *Catcher*

in the Rye when they think, "Ah, poor, sweet Holden." Actually I think
Salinger was directing a lot of dry irony at Holden. I certainly meant
to suggest that Charles was neurotic, obsessive, extremely defensive,
and that anything that fit his purpose—such as the view that "Oh,
there was once a romantic past and now it's gone"—was a good cover
for him. So I was more interested in him as a case study than as
somebody who could really be representative of some sort of past. I
mean, Charles will take *anything* as an excuse, he's compulsive; but
this nostalgia for the '60s is a very easy excuse. People today evoke
the '60s all the time and try to pretend to feel some sort of romantic
bond with them, but this is falling flatter and flatter.

SG: Why do you think so many readers and critics have missed the
irony in your presentation of the romantic dreams of Charles and Sam?

AB: Today we've got a lot of books that seem recognizably "'60s
books"—there are a lot of them on publishers' desks, they're what
people are writing today—but that wasn't true in 1976. People *wanted*
a book about the '60s when *Chilly Scenes* appeared, so their reactions
to the book were colored by these desires. They didn't really get what
they wanted, but they seemed to want it badly enough to misrepresent
my intentions. Had I known they wanted it that much, I don't know
if I wouldn't have sold out and given it to them. But it gets tiresome,
protesting that I *didn't*.

LM: You say of one of your characters in "Friends" that he "still
berated himself for still believing that the most honorable activity was
working from nine to five." This seems to be a problem for a number
of your characters—that is, trying to cope with what are essentially
ordinary lives. Don't you find this kind of thing all the time—that,
after all the build-ups the people of our generation went through, it's
especially difficult for us to accept life as it comes to be for most people?

AB: I think I believe more in the Chinese curse: "May you have an
interesting life." What I like to fall back on, since it's not what I have,
is thinking that life would be a lot easier if I had a lawyer husband
supporting me in Morristown and my main worries were about Mon-
tessori schools. I'm sure that this romantic illusion is something I hold
onto because it's so impossible. I would probably stop it if it started
becoming possible. Most people would say that the kind of life I lead
is very enviable, and I wouldn't change it; it *is* enviable in many ways,
and even though some people can't imagine the disadvantages of such
a life, I'm willing to pay the price. As for my characters, I'm afraid
the whole question of what they do for jobs is actually less of a
philosophical issue for me than it is a technical problem, because they
have to have money to have mobility and I don't know how people
get money. I know how you can have people not go to the bathroom

in a novel now, because I've become technically good at dodging the mundane when I want to as a writer. The bathroom used to be a problem. You want to be honest about these things: In twenty-four hours, when does somebody pee? But it's not as easy for me to explain mobility. So I give them trust funds or something.

SG: You went to graduate school for a while. What were you there for?

AB: Mainly to avoid working nine to five.

SG: You were studying English, right? Not creative writing?

AB: I wasn't studying any one thing in particular. I was taking professors that I liked, more than caring about the authors in the courses they taught. This got me into great trouble, and I never did get the Ph.D. You had to take five area exams in literature, and I didn't know areas. I would know certain novels and writers, but I wouldn't think of them together. I wouldn't think of Sterne along with Fielding or whatever. I would actually have to walk into my advisor's office and ask, "Who wrote in the eighteenth century?" and get a list and go out and study for three months and then read what it was in vogue to think about eighteenth-century literature and then go and regurgitate it. I thought this whole process was extremely demeaning and boring because I never thought about literature that way.

LM: What turned you into a writer?

AB: I was so goddamn bored in graduate school that I turned into a writer. Why that, as opposed to being turned into a dancer? I suppose because I could do it on my own and I was living in a place where there was no way to study dance.

SG: You hadn't been writing before, in high school or college?

AB: A little bit. I was the editor of the literary magazine at American University. I liked writing. I liked painting. I was an artsy little thing. But I don't really know why writing rather than anything else.

LM: Were there any specific literary influences when you started writing? One writer who comes to mind is Hemingway—there seems to be a similar quality to your prose.

AB: Yes, Hemingway. I didn't read much contemporary literature at all while I was starting out. I occasionally read *Esquire*, but when I started graduate school I was more interested in the writers of the 1920s. I see stylistically that Hemingway is there in my work, and I'm glad that he is, but overall I don't see a great influence of anyone on my work. I hate to answer this question because I hate to sound like an egomaniac, as though I came full-born with my brilliance from the forehead of Zeus. No doubt other people are right—they've found other influences. But when I started writing seriously, I was actually not at all widely read.

LM: So you didn't look to another writer as a kind of model?

AB: Not only was there no model, but I didn't really think of writing as a career when I was starting out. It would have made no more sense than drinking wine and wondering if Claiborne would like to come over and have a drink. In my case, I'd say the whole question of models was moot. I certainly didn't know any writers personally, and I didn't think they had romantic lives. I didn't wish to be a writer and I barely understood that I was becoming one, so there was no reason to look for models.

SG: In an interview in the *New York Times Book Review*, you respond to the comment made by Maynard that you are primarily a chronicler of the '60s counterculture by saying, "It's certainly true that the people I write about are essentially my age, and so they were a certain age in the '60s and had certain common experiences and tend to listen to the same kind of music and get stoned and wear the same kind of clothes, but what I've always hoped for is that somebody will then start talking more about the meat and bones of what I'm writing about." The "meat and bones" that you refer to seems to me to involve the difficulties involved in people understanding each other—the difficulty of saying what we feel, of making ourselves clear, of having the courage or honesty to say what we mean.

AB: Yes, my fiction often has to do with that. A direct result of this breakdown of communication is the breakdown of relationships. I don't think the people in my stories are representative, by the way—that's really off the point of what you just asked me, but it's behind Maynard's comment, and behind what a lot of people have said about my work. I'd say that the people in my fiction reflect some of my own personal problems and concerns, perhaps to an exaggerated degree, but I don't mean them to be taken as representative of the culture. So that's part one of the answer. As to part two, what you're saying sounds perfectly insightful to me—I'd agree that these breakdowns *do* have a lot to do with my work. But even this, I think, tends to generalize a great deal. If I were to ask you to be specific and cite the common denominator between two different stories of mine, I wonder what it would be?

SG: I'd probably say that a lot of your stories seem to focus on relationships in the process of breaking down.

AB: OK, fair enough. But often the people in my stories are unstable in some way even before the relationship. There's no reason to think the breakdown is a *consequence* of the relationship itself.

LM: The other common denominator I'd point to is one Sinda mentioned: in quite a few of your stories you seem to imply that people's relationships break down because they can't express themselves. You don't always explain *why* they are unable to talk to each other, but often your stories have scenes with characters who are totally cut off from or who misunderstand each other.

SG: A good example of this is the scene in *Falling in Place* when John has taken the whole family out for dinner and they're sitting around the table. Each one of them makes a gesture of generosity toward the others that is misconstrued and rejected, so they draw back.

AB: Yes, I'll have to agree that these communication-breakdown scenes do appear in my work, in one form or another. But this is not something I'm doing deliberately. Personally, of course, I believe that many people have a lot of trouble communicating, but I'm afraid this sounds so banal that I hate to dwell on it. When I was working on the scene that Sinda just mentioned, for instance, I was mainly thinking of the literary effect—the tension it creates—and not the general issue involved. If you're mainly interested in showing people not communicating, you ought to be at least as interesting as Harold Pinter.

LM: What I really tend to notice in your fiction is not so much the issues you raise but the *specific people* you place into your stories. What interests *you* about your characters?

AB: I'm often interested in my characters because they can't break away from the situation in which they find themselves. If they can't communicate to begin with, you'd think even more of them would fly off. Part of this interest is a reflection of my own experiences with people. I find it very hard to envy most of the couples I know. I can't imagine exchanging places with those that are together, even those that are happy, because it seems to me they have made so many compromises to be together. So I'm very interested in the fact that there are these personalities who have compromised in so many ways. On the other hand, there are so many people who are together for all the obvious reasons: they don't want to be lonely, or they are in the habit of being together, or this whole Beckettian thing—I can't stay and I can't go. This tug interests me more than the fact that they're not communicating—I want to find out why they're staying and not going.

LM: A lot of your characters are very self-conscious—about their roles, about the clichés they use to express themselves, about almost everything. But this self-awareness inhibits spontaneity or whatever it is that is "natural" in relationships.

AB: Intellectualizing or self-consciousness usually simply allows you to hide from yourself, maybe permanently. People can easily fall into the trap of thinking that to label something is to explain it. If you'll notice, the insights that my characters arrive at aren't very profound. Usually in my stories I've set things up so that one person is basically insightful and the other person isn't. They end up in a tug-of-war when it becomes inconsequential whether they're insightful or not. In "Colorado," Robert knows what the score is with Penelope, but so what? She understands why they've ended up in Vermont, but her understanding doesn't matter. Charles Manson said there was a particular voice telling him to do something, and David Berkowitz said it was a dog, Sam, up in the sky motivating him. Don't people always say that what motivates them is logical? What matters is that they're getting through life and they're unhappy and there's something missing. If I knew what was missing, I'd write about it. I'd write for Hallmark Cards. That would please a lot of my critics.

LM: Some critics have complained that your stories don't offer resolutions to your characters' problems. How do you respond to the idea that writers need to supply answers and not simply to describe problems or situations?

AB: I don't expect answers of anyone other than a medical doctor. No, it wouldn't occur to me that writers should have to supply answers. I certainly don't feel that it's the obligation of any artist to supply answers.

LM: One reviewer said, half-jokingly I think, that no time before 1968 exists in your work. Are you ever tempted to write about a historical period other than the present?

AB: No, I've never tried that type of work, because that would require research and I fear libraries. No kidding, I don't know if I could do it or not, so I've not been tempted in that direction. I'm very much interested in writers who are tempted and do it. Mary Lee Settle is one of my favorite writers, and the background research she undertakes is amazing: she gets herself in a rowboat and goes down a river in West Virginia to see the way it curves at a particular point; then she studies topographical maps, circa 1890, to see if that bend was in the river at that time; then she flies to Boston to listen to a speech JFK gave in a particular town in West Virginia to see how this relates to her material. I'm fascinated with this approach, but it seems like Perry Mason stuff to me. Sleuthing and trying to keep all that in one's mind would be impossible for me. I hate writing novels to begin with because I can't remember what the character did five days ago; so I write everything quickly, including novels. Complexity fouls me up. If I can't remember in a fifteen-page story what one of my characters did on page five, I can take a few minutes and look it up and make sure that the X who walked in on page five was a shit. But if I can't remember whether this character is a shit or not, and I have to take the time to go through chapters one through nineteen to find his off-the-wall comment that *showed* he was a shit, my train of thought is gone. So for me it would be just agonizing to try to go back and write from research and then imagine something. I have a touchstone in that I'm writing out of what happened yesterday.

SG: You just said that you work very quickly. What kinds of writing habits do you have—have you always worked in spurts like this?

AB: No. At first, when I found out there was something I could do—I was learning, teaching myself, mostly, how to write—I wrote a lot more than I do today. Those stories were more speculative and funnier than what I write now. I don't think I have as much to say today. Some of the things that interested me when I was starting out don't interest me as much now, or they interest me in a different way. I've always had what people call "writer's block," but it's never scared me because I never thought of it as that. My total output is pretty large, and I can't be too frightened about deviating from work habits that have always been erratic.

SG: What about the mundane details, like whether or not you work at a typewriter, or during the day?

AB: I always work at a typewriter. I can make some revisions or do fine editing in longhand, but if I'm revising a whole page I always go back to the typewriter. When I lived in the country I usually worked at night, although this isn't true any longer. I find that I'm very lethargic during the day; everything seems distracting, and it's very hard to concentrate. Of course, now I do different kinds of work—when a revised script for PBS is due in forty-eight hours, what are you going to do? Explain that you don't start writing until after midnight? I get in there and start writing right after breakfast. I'm also very neurotic about my work habits. To this day I have my mother mail to me, from Washington, a special kind of typing paper—which isn't even particularly *good* typing paper—from People's Drug Store. It costs about $1.29 a pack. I always used to work in my husband's clothes. He's not my husband any longer, but I still occasionally put on the essential plaid shirt.

LM: What seems to get you to sit down at the typewriter in the first place? Do you have a specific scene or character or sentence in mind?

AB: My stories always seem to begin with something very small, whether it be one or the other of those things you've just mentioned. If I were to say I usually begin with a character, that wouldn't mean that I know the character's occupation or age or whether the character is happy or sad. I *would* know that the character is named Joe. Yes, sometimes the idea that the character's name is Joe has gotten me to the typewriter. More often it's really a physiological feeling that I should write something. This feeling doesn't always work out.

LM: What do you mean by a "physiological feeling"?

AB: I don't know how to talk about this without sounding like Yeats saying that the "Voices" were driving him into a room and dictating to him, but it's almost like that. Something in me has built up, and this is a compulsion to go and write something at the typewriter. It's not totally amorphous. There is something in the back of my mind: a sentence, a sense of remembering what it is like to be in the dead of winter and wanting to go to the beach in the summer, some vague notion like that. It's never more than that. I've never in my life sat down and said to myself, "Now I will write something about somebody to whom such-and-such will happen."

SG: Most people probably assume that, because your characters are so particularized and "real-seeming," they must be based on people you've actually known. Are they right?

AB: Given the nature of most of my characters, it wouldn't be much to my advantage to admit it if I did draw them from my own experience. There have been some instances when I thought I've come very close to capturing the essence of somebody, even though I always make some small change in their clothing or in the location of the story. These changes are made subconsciously, not deliberately, but they are always enough to throw people off. I don't think anyone has ever said to me, "Hey, that's me," and been right, not even when I thought it was most obvious. On the other hand, in places where a character I've created has nothing to do with anyone I know, people have insisted that a particular line is something they've said.

SG: You've said that, when you began *Falling in Place*, you had no idea where it was heading; you only knew you wanted it to be about children.

AB: That wasn't quite true. I knew the beginning of the first sentence: "John Joel was high up in a tree. . . ." And *then* it occurred to me that if somebody was high up in a tree, it would probably be a child, and it was likely that there would be a family surrounding him. With that as an idea I proceeded to write the novel. I had seven weeks to go with this deadline at Random House. I understand that, in the real world, people don't come after you with whips that say "Random House" on the handles, but it still makes me very nervous. I don't like to have deadlines, and I've organized my life so that I don't have deadlines very often. But in this case I did, and I looked out my window and there was this wonderful peach tree out there. That's what started *Falling in Place*.

LM: Despite being written in seven weeks under the pressure of these Random House whips, *Falling in Place* seems to me to have a much greater sense of structure or plot than, say, *Chilly Scenes*. That is, it seems to be working toward that climax, the shooting of Mary by John Joel.

AB: I was totally surprised when that shooting happened.

LM: How far in advance had you realized that this was where the book was heading?

AB: I didn't realize it until I wrote the scene. I was totally amazed to find the gun in that kid's hands. But then I remembered that odd box that had belonged to Parker's grandfather.

SG: You hadn't *planted* that box there with the gun in it?

AB: No; in fact, after the shooting happened I thought, "Oh, my God, we're only three weeks into the book and here Mary is dead on the ground—what am I going to do to resurrect her?" So I resurrected her. Really, I was very upset when that shooting happened.

LM: Despite these kinds of surprises, wouldn't you agree that *Falling in Place* is a more "writerly novel" than *Chilly Scenes of Winter*—that it has a tighter structure and is governed by a more coherent set of images and metaphors?

AB: Sure. Remember, *Falling in Place* was written several years after my first novel. I wrote *Chilly Scenes* in 1975, and it was all dialogue, basically; it was really more like a play than a novel. And that book was written in *three* weeks. I hope I knew more about writing in the summer of 1979 than I did four years earlier. Of course, things happen to you that also help create a focus for your work. I was living in Redding, Connecticut, when I wrote *Falling in Place*, and I had been living there about a year. While I was actually working on *Falling in Place* I didn't really realize how much of Redding—a commuter community and all that sort of thing—had gotten into my head. Actually I guess I had grown very hostile to Redding and was very upset by being there, so in a way it was almost a relief to write *Falling in Place* and sort of purge myself of these feelings. I had been watching these children who seemed to me to be both monstrous and pathetic. These were kids riding the commuter trains into New York; I had never personally met a ten-year-old in Redding. There were only two couples who were friends of ours in Redding, and that was only toward the end, so we had had more than a year of very bad times and total isolation in this wealthy commuter community. I kept doing things like watching the people at the market and the sensation was like when you're sick and have a fever and everything seems in sharper focus. I went around with that kind of fever for about a year, and then I had this deadline, so I wrote *Falling in Place*. I don't think that it follows that this is the way I always work—if you put me in Alaska for a year, I'm not sure I'd write about igloos—but it did happen that way in Redding, Connecticut. There was so much more that I had subconsciously stored away that I wanted to get out than there had been about anywhere else I've lived.

SG: Why did you have every other chapter take the form of a brief italicized section?

AB: I started out writing chapters—I would write a chapter a day. But after I wrote the first chapter—it was the opening chapter that's there now—I realized that I had forgotten to put any background information in it, so I made notes on what I had to go back and include in that first chapter. The second day I wrote a chapter and then thought, "Here's what I left out of this one." The third day I thought, "I wonder if anyone has ever written a whole book like this. I wonder if this isn't too artsy?" Then I thought, "Who cares?" Eventually I went back and made these lists a little more articulate; they became the italicized chapters. If I were teaching this book, I could imagine myself making any number of pretentious guesses about why the book is structured this way, but in point of fact the book is structured this way because I left in these notes and comments to myself. Another thing I should mention is that I'll do anything to trick myself into thinking that I'm not writing a novel. If I just think in terms of chapter one, chapter two, chapter three, I can deal with that. So I thought of the italics at the end of Chapter One in *Falling in Place* as being a kind of coda. Of course, the chapters in that book don't all function in the same way: some of them repeat what you already know, some of them tell you what you know is an absolute lie, some of them tell you what to anticipate later on.

LM: One of the things I like about your fiction is precisely the thing that some critics seem most troubled by—that is, your work often seems to re-create a sense of modern life's aimlessness. Is this a conscious strategy on your part—a desire to suggest that life isn't shaped like most well-made stories and novels? Or does this sense emerge mainly as a function of your writing habits?

AB: There are at least two honest answers to that question. One is to repeat what I've said before: I've never known beforehand what I'm setting out to write, so even when I write the ending to a piece it's only *at that point* that I know how it ends. I do agree with your characterization of my endings—the sense of them is aimless, but the language used to create this sense isn't. I imagine, though, that subconsciously this is aesthetically what I believe in.

LM: You mean that incidents in people's lives can't be wrapped up neatly with a climax and denouement?

AB: Not the people and situations that I'm writing about. I don't hate books in which this happens; in fact, I rather admire them. One of my favorite books is nonfiction, *Blood and Money* by Thomas Thompson. The last page is so apocalyptic and satisfying. If I could do anything like that—see things with such an overview—I would wrap things up neatly. But it's not the way my mind works; it would seem inappropriate to what I've done, and I've never been able to overhaul a story. In fact, stories often get thrown away in the last paragraph, even the last sentence, because I don't know how it can end. It seems to me most honest personally to write something that still implies further complexity. I'm not writing confessionally. If I want to do that, I can write to my grandmother and say, "The day began here and it ended here." But it wouldn't occur to me that this approach would be pleasurable or meaningful in a story.

SG: You've mentioned how *Falling in Place* started. Do you recall the opening image in *Chilly Scenes of Winter*?

AB: No, not really. All I remember is that I had an idea about the -friendship between two men, Charles and Sam. I wrote quite a bit of background about them, and I showed it to a good friend. When he handed it back to me, there was only a little shred of paper left—the remains of page 51, with Charles saying, "Permittez-moi de vous presenter Sam McGuire." Everything about how Charles came to meet Sam, what town they lived in, everything else had been scissored away. And I thought, He's right, I should just jump in. So whatever had been my original intention was gone, and the book that now stands is what took over. He had done the perfect job of editing.

My friend, J. D. O'Hara, to whom *Falling in Place* is dedicated and who teaches at the University of Connecticut, used to take the scissors to the ends of my stories. Maybe I'm just a victim of my friends' Freudian obsessions, but in both cases they were right. It was really O'Hara who, in literally taking the scissors to my pages, suggested that more elliptical endings might be advantageous.

LM: You seem to omit the kinds of background and psychological information that most writers include. You just put your characters in a situation and show the reader that situation.

AB: I don't think my characters are what they are because of interesting psychological complexities. They're not clinical studies to me. For instance, I like *you*, but I don't care about your childhood; if we know each other for the next ten years, I would no doubt be interested if you were to tell me about your childhood, but I don't think that having known you at some point in time would change my impression, help me to uncover what I'm looking for in our personal relationship. For whatever reasons, I just seem to react to what is right there in front of me. So that's usually the way I write. There is often background information—though I supply it late in the story.

LM: One of the things that everyone seems to notice about your work is your ability to pick out exactly the right details to help identify your characters, to make them seem real. When I first began reading your stories I did what comes naturally to all former graduate students: I tried to assign a specific symbolic significance to these details. But you don't seem to use details symbolically.

AB: A couple of times I do, but I don't think my details are so much "perfect" or "symbolic" as inherently meaningful. If you were to say something about what I am wearing tonight, just about any of the things you pick would be equally telling. I don't think my cowboy boots are any more significant than my long nails. Often for me, artistically speaking, something will build up meaning in the back of my mind or become—I hate to say this because I don't think of myself as writing symbolically—a kind of motif in a story. The sense you're talking of results from the quantities of details that I notice, not from those details being so "perfect." Other writers are far more perfect, in that sense, about details—Raymond Carver's details are *perfect*. I'm aiming for texture, mainly. I'm trying to do what a painter does, in a way, by putting a line on the diagonal instead of straight. It has to do with my trying to re-create a very personal vision.

LM: That phrase—personal *vision*—reminds me that you're obviously very interested in painting. I say this not just because of the prominence of the Segal exhibit in *Falling in Place*, but because a lot of your other stories have references to painting. A few are even about painters. It's occurred to me that your stories have something in common with both superrealism and with the notion of found art—the way you seem to pick out ordinary objects from the landscape, re-create them meticulously, and then plant them in your stories. Both superrealism and found art often seem able to skirt the issue of symbolism, too.

AB: I am very much interested in both superrealism and found art. Of course, no one can totally reject symbolism. There was a show at the Guggenheim of photorealists, and there was one painting that I thought was really incredible: it was of a family posed in front of a car. My response was almost like what I was referring to in *Falling in Place*, when John is looking at the picture on his desk and thinking that the way a shadow falls suddenly means more in retrospect than all of his memories of a family vacation. The same thing happened in this painting—something introduced itself into that scene that is far more interesting than the essential composition of the scene, or the reality of it, or anything else I might imagine about it. It forces you *not* to imagine. You might want to think it's *this* kind of day, but this little shadow says it's not. The fact that photorealists can't edit out fascinates me. I like live television for the same reason. If I had my career to do all over again, I'd be a photorealist.

SG: Your use of certain details in *Falling in Place*, like the Skylab falling or the Segal show in New York, seems like a good example of these found objects which still seem to function symbolically.

AB: To tell you the truth, if I had written that book the following summer it would have been the Picasso exhibit instead of the Segal show; instead of Skylab, it would have been the garbage or subway strikes. These details are almost interchangeable, more interchangeable than people realize. I'm not so super-bright that I'm finding these details that other people don't perceive. I'm simply good at noticing that there are *a lot* of details in the landscape and then throwing them into my work. Last year's T-shirt had the Picasso exhibit on it; the year before it was Chicken Little saying that Skylab was falling. The fact is that people buy these things that are manufactured and then they go around with these slogans on their chests. It's as simple as that. It doesn't really matter *what* the slogan of the moment is. In my novels, nothing works against me, unless the thing is too obvious in a literary sense.

LM: References to pop music are everywhere in your work—it's one of your trademarks by now. You seem to rely on the public's awareness of pop music in much the same way that a previous generation's writers relied on their audience's familiarity with poetry and classical literature. I've seen your claim that you don't really bother much with choosing exactly the right music, but this seems hard to believe, since your references are inevitably appropriate. Could you describe this selection process? Is it really just a matter of what song is playing in the background while you're writing?

AB: Almost always. Honest. Of course, sometimes terribly inappropriate things can be playing because the radio has changed programs or the station has gotten switched so that Frank Sinatra is crooning— and that might be an irony I don't want in the middle of a story like "Colorado." I don't listen to music so much now, but I used to when I was married. My husband was a musician and I would be writing these stories while the band was rehearsing in the house. My husband sometimes listened to music from morning until night, and I would be up writing at some point during this period, and whatever was playing at the time I would often use. I simply sensed that at a certain point I needed to have music come in.

SG: Doesn't Charles say in *Chilly Scenes* that music seems to be appropriate to what's going on?

AB: Yes, and what a cover for me! I finally realized that I had to put that in there so it didn't look like the writer concocted the music. Again, it's a technical thing. I would look like the worst writer imaginable if one of my characters is just putting his arms around the woman in the car and "If I Fell" by the Beatles comes on the radio. But this does happen all the time in real life. Think of the appropriateness of Muzak in elevators. To my knowledge nobody before me had a character comment that music was always appropriate, so I put that statement in Charles's mouth. But I was using music more for tempo and texture than to plug my favorite song or to make some comment about the role of music in our society. In other words, I use songs partially to help keep myself going.

SG: You even chose the title *Chilly Scenes of Winter* because of a song, didn't you?

AB: Actually, I didn't choose that title—my husband did. I didn't have a title and I was sitting around wondering, "What am I going to call this thing?" So my husband mentioned this song by Cousin Emmy, who really is the way I describe her—you know, Joan Crawford gone country—and the song seems a little oblique but appropriate. So that's how I got the title. I usually don't title my own stuff. Roger Angell, my editor at the *New Yorker*, titles most of my stories, but if I'm left to do it I usually just pick out the most likely word in the story, which is why a lot of them have one-word titles.

LM: Despite your disclaimers about symbolism, one thing that must be conscious on your part is your use of the color blue. It's almost a personal signature, like John Irving's bears.

AB: Really? I never noticed it.

LM: This is even harder to believe than your not knowing the words to all those songs.

AB: Really, I swear I haven't ever noticed it. I'm doing a double take right now because I just wrote a story called "Blue." Blue isn't even my favorite color—green is.

Now that I think about it, I can see what you mean. *Falling in Place* was based, imaginatively and truly, on the house I was living in—a rented house where people had once searched for the ideal shade of blue. So the porch roof was painted one shade of blue, the woodwork in the kitchen another shade of blue, the front door yet another shade of blue, and so on. Since I don't find blue an unpleasant color, it wouldn't have occurred to me, in re-creating the house in my novel, to say, "Oh, my God, let's paint the cabinet white." But as far as using the color blue as a conscious device, it's never occurred to me until just now. Of course, my being unaware of this doesn't really mean anything.

LM: Even as you're talking I'm planning my next essay: an analysis of Ann Beattie's use of blue, very convincing, very erudite, with this interview tacked on at the end.

AB: Discovering something like this about my work doesn't bother me at all because, since it's obviously been subconscious all along, it'll never stop me from using the color blue. Today I feel like I understand a lot more about the structures of my stories than I did when I first started writing. Unfortunately, this understanding will never *teach me* how to structure a story. One critic who wanted to put me down said that reading my stories was like watching a dog go round and round until it succeeded in catching its tail. He was saying that my writing lacked structure, and when I read that I thought, "Wow, he's right." But I took what he said as a compliment. Roger Angell once brought it to my attention that my characters go out in restaurants and bars to mark time. I could have killed him for that because it made me self-conscious. No, don't worry; the color blue I can handle. Now I'm embarrassed to send a character into a restaurant or bar. But you tell me what to do with a character who's got hours to kill—a situation in which you find yourself during the course of a long novel—except to send him into a bar or someplace to eat.

SG: Your prose style has been characterized as "deadpan" or "emotionless." Are you consciously aiming for a certain effect?

AB: That's the way people talk. I know I think that way—in short sentences. If I didn't describe things neutrally, I would be editorializing, which is not at all what I mean to do. It may be that I have gone *too* far with my prose style. It's a very mannered style, really—or the effect of it is very mannered—but that effect is no more conscious on my part than these other things we've been talking about. I write so fast that I couldn't possibly think about whether or not I'm putting compound or complex sentences into my prose, or whether I'm writing like a dope, or whatever. I mean, we're talking about writing a whole story in two or three hours.

LM: I take it that you are conscious about trying to eliminate an intrusive, editorializing narrator?

AB: Usually, but not always. There's a story of mine called "Greenwich Time," which was in the *New Yorker*; it doesn't exactly have editorializing, but it does have what is purple prose for me. So I won't say I never change my prose style or point of view. I don't think you would even recognize that "Greenwich Time" is by me, except maybe in terms of the characters. It's full of analogies, it's constructed like a prism, the language is extremely deliberate and insistent; it's ostensibly seen through the main character's eyes, but the author is so completely and obviously *there* that you couldn't possibly remove her.

SG: Is this different approach just an isolated incident?

AB: It's something I realize more that I can do now, but it would be damn hard for me to do it all the time. And, of course, the most important thing is that this different approach seemed appropriate for that story, whereas it wouldn't be in others.

SG: When you say that you write the way you do because it's too hard to write in other ways, what do you mean?

AB: I don't think I have an overall view of things to express.

SG: So you focus on trying to observe small things . . .

AB: Not so much small *things* as small *moments*. I wish that writing these stories would suddenly lead me to some revelation that could help me as well as existing as art, as well as pleasing others. But I don't think I've ever written anything that's allowed me to put pieces together. Or maybe I have a psychological problem that makes me resist putting pieces together. But one or the other is true.

SG: It's interesting that you relate this to your own psychological makeup, because your characters often have moments where they seem unable to put their lives together, to understand their own or others' motivations.

AB: This problem may indeed be peculiar to me. Based on what I've experienced, even with the people I'm closest to, I can't predict or always find consistency to others' behavior—and I don't think I'm especially bad about reading people. What I'm perceiving, though, is probably correct: people *are* unpredictable. What I tend to think about someone is not, "X will always be cheerful on a given evening; therefore I should call X and we'll go out and get a pizza." Rather, I think, "I'll call X—*anything* might happen." I think this way even if I've known X for fifteen years. Obviously this attitude works its way into my fiction.

LM: What other contemporary writers do you especially admire?

AB: This is a hard question because it makes me seem like a fool to like so many. I do read a lot these days, whereas years ago I didn't. If you asked me, "Who do you think is *always* good?" that would be really hard—I'd say, "Almost nobody, me included." But for individual moments or books or stories, there are so many. Obviously one writer I like is Mary Lee Settle. Donald Barthelme—I think he's the true genius of our time. Anne Tyler is really good. Joy Williams is one of the best short story writers in America; she has a collection called *Taking Care* that is great. I just read a Tobias Wolff collection called *In the Garden of the North American Martyrs*, a terrible title but the first story in it is absolutely magnificent and the whole book is really first rate. Raymond Carver. If there's one story I could die happy having written, it's "What Is It?" by Raymond Carver. If there's one novel I would love to have written, it would have been Steven Millhauser's *Edwin Mullhouse*. Stanley Crawford's *Some Instructions for My Wife* is bitterly witty; my favorite book of his is *Log of the S.S. The Mrs. Unguentine*. I also read a lot of poetry. I'm a great admirer of Louise Gluck, Jay Parini, Gregory Orr, Michael Ryan, Sydney Lea.

LM: In "A Reasonable Man" one of your characters points to all the books lining his walls and then wonders whether any of them were written by happy people. Has writing made *you* happy? Or does it tend to aggravate things, open up wounds, the way it apparently does for some writers?

AB: Writing doesn't open up wounds for me; during the writing it has made me happy. There have been a couple of times, only three I can think of, where I have finished a story—and remember, when I start to write something I don't know what I'm going to write—and have thought, "I really wish I had never had to put these pieces together." These were "The Burning House," a story in *Vogue* called "Playback," and a story in the *New Yorker* called "Desire."

SG: Why did you regret finishing these?

AB: Each made me realize that I had kept at bay and deliberately misinterpreted painful truths. But it is worth the price of discovering what you don't want to know, because you can also have the sheer pleasure of writing something absurd like "It's Just Another Day at Big Bear City, California," and deciding to have spacemen take pornographic pictures. That's *fun*, and I basically write because I think it's fun. There are a few things I wish I had never written only because I wish I hadn't found out the things I found out.

LM: So at least occasionally you feel that the process of writing allows you to discover things about yourself.

AB: Yes, but always in retrospect. I don't ever sit down thinking that. I just *do it*, the way I get my groceries.

Jerry Bauer

An Interview with
Raymond Carver

To be inside a Raymond Carver story is a bit like standing in a model kitchen at Sears—you experience a weird feeling of disjuncture that comes from being in a place where things *appear* to be real and familiar, but where a closer look shows that the turkey is papier-mâché, the broccoli is rubber, and the frilly curtains cover a blank wall. In Carver's fiction things are simply not as they appear. Or, rather, things are *more* than they appear to be, for often commonplace objects—a broken refrigerator, a car, a cigarette, a bottle of beer or whiskey—become transformed in Carver's hands, from realistic props in realistic stories to powerful, emotionally charged signifiers in and of themselves. Language itself undergoes a similar transformation. Since there is little authorial presence and since Carver's characters are often inarticulate and bewildered about the turns their lives have taken, their seemingly banal conversations are typically endowed with unspoken intensity and meaning. Watching Carver's characters interact, then, is rather like spending an evening with two close friends who you know have had a big fight just before you arrived: even the most ordinary gestures and exchanges have transformed meanings, hidden tensions, emotional depths.

Although Carver published two books of poetry in the late 1960s and early '70s (*New Klamath* in 1968 and *Winter Insomnia* in 1970), it was his book of stories, *Will You Please Be Quiet, Please*, published in 1976 and nominated for the National Book Award, that established his national reputation as a writer with a unique voice and style. Pared down, stark, yet intense, these stories can perhaps best be compared in their achievement to work outside literature, Bruce Springsteen's album *Nebraska*. Like Springsteen, Carver writes about troubled people on the outs—out of work, out of love, out of touch—whose confusion, turmoils, and poignancy are conveyed through an interplay of surface details. His next collection, *What We Talk About When We Talk About Love* (1981), takes this elliptical, spare style even further. With just enough description to set the scene, just enough interpretation of motivation to clarify the action, these stories offer the illusion of the authorless story in which "reality" is transcribed and meaning arises without mediation. This move toward greater and greater economy was abandoned by Carver in *Cathedral* (1983); as the following conversation indicates, changes in his personal life affected his aesthetics. While still written in his distinctive voice, these stories explore more interior territory using less constricted language.

This change (mirrored as well in his most recent collection of poems, *Ultramarine* [1986]) is apparent not just in style but in the themes found in *Cathedral*, which contains several stories of hope and spiritual communion. As we drove to Carver's home outside Port Angeles, Washington, we were still formulating questions designed to reveal why *Cathedral* was less bleak, less constricted. But nothing very devious or complex was required. Sitting in his living room, which offers an amazing vista of the blustery Strait of Juan de Fuca, Carver was obviously a happy man—happy in the homelife he shares with Tess Gallagher, his work, his victory over alcohol, and his new direction. Replying to our questions in a soft, low voice with the same kind of direct honesty evident in his fiction, Carver seemed less like an author of three collections of stories; a book of essays, short stories, and poems (*Fires*, 1983); and three volumes of poetry than he did a writer starting out, eager to begin work, anxious to see where his life would lead.

Larry McCaffery: In an essay in *Fires* you say, "To write a novel, a writer should be living in a world that makes sense, a world that the writer can believe in, draw a bead on, and then write about accurately. A world that will, for a time anyway, stay fixed in one place. Along with this there has to be a belief in the essential *correctness* of that world." Am I right in assuming that you've arrived at a place, physically and psychologically, where you can believe in the "correctness" of your world enough to sustain a novel-length imaginary world?

Raymond Carver: I do feel I've arrived at such a place. My life is very different now than it used to be; it seems much more comprehensible to me. It was previously almost impossible for me to imagine trying to write a novel in the state of incomprehension, despair, really, that I was in. I have hope now, and I didn't have hope then—"hope" in the sense of belief. I believe now that the world will exist for me tomorrow in the same way it exists for me today. That didn't used to be the case. For a long time I found myself living by the seat of my pants, making things terribly difficult for myself and everyone around me by my drinking. In this second life, this post-drinking life, I still retain a certain sense of pessimism, I suppose, but I also have belief in and love for the things of this world. Needless to say, I'm not talking about microwave ovens, jet planes, and expensive cars.

LM: Does this mean you have plans to try your hand at a novel?

RC: Yes. Maybe. Maybe after I finish this new manuscript of poems. Maybe then I'll return to fiction and do some longer fiction, a novel or a novella. I feel like I'm reaching the end of the time of writing poetry. In another month or so I'll have written something like 150–180 poems during this period, so I feel like I'm about to run out this string, and then I can go back to fiction. It's important to me, though, to have this new book of poems in manuscript in the cupboard. When *Cathedral* came out, that cupboard was absolutely bare; I don't want something like that to happen again. Tobias Wolff recently finished a book of stories that he turned in to Houghton Mifflin; he asked me if it was hard for me to start work again after finishing a book, because he was having a hard time getting going again. I told him not to worry about it *now*, but that he should make sure he's well along on something by the time his book is ready to come out. If you've emptied all your cupboards, the way I had after *Cathedral*, it can be difficult to catch your stride again.

Sinda Gregory: Your newfound "belief in love for the things of this world" is very evident in some of the stories in *Cathedral*, especially in the title story.

RC: That story was very much an "opening up" process for me— I mean that in every sense. "Cathedral" *was* a larger, grander story than anything I had previously written. When I began writing that story I felt that I was breaking out of something I had put myself into, both personally and aesthetically. I simply couldn't go on any farther in the direction I had been going in *What We Talk About When We Talk About Love*. Oh, I *could* have, I suppose, but I didn't want to. Some of the stories were becoming too attenuated. I didn't write anything for five or six months after that book came out. I literally wrote nothing except letters. So it was especially pleasing to me that, when I finally sat down to write again, I wrote *that* story, "Cathedral." It felt like I had never written anything that way before. I could let myself *go* in some way, I didn't have to impose the restrictions on myself that I had

in the earlier stories. The last story I wrote for the collection was "Fever,"
which was also just about the longest story I've ever written. And it's
affirmative, I think, positive in its outlook. Really, the whole collection
is different, and the next book is going to be different as well!

LM: What does it mean to a writer like you to find yourself, relatively
suddenly, in such a different frame of mind? Do you find it difficult
today to write about the despair, emotional turmoil, and hopelessness
that is so much a part of the vision of your earlier fiction?

RC: No, because when I need to open this door to my imagination—
stare out over the window casement, what Keats called his "magic
casements"—I can remember exactly the texture of that despair and
hopelessness, I can still taste it, feel it. The things that are emotionally
meaningful to me are still very much alive and available to me, even
though the circumstances of my personal life have changed. Merely
because my physical surroundings and my mental state are different
today doesn't mean, of course, that I still don't know exactly what I
was talking about in the earlier stories. I can bring all that back if I
choose to, but I'm finding that I am not driven to write about it
exclusively. That's not to say I'm interested in writing about life here,
where I live in Four Seasons Ranch, this chichi development. If you
look carefully at *Cathedral*, you'll find that many of those stories have
to do with that other life, which is still very much with me. But not
all of them do, which is why the book feels different to me.

LM: A striking example of the differences you're referring to can be
seen when you compare "A Small Good Thing" (in *Cathedral*) with
the earlier version, "The Bath," which appeared in *What We Talk About*.
The differences between the two versions are clearly fundamental.

RC: Certainly there's a lot more optimism in "A Small Good Thing."
In my own mind I consider them to be really two entirely different
stories, not just different versions of the same story; it's hard to even
look on them as coming from the same source. I went back to that
one, as well as several others, because I felt there was unfinished
business that needed attending to. The story hadn't been told originally;
it had been messed around with, condensed and compressed in "The
Bath" to highlight the qualities of menace that I wanted to emphasize—
you see this with the business about the baker, the phone call, with
its menacing voice on the other line, the bath, and so on. But I still
felt there was unfinished business, so in the midst of writing these
other stories for *Cathedral* I went back to "The Bath" and tried to see
what aspects of it needed to be enhanced, redrawn, reimagined. When
I was done, I was amazed because it seemed so much better. I've had
people tell me that they much prefer "The Bath," which is fine, but
"A Small Good Thing" seems to me to be a better story.

SG: Many of your stories either open with the ordinary being slightly disturbed by this sense of menace you've just mentioned, or they develop in that direction. Is this tendency the result of your conviction that the world *is* menacing for most people? Or does it have more to do with an aesthetic choice—that menace contains more interesting possibilities for storytelling?

RC: The world is a menacing place for many of the people in my stories, yes. The people I've chosen to write about *do* feel menace, and I think many, if not most, people feel the world is a menacing place. Probably not so many people who will see this interview feel menace in the sense I'm talking about. Most of our friends and acquaintances, yours and mine, don't feel this way. But try living on the other side of the tracks for a while. Menace is there, and it's palpable. As to the second part of your question, that's true, too. Menace does contain, for me at least, more interesting possibilities to explore.

SG: When you look back at your stories, do you find "unfinished business" in most of them?

RC: This may have to do with this newfound confidence, but I feel that the stories in *Cathedral* are *finished* in a way I rarely felt about my stories previously. I've never even read the book since I saw it in bound galleys. I was happy about those stories, not worried about them; I felt there was simply no need to mess around with them, make new judgments about them. A lot of this surely has to do with this whole complicated business about the new circumstances in my life, my sense of confidence in what I'm doing with my life and my work. For such a long time, when I was an alcoholic, I was very *un*-confident and had such very low self-esteem, both as a person and as a writer, that I was always questioning my judgments about everything. Every good thing that has happened to me during the last several years has been an incentive to do more and do better. I know I've felt that recently in writing all these poems, and it's affecting my fiction as well. I'm more sure of my voice, more sure of *something*. I felt a bit tentative when I started writing those poems, maybe partly because I hadn't written any for so long, but I soon found a voice—and that voice gave me confidence. Now when I start writing something, and I mean *now* in these last few years, I don't have that sense of fooling around, of being tentative, of not knowing what to do, of having to sharpen a lot of pencils. When I go to my desk now and pick up a pen, I really know what I have to do. It's a totally different feeling.

SG: What was it that made you return to poetry after all those years of focusing exclusively on fiction?

RC: I came out here to Port Angeles with the intention of bringing to completion a long piece of fiction I had started back at Syracuse.

But when I got out here, I sat around for five days or so, just enjoying the peace and quiet (I didn't have a television or radio), a welcome change from all the distractions going on at Syracuse. After those five days I found myself reading a little poetry. Then one night I sat down and wrote a poem. I hadn't written any poetry in two years or more, and somewhere in the back of my mind I was lamenting the fact that I hadn't written any—or really even given any serious thought to poetry writing for a long time. During the period when I was writing the stories that went into *Cathedral*, for example, I was feeling I couldn't have written a poem if someone had put a gun to my head. I wasn't even *reading* any poetry, except for Tess's. At any rate, I wrote this first poem that night, and then the next day I got up and wrote another poem. The day after that I wrote *another* poem. This went on for ten straight weeks; the poems seemed to be coming out of this wonderful rush of energy. At night I'd feel totally empty, absolutely whipped out, and I'd wonder if anything would be left the next morning. But the next day there *was* something—the well hadn't gone dry. So I'd get up, drink coffee, and go to my desk and write another poem. When it was happening I felt almost as if I were being given a good shaking, and suddenly my keys were falling out of my pockets. I've never had a period in which I've taken such joy in the act of writing as I did in those two months.

LM: You've said that it no longer matters where you are living as far as your writing is concerned. Has that feeling changed?

RC: I'd certainly retract that statement nowadays. Having this place here in Port Angeles has been very important to me, and I'm sure coming out here helped me get started writing poetry. I think it was getting clear away from the outdoors and my contact with nature that made me feel I was losing whatever it was that made me want to write poetry. I had spent the summer of 1982 out here (not in this house, but in a little cabin a few miles from here), and I wrote four stories in a fairly short period of time, although they took place indoors and didn't have anything specifically to do with this locale. But without question my poetry came back to me because of this relocation. It had been increasingly difficult for me to work in Syracuse, which is why I pulled up stakes and came out here. There was just too much going on back in Syracuse, especially after *Cathedral* came out and there was so much happening in connection with the book. There were people coming in and out of the house, and a lot of other business that never seemed to end. The telephone was ringing all the time, and Tess was teaching, and there were a certain number of social obligations. This might only mean having an occasional dinner with dear friends, whom it was always a pleasure to see, but all this was taking me away from my work. It got to the point where even hearing the cleaning woman, hearing her make the bed or vacuum the rug or wash the dishes, bothered me. So I came out here, and when Tess left to go back to Syracuse on September 1, I stayed on for another four weeks to write and fish. I did a lot of work during those weeks, and when I got back to Syracuse I thought I could keep up that rhythm. I did manage to for a few days, but then I found myself limited to editing the stuff I had written out here. Finally, the last few weeks or so, it was all I could do to make it from day to day. I would consider it a good day if I could take care of my correspondence. That's a hell of a situation for a writer to be in. I wasn't sorry to leave, even though I have some dear friends there.

SG: In the *Esquire* article you wrote about your father, you mention a poem you wrote, "Photograph of My Father in His 22nd Year," and comment that "the poem was a way of trying to connect up with him." Does poetry offer you a more direct way of connecting to your past?

RC: I'd say it does. It's a more immediate way, a faster means of connecting. Doing these poems satisfies my desire to write something, and tell a story, every day—sometimes two or three times a day, even four or five times a day. But in regard to connecting up to my past, it must be said of my poems (and my stories, too) that even though they may all have some basis in my experience, they are also *imaginative*. They're totally made up, most of them.

LM: So even in your poetry that persona who is speaking is never precisely "you"?

RC: No. Same as in my stories, those stories told in the first person, for instance. Those "I" narrators aren't me.

SG: In your poem "For Semra, with Martial Vigor," your narrator says to a woman, "All poems are love poems." Is this true in some sense of your own poetry?

RC: Every poem is an act of love, and faith. There is so little other reward for writing poems, either monetarily or in terms of, you know, fame and glory, that the act of writing a poem has to be an act that justifies itself and really has no other end in sight. To *want* to do it, you really have to love doing it. In that sense, then, every poem *is* a "love poem."

LM: Have you found it a problem to move back and forth between genres? Is a different composition process involved?

RC: The juggling has never seemed a problem. I suppose it would have been more unusual in a writer who hadn't worked in both areas to the extent that I have. Actually I've always felt and maintained that the poem is closer in its effect and in the way it is composed to a short story than the short story is to a novel. Stories and poems have more in common in what the writing is aiming for, in the compression of language and emotion, and in the care and control required to achieve their effects. To me, the process of writing a story or a poem has never seemed very different. Everything I write comes from the same spring, or source, whether it's a story or an essay or a poem or a screenplay. When I sit down to write, I literally start with a sentence or a line. I always have to have that first line in my head, whether it's a poem or a story. Later on everything else is subject to change, but that first line rarely changes. Somehow it shoves me on to the second line, and then the process begins to take on momentum and acquire a direction. Nearly everything I write goes through many revisions, and I do a lot of backing up, to-and-froing. I don't mind revising; I actually enjoy it, in fact. Don Hall has taken seven years to write and polish the poems that make up his new book. He's revised some of the poems a hundred and fifty times or so. I'm not *that* obsessive, but I do a lot of revising, it's true. And I think friends of mine are a bit dubious about how my poems are going to turn out. They just don't think poems can or should be written as fast as I wrote these. I'll just have to show them.

LM: One possible source of interaction between your poetry and fiction has to do with the way the impact of your stories often seems to center on a single image: a peacock, a cigarette, a car. These images seem to function like poetic images—that is, they organize the story, draw our responses into a complex set of associations. How conscious are you of developing this kind of controlling image?

RC: I'm not consciously creating a central image in my fiction that would control a story the way images, or an image, often control a work of poetry. I have an image in my head but it seems to emerge out of the story in an organic, natural fashion. For instance, I didn't realize in advance that the peacock image would so dominate "Feathers." The peacock just seemed like something a family who lived in the country on a small farm might have running around the house. It *wasn't* something I placed there in an effort to have it perform as a symbol. When I'm writing I don't think in terms of developing symbols or of what an image will do. When I hit on an image that seems to be working and it stands for what it is supposed to stand for (it may stand for several other things as well), that's great. But I don't think of them self-consciously. They seem to evolve, occur. I truly invent them and *then* certain things seem to form around them as events occur, recollection and imagination begin to color them, and so forth.

SG: In an essay in *Fires*, you make a remark that perfectly describes for me one of the most distinctive things about your fiction: "It's possible, in a poem or a short story, to write about commonplace things and objects using commonplace language and to endow those things—

a chair, a window curtain, a fork, a stone, a woman's earring—with immense, even startling power." I realize that every story is different in this regard, but how *does* one go about investing these ordinary objects with such power and emphasis?

RC: I'm not given to rhetoric or abstraction in my life, my thinking, or my writing, so when I write about people I want them to be placed within a setting that must be made as palpable as possible. This might mean including as part of the setting a television or a table or a felt-tipped pen lying on a desk, but if these things are going to be introduced into the scene at all, they shouldn't be inert. I don't mean that they should take on a life of their own, precisely, but they should make their presence *felt* in some way. If you are going to describe a spoon or a chair or a TV set, you don't want simply to set these things into the scene and let them go. You want to give them some weight, connecting these things to the lives around them. I see these objects as playing a role in the stories; they're not "characters" in the sense that the people are, but they are *there* and I want my readers to be aware that they're there, to know that this ashtray is here, that the TV is there (and that it's going or it's not going), that the fireplace has old pop cans in it.

SG: What appeals to you about writing stories and poems, rather than longer forms?

RC: For one thing, whenever I pick up a literary magazine, the first thing I look at is the poetry, and then I'll read the stories. I hardly ever read anything else, the essays, reviews, what have you. So I suppose I was drawn to the *form*, and I mean the brevity, of both poetry and short fiction from the beginning. Also, poetry and short fiction seemed to be things I could get done in a reasonable period of time. When I started out as a writer, I was moving around a lot, and there were daily distractions, weird jobs, family responsibilities. My life seemed very fragile, so I wanted to be able to start something that I felt I had a reasonable chance of seeing through to a finish—which meant I needed to finish things in a hurry, a short period of time. As I just mentioned, poetry and fiction seemed so close to one another in form and intent, so close to what I was interested in doing, that early on I didn't have any trouble moving back and forth between them.

LM: Who were the poets you were reading and admiring, perhaps being influenced by, when you were developing your notions of the craft of poetry? Your outdoor settings may suggest James Dickey, but a more likely influence seems to me to be William Carlos Williams.

RC: Williams was indeed a big influence; he was my greatest hero. When I started out writing poetry I was reading his poems. Once I even had the temerity to write him and ask for a poem for a little magazine I was starting at Chico State University called *Selection*. I think we put out three issues; I edited the first issue. But William Carlos Williams actually sent me a poem. I was thrilled and surprised to see his signature under the poem. That's an understatement. Dickey's poetry did not mean so much, even though he was just coming into his full powers at about the time when I was starting out in the early '60s. I liked Creeley's poetry, and later Robert Bly, Don Hall, Galway Kinnell, James Wright, Dick Hugo, Gary Snyder, Archie Ammons, Merwin, Ted Hughes. I really didn't know anything when I was starting out, I just sort of read what people gave me, but I've never been drawn to highly intellectualized poetry—the metaphysical poets or whatever.

LM: Is abstraction or intellectualism something that usually turns you off in a work?

RC: I don't think it's an anti-intellectual bias, if that's what you mean. There are just some works that I can respond to and others operating at levels I don't connect with. I suppose I'm not interested in what you might call the "well-made poem," for example. When I see one I'm tempted to react by saying, "Oh, that's just poetry." I'm looking for something else, something that's *not just* a good poem. Practically any good graduate student in a creative writing program can write a good poem. I'm looking for something beyond that. Maybe something rougher.

SG: A reader is immediately struck with the "pared down" quality of your work, especially your work before *Cathedral*. Was this style something that evolved, or had it been with you from the beginning?

RC: From the very beginning I loved the rewriting process as much as the initial execution. I've always loved taking sentences and playing with them, rewriting them, paring them down to where they seem solid somehow. This may have resulted from being John Gardner's student, because he told me something I immediately responded to: If you can say it in fifteen words rather then twenty or thirty words, then say it in fifteen words. That struck me with the force of revelation. There I was, groping to find my own way, and here someone was telling me something that somehow conjoined with what I already wanted to do. It was the most natural thing in the world for me to go back and refine what was happening on the page and eliminate the padding. The last few days I've been reading Flaubert's letters, and he says some things that seem relevant to my own aesthetic. At one point when Flaubert was writing *Madame Bovary*, he would knock off at midnight or one in the morning and write letters to his mistress, Louise Colet, about the construction of the book and his general notion of aesthetics. One passage he wrote her that really struck me was when he said, "The artist in his work must be like God in his creation—

invisible and all powerful; he must be everywhere felt but nowhere seen." I like the last part of that especially. There's another interesting remark when Flaubert is writing to his editors at the magazine that published the book in installments. They were just getting ready to serialize *Madame Bovary* and were going to make a lot of cuts in the text because they were afraid they were going to be closed down by the government if they published it just as Flaubert wrote it, so Flaubert tells them that if they make the cuts they can't publish the book, but they'll still be friends. The last line of this letter is: "I know how to distinguish between literature and literary business"—another insight I respond to. Even in these letters his prose is astonishing: "Prose must stand upright from one end to the other, like a wall whose ornamentation continues down to its very base." "Prose is architecture." "Everything must be done coldly, with poise." "Last week I spent five days writing one page." One of the interesting things about the Flaubert book is the way it demonstrates how self-consciously he was setting out to do something very special and different with prose. He consciously tried to make prose an art form. If you look at what else was being published in Europe in 1855, when *Madame Bovary* was published, you realize what an achievement the book really is.

LM: In addition to John Gardner, were there other writers who affected your fictional sensibility early on? Hemingway comes immediately to mind.

RC: Hemingway was certainly an influence. I didn't read him until I was in college and then I read the wrong book (*Across the River and into the Trees*) and didn't like him very much. But a little later I read *In Our Time* in a class and I found that he was marvelous. I remember thinking, This is *it*; if you can write prose like this, you've done something.

LM: In your essays you've spoken out against literary tricks or gimmicks—yet I would argue that your own works are really experimental in the same sense that Hemingway's fiction was. What's the difference between literary experimentalism that seems legitimate to you and the kind that isn't?

RC: I'm against tricks that call attention to themselves in an effort to be clever or merely devious. I read a review this morning in *Publishers Weekly* of a novel that is coming out next spring; the book sounded so disjointed and filled with things that have nothing to do with life, or literature as I know it, that I felt certain I wouldn't read it except under pain of death. A writer mustn't lose sight of the story. I'm not interested in works that are all texture and no flesh and blood. I guess I'm old fashioned enough to feel that the reader must somehow be involved at the human level. And that there is still, or ought to be, a compact between writer and reader. Writing, or any form of artistic endeavor, is not just expression, it's communication. When a writer stops being truly interested in communicating something and is only aiming at expressing something, and that not very well—well, they can express themselves by going out to the streetcorner and hollering. A short story or a novel or a poem should deliver a certain number of emotional punches. You can judge that work by how strong these punches are and how many are thrown. If it's all just a bunch of head trips or games, I'm not interested. Work like that is just chaff: it'll blow away with the first good wind.

LM: Are there out-and-out experimentalists whom you *do* admire? I was wondering about your reaction to Donald Barthelme's work, for example.

RC: I like his work. I didn't care much for it when I first started reading it. It seemed so strange that I stopped reading him for a while. Also, he was, or so it seemed to me, the generation right ahead of mine, and it wouldn't do at the time to like it all that much! But then I read *Sixty Stories* a couple of years ago. He's terrific! I found that the more I read his stories, the more regard I began to have for them. Barthelme has done a *world* of work, he's a true innovator who's not being devious or stupid or mean spirited or experimenting for experimenting's sake. He's uneven, but then who isn't? Certainly his effect on creative writing classes has been tremendous (as they say, he's often imitated but never duplicated). He's like Allen Ginsberg in that he opened a gate, and afterward a great flood of work by other people poured through, some of it good and a lot of it awful. I'm not worried that all that bad stuff which has followed after Barthelme or Ginsberg will push the good stuff off the shelves. It will just disappear on its own.

SG: One of the nontraditional aspects of your own fiction is that your stories don't tend to have the "shape" of the classically rendered story: the introduction/conflict/development/resolution structure of so much fiction. Instead there is often a static or ambiguous, open-ended quality to your stories. I assume you feel that the experiences you are describing simply don't lend themselves to being rendered within the familiar framework.

RC: It would be inappropriate, and to a degree impossible, to resolve things neatly for these people and situations I'm writing about. It's probably typical for writers to admire other writers who are their opposites in terms of intentions and effects, and I'll admit that I greatly admire stories that unfold in that classic mode, with conflict, resolution, and denouement. But even though I can respect those stories, and sometimes even be a little envious, I can't write them. The writer's job, if he or she has a job, is not to provide conclusions or answers. If the story answers *itself*, its problems and conflicts, and meets its *own* requirements, then that's enough. On the other hand, I want to make certain my readers aren't left feeling cheated in one way or another when they've finished my stories. It's important for writers to provide enough to satisfy readers, even if they don't provide "the" answers, or clear resolutions.

LM: Another distinctive feature of your work is that you usually present characters that most writers don't deal with—that is, people who are basically inarticulate, who can't verbalize their plights, who often don't seem to really grasp what is happening to them.

RC: I don't think of this as being especially "distinctive" or nontraditional because I feel perfectly comfortable with these people while I'm working. I've known people like this all my life. Essentially, I *am* one of those confused, befuddled people, I come from people like that, those are the people I've worked with and earned my living beside for years. That's why I've never had any interest whatsoever in writing a story or a poem that has anything to do with the academic life, with teachers or students and so forth. I'm just not that interested. The things that have made an indelible impression on me are the things I saw in lives I witnessed being lived around me, and in the life I myself lived. These were lives where people really *were* scared when someone knocked on their door, day or night, or when the telephone rang; they didn't know how they were going to pay the rent or what they could do if their refrigerator went out. Anatole Broyard tries to criticize my story "Preservation" by saying, "So the refrigerator breaks—why don't they just call a repairman and get it fixed?" That kind of remark is dumb. You bring a repairman out to fix your refrigerator and it's sixty bucks to *fix* it; and who knows how much if the thing is completely broken? Well, Broyard may not be aware of it, but some people can't afford to bring in a repairman if it's going to cost them sixty bucks, just like they don't get to a doctor if they don't have insurance, and their teeth go bad because they can't afford to go to a dentist when they need one. That kind of situation doesn't seem unrealistic or artificial to me. It also doesn't seem that, in focusing on this group of people, I have really been doing anything all that different from other writers. Chekhov was writing about a submerged population a hundred years ago. Short story writers have always been doing that. Not all of Chekhov's stories are about people who are down and out, but a significant number of them deal with that submerged population I'm talking about. He wrote about doctors and businessmen and teachers sometimes, but he also gave voice to people who were not so articulate. He found a means of letting those people have their say as well. So in writing about people who aren't so articulate and who are confused and scared, I'm not doing anything radically different.

LM: Aren't there formal problems in writing about this group of people? I mean, you can't have them sit around in drawing rooms endlessly analyzing their situations, the way James does, or, in a different sense, the way Bellow does. I suppose setting the scene, composing it, must be especially important from a technical standpoint.

RC: If you mean literally just setting the scene, that's the least of my worries. The scene is easy to set: I just open the door and see what's inside. I pay a lot of attention to trying to make the people talk the right way. By this I don't mean just *what* they say, but *how* they say it, and *why*. I guess *tone* is what I'm talking about, partly. There's never any chit-chat in my stories. Everything said is for a reason and adds, I want to think, to the overall impression of the story.

SG: People usually emphasize the realistic aspects of your work, but I feel there's a quality about your fiction that is *not* basically realistic. It's as if something is happening almost off the page, a dreamy sense of irrationality, almost like Kafka's fiction.

RC: Presumably my fiction is in the realistic tradition (as opposed to the really far-out side), but just telling it like it is bores me. It really does. People couldn't possibly read pages of description about the way people *really* talk, about what *really* happens in their lives. They'd just snore away, of course. If you look carefully at my stories, I don't think you'll find people talking the way people do in real life. People always say that Hemingway had a great ear for dialogue, and he did. But no one ever talked in real life like they do in Hemingway's fiction. At least not until after they've *read* Hemingway.

LM: In "Fires," you say that it is not true for you, as it was with Flannery O'Connor or Gabriel García Márquez, that most of the stuff that has gone into your fiction had already happened to you before you were twenty. You go on to say, "Most of what now strikes me as story 'material' presented itself to me after I was twenty. I really don't remember much about my life before I became a parent. I really don't feel that anything happened in my life until I was twenty and married and had kids." Would you still agree with that statement? I say this because we were both struck, after we read the piece about your father in *Esquire*, with how much your description of your childhood and relationship with your father seemed relevant to your fictional world in various ways.

RC: That statement certainly felt true when I wrote it—it simply didn't seem that much had truly happened to me until I became a father, at least the sorts of things I could (or wanted to) transform in my stories. But I was also just gaining some perspective on various aspects of my life when I wrote "Fires," and by the time I wrote the piece on my father for *Esquire* I had even more perspective on things. But I see what you're saying. I had touched on something in a very close way in regard to my father when I wrote that essay, which I wrote very quickly and which seemed to come to me very directly. I still feel, though, that the piece on my father is an exception. In that instance I could go back and touch some "source material" from my early life, but that life exists for me as through a scrim of rain.

SG: What kind of a kid were you in that earlier life?

RC: A dreamy kid. I wanted to be a writer and I mostly followed my nose as far as reading was concerned. I'd go to the library and check out books on the Spanish conquistadors, or historical novels, whatever struck my fancy, books on shipbuilding, anything that caught my eye. I didn't have any instruction in that regard at all; I'd just go down to the library once a week and browse. All in all, I'd say my childhood was fairly conventional in many respects. We were a poor family, didn't have a car for the longest while, but I didn't miss not having a car. My parents worked and struggled and finally became what I guess you'd call lower middle class. But for the longest while we didn't have much of anything in the way of material goods, or spiritual goods or values either. But I didn't have to go out and work in the fields when I was ten years old or anything of that sort. Mainly I just wanted to fish and hunt and ride around in cars with other guys. Date girls. Things like that. I sponged off my folks as long as I could. The pickings were slim at times, but they bought me things. They even bought me my cigarettes the first year or two I was smoking; I didn't have a job and I guess they knew I would have gone out and stolen them if they didn't buy them for me. But I did want to write, which might have been the only thing that set me apart from my friends. There was one other kid in high school who was my friend and who wanted to write, so we would talk about books. But that was about it. An undistinguished childhood.

SG: Was your father much of a storyteller?

RC: He read to me a little when I was a kid. Mainly Zane Grey stories that he'd read when I'd ask him to (he had a few of those books in the house). But he also told me stories.

LM: You've referred to the bad times you went through with your drinking in the '60s and '70s. In retrospect, was there anything positive at all that came out of those experiences?

RC: Obviously my drinking experiences helped me write several stories that have to do with alcoholism. But the fact that I went through that and was able to write those stories was nothing short of a miracle. No, I don't see anything coming out of my drinking experiences except waste and pain and misery. And it was that way for everybody involved in my life. No good came out of it except in the way that someone might spend ten years in the penitentiary and then come out of that and write about the experience. Despite that comical remark Richard Nixon made about writing and prison at the time when he was about to be impeached, you have to take it on faith that prison life is not the best for a writer.

LM: So you never used any of those confessional stories that one hears at AA meetings as the starting point for one of your stories?

RC: No, I never have. I've heard a lot of stories in AA but most of them I forgot immediately. Oh, I recall a few, but none of them ever struck me as material I wanted to use for a story. Certainly I never went to those meetings thinking of them as possible source materials for my work. To the extent that my stories have to do with drinking, they all pretty much have some starting point in my own experience rather than in the funny, crazy, sad stories I heard at AA. Right now I feel there are enough drinking stories in my work, so I'm not interested in writing them anymore. Not that I have a quota in the back of my mind for any particular type of story, but I'm ready to move on to something else.

SG: I wonder if you're ready to move on to writing more about the outdoors or nature once again. Those elements seem to be missing from your recent work.

RC: I began writing by wanting to write about those things like hunting and fishing that played a real part in my emotional life. And I did write about nature quite a lot in my early poems and stories: you can find it in many of the stories in *Furious Seasons* and in some of the ones in *Will You Please Be Quiet, Please* and in a lot of the poems. Then I seemed to lose that contact with nature, so I haven't set many of my recent stories in the outdoors—although I suspect I will in the time to come, since a lot of the poems I've recently been writing are set outside. The water has been coming into these poems, and the moon, and the mountains and the sky. I'm sure this will make a lot of people in Manhattan laugh! Talk of tides and the trees, whether the fish are biting or not biting. These things are going to work their way back into my fiction. I feel directly in touch with my surroundings now in a way I haven't felt in years. It just so happened that this was channeled into what I was writing at the time, which was poetry. If I had started a novel or some stories, this contact I've reestablished would have emerged there as well.

SG: Who are the contemporary writers you admire or feel some affinity with?

RC: There are many. I just finished Edna O'Brien's selected stories,

A Fanatic Heart. She's wonderful. And Tobias Wolff, Bobbie Ann Mason, Ann Beattie, Joy Williams, Richard Ford, Ellen Gilchrist, Bill Kittredge, Alice Munro, Frederick Barthelme. Barry Hannah's short stories. Joyce Carol Oates and John Updike. So many others. It's a fine time to be alive, and writing.

Sutor & Lindsey

An Interview with
Samuel Delany

By the time of the interview, when we first see the living writer, we've already roamed around in some very intimate parts of his or her mind. We've decided some basic things about the person's concerns, anxieties, and vision of an ideal world. In some ways we know this person we've never met better than we know our mother-in-law, our son. In the case of Samuel Delany (who becomes Chip as soon as you meet him), our preconceptions seemed bound to influence our view of a man who is black, gay, and a science fiction writer. In New York City during August 1983 Delany blasted through those preconceptions in a five-hour interview at his Upper West Side apartment.

Few writers are as rigorous as Delany in analyzing the cultural, sexual, linguistic, and aesthetic biases that control our lives. What follows is a much abbreviated version of our conversation. Chip talks faster than most people read; and he commands an encyclopedic range of disciplines that allows him to discuss his debts to the poststructuralists and deconstructionists at one moment, the aesthetic implications of how time can be frozen in comic books at the next, and—minutes later—why Rimbaud, Huysmans, and Proust have been such problematic models for certain postmodernists.

Summarizing the personal, intellectual, and artistic influences on Delany's career is difficult because of the many interactions and paradoxes involved. Imagine a personality shaped equally by Harlem (where Delany was born in 1942 and where he grew up) and one of New York City's most prestigious schools for the gifted, the Bronx High

School of Science—on top of a lifetime battle with dyslexia. Add the counterculture revolution of the 1960s, a writerly imagination that has been affected in equal measure by pulp science fiction and by the textual explorations of Roland Barthes, by French Symbolism, by the linguistic investigations of Saussure, Wittgenstein, Quine, and the mathematics of G. Spencer Brown; by both rock and contemporary classical music, and (of increasing importance) by structuralist and poststructuralist thinkers such as Lacan, Kristeva, Derrida, Felman, and Foucault. This unlikely confluence of influences supports a body of science fiction that is probably unrivaled in terms of intellectual sophistication and formal ingenuity.

In Delany's work perverse, primordial passions collide headlong with intellectual abstractions, and science fiction's exotic alien encounters become multilayered vehicles for exploring sexuality (who else would write a sword-and-sorcery tale about AIDS?), the effects of language on perception and identity (like the Neo-Empiricists, Delany believes that there's no such thing as this last), and the way artists can generate beauty and meaning in our random, ambiguous cosmos governed by the second law of thermodynamics—and the similarity of the whole artistic process to crime. What chiefly characterizes Delany's work is both the rigor of his methods and his impressive invention of otherworldly cultures that critique our societal givens, cultures that demand that we recognize all *meanings* as (first) social and (second) part of a larger play of *différances*.

Most critics divide Delany's career into two phases. During the 1960s, between age 19 and age 25, Delany wrote nine science fiction novels, including *Babel-17* (1966) and *The Einstein Intersection* (1967)—both of which won the prestigious Nebula Award—and *Nova* (1968). In the second phase, signaled seven years later by the publication of *Dhalgren*, his magnum opus, Delany's fiction had become more textured, more dense, more difficult, and more clearly influenced by critical theory.

Dhalgren remains the pivotal book in Delany's career. This massive (almost 900 pages), ambitious, unclassifiable novel presented unparalleled challenges for science fiction readers. *Dhalgren* transfers the exoticism of other worlds to a surreal, nightmarish urban landscape, a twisted, disrupted vision of Harlem and America's other decaying inner cities. Like all of Delany's major novels, *Dhalgren* explores the relation of men and women to the systems and codes around them. His central character is an artist whose doomed efforts to make sense of the chaos become an emblem of all our similar attempts. What is especially interesting about *Dhalgren* is the way its phantasmagoric, prismatic approach to its own structure defeats the reader's efforts to create a single interpretation of what occurs. The book is part myth, part dream, part verbal labyrinth.

Delany's newer fiction also includes *Triton* (1976), which rivals Ursula Le Guin's *The Left Hand of Darkness* as one of the most interesting science fictional treatments of sexuality. More recently he has explored the sword-and-sorcery subgenre in *Tales of Neveryon* (1979), *Neveryona* (1983), and *Flight from Neveryon* (1985). In 1984 he returned to space opera with *Stars in My Pocket Like Grains of Sand*, the first volume of a projected diptych.

Larry McCaffery: Science fiction would seem to provide ideal territory for exploring racial issues, but you are one of the few black SF writers. Is this mainly a sociological situation, as with golfers or tennis players?

Samuel Delany: Well, black golfers and tennis players are actively not wanted by an overwhelmingly white audience and white administration that considers both sports highly elite. Althea Gibson, the first black to play—and win—at Wimbledon, had some pretty hairy stories about her road there. But it's an interesting comparison.

SF starts in most people's minds as something highly technical, full of dials, switches, and things that glitter. Images like that serve as social signs. People learn to read them very quickly. They're like placards on the clubhouse door: "No girls allowed." They say very clearly: We don't want any blacks, we don't want the poor, we don't want Hispanics; but finally the door gets broken in when somebody says, "Wait. *I* want to see what's going on in there."

Because science fiction, unlike the world of professional golf and tennis, is not a real club where people are pushing on a tangible door, nothing stops people from reading SF if they want to. Still, in something as complex as a specific practice of writing, you can't have minority writers until you have minority readers. Once you have the readers, the writers start tumbling out the door. Having said that, I've got to add there *are* black—and native American, and Asian-American, and a whole lot more non-Caucasian—SF writers working in the U.S.A., many of them spectacularly good: Octavia Butler, Steve Barnes, Charles Saunders, Creig Street, Russel Bates, Lawrence Yep, Samtow Suchkeritkil . . . Still not as many as there should be, when you consider that SF makes up nearly 16 percent of *all* new fiction published in this country each year.

LM: Let me quote a comment you once made to a white critic. You told him, "If you wrote, 'Behind a deceptively cool, even disinterested, narrative exterior you can hear the resonances of the virulent anti-

white critique that informs all aware black writing in America,' I would
think you were a downright perceptive reader." Early on this critique
seems to inform your work by your almost casual inclusion of black
characters in positions of power. But later, in *Dhalgren*, for instance,
and in the Neveryon books, you take up the issue of racism more
directly. Was this a conscious shift?

SD: You're really asking, What's the relation of politics to art? Or,
at least, how do I perceive that relation? The aesthetic bias I share with
a lot of others is that you can't propagandize directly in fiction. You
have to present politics by indirection, by way of allegory—and complex allegory at that. You have to resort to figurative means. When you
just break out and start preaching, however right your sermon might
be, it's still propaganda and hence awkward art. You're stuck with the
need to allegorize, but you have to do so in a rich way, not in a
simplistic way.

Certainly the *way* I allegorize has shifted. (I wasn't yet twenty-five
when I wrote most of those earlier books.) In my Neveryon stories,
for example, it should slowly creep up on readers that the barbarians,
who have just come to the city and who are creating many social
problems, are blond and blue-eyed, while the indigenous citizens are
dark. The dark-skinned citizens learn to live with and/or ignore the
blond barbarians in some public space that's, say, the prehistoric equivalent of a bus terminal, as if the barbarians weren't there—like middle-
class New Yorkers avoiding the many people who hang out and even
live in the Port Authority bus station. This kind of reversal serves to
distance the contemporary situation. At the same time one recognizes
it as *structure*, rather than as *content*; the reader sees a set of relationships, largely economic, a set of positions that anyone might fill, re-
gardless of color—rather than a collection of objects, dark-skinned
folks and light-skinned folks, each with an assigned value.

Of course, from a certain standpoint, everything one writes is propaganda. (Wittgenstein used to say that his writings were propaganda
for his particular way of thinking.) Certainly the fact that I'm black
and have had certain kinds of experiences, not only as a black person
growing up in Harlem and New York, but also as a black person going
down to the Port Authority, is why I've chosen to write about the
particular relationships I've seen. Someone with a different background
and a different experience is going to write about something else.

Sinda Gregory: So there was never a moment in your career when
you sat down and thought, I want to deal with racial issues more
directly?

SD: A moment? No. A period, perhaps. Also, some work just demands a more direct approach. If, as in the Neveryon stories, I'm

writing about a culture where there's still real slavery, since most of my great-grandparents were slaves and I grew up with my grandmother telling me tales of slavery times that her mother told her, then even if I don't use any of her specific stories, I *have* to handle the racial aspects of the situation more directly. The work requires it.

SG: Your view that allegory and indirection are the most likely means of getting people to respond to political issues seems a far cry from what we heard in the '30s—when most politically committed writers seemed to feel the need to deal with issues directly, in socially realistic terms.

SD: True. But there's another side of the subject that can't be forgotten. Because of all the social pressures placed on black people, the structure of black life is very different, especially at the lower economic levels. I'm talking about the experiential specificity of black life. If we— the black writers—are writing directly about the black situation, we use this experience directly. But if we're writing in a figurative form, as I am most of the time with SF or sword-and-sorcery, we have to tease out the structure from the situation, then replace the experimental terms with new, or sometimes opaque, terms that nevertheless keep the structure visible. The new terms change the value of the structure. Often they'll even change its form. I think the figurative approach is more difficult, but it's the best way to say something *new*.

SG: Your exploration of gay and bisexual relations seems more open from *Dhalgren* onward. Was this a reflection of your own sexual development?

SD: Mainly it's a reflection of what was going on in American culture —certainly not just with me. Sexual areas have been opened up for more discussion on every level. One thing that opened them up was, of course, the women's movement, which created a damning critical dialogue with the so-called sexual revolution. In the late '60s and early '70s, as the women's movement was getting itself together, I was very aware of the similarities between its problems and the problems of the black movement some years before. You saw a lot of the same arguments going down, both pro and con, and you recognized the form. It took a very small leap to see that the movement for gay rights was going to have to go through similar arguments. The gay rights movement probably went through the early stages more rapidly, because it had those two examples to use as models. Not that any of the three situations have been solved. But some progress has been made in all of them.

SG: Probably the most famous science fiction treatment of sexuality, after the early days of Sturgeon and Farmer, is Le Guin's *The Left Hand of Darkness*. It's received some heavy criticism recently.

SD: There's much in it that's extraordinarily good, and we should keep this in mind when we criticize its shortcomings—especially since it wasn't written as a tract. It's a novel. Certainly you can question its presentation of sexual roles. Ideology (at least in readerly or writerly matters) is a set of questions you're predisposed to ask *of* the text, not something materially situated *within* the text itself; and there's nothing to stop you from asking those questions that reveal the book's lacks: Who, in this ambisexual society, takes care of the children? Why, in a society where everyone can get pregnant and deliver and nurse a child, is everyone called *he*? And, yes, it's terribly easy to read some of the novel's situations as ordinary clichés about homosexuals—from the intrigues and backbiting at the Court of Karhide to the scene with Genly and Estraven on the ice. There were an awful lot of '50s gay novels with terribly similar sections, where the hero discovers he just can't make it with the other guy, at which point one character crashes his car into a tree and conveniently and tragically dies, thus solving the problem.

On the other hand, Le Guin has created a true three-handkerchief climax that's made a million-plus readers weep their hearts out; and it's not easy to write one of those. In that sense, I think she did what she wanted. But more to the point, the book starts its younger readers *thinking*—as well as feeling. Young gay readers who come to *this* book are *not* wondering where in the world they can sneak off to find *any* novel about gay life at all, the way I had to when I was a kid. The novels that ended with the car crashes (or the electrocutions, or whatever) were the closest you could get to any rich literary description of gay life in 1955. It was that or read the appendix to some bizarre self-help book by Erich Fromm, which told you in its final pages that, if you *were* gay, you could expect to die of alcoholism—if you hadn't already committed suicide, thanks to your miserable, meaningless life. The paperback novels and Fromm were, of course, both telling us the same thing. But today we have the option of being blown away at the desk of our City Hall office by some psychotic twit who's just wandered across the corridor and shot the mayor. I *guess* it's an improvement.

LM: In all fairness to Le Guin, when we talked with her about this issue, she mentioned that she now realizes the limitations of *The Left Hand of Darkness*. She said that it was written during a period when her own consciousness was just being raised, and that from today's perspective it could have been handled more effectively. But she did the best she could at the time.

SD: And that's one reason why she's a fine science fiction writer. She has a sense that there *is* a potential political dimension to a text that may sprout later on. It suggests that the seeds of growth are there in her book, too—even if they haven't necessarily flowered in that particular story. Having made perfectly valid criticisms of Le Guin's book, I think there are much richer answers suggested in the book than *some* of the people who are looking only for right answers have seen. And she opens up a lot of questions that many writers don't even acknowledge to exist, which puts her books head and shoulders above many, many novels written in the years just before and after them. Besides, you don't castigate Jane Austen for her appalling classism in *Emma*; you extol her for her astonishing and satisfying novelistic dance.

LM: Unlike Kurt Vonnegut, you have openly and proudly proclaimed your writing to be science fiction. Indeed, in your critical writings you have suggested that SF is a genre in its own and not merely a subgenre of "mainstream" fiction, or of the romance, or whatever. You have resisted the notion that recent SF is "reentering" the realm of serious fiction. Could you talk about these controversial notions, explain how you arrived at them, and why you feel they're important?

SD: The bottom line, of course, is that distinctions are important. The ability to make *significant* distinctions—and to avoid dumb ones— is the only way to organize the vast amounts of information we have to deal with today. There are clear differences between SF and other kinds of writing, differences in the way people learn to read it, and interpret it, differences between it and other kinds of writing as particular socially and economically grounded writing practices. Many people are comfortable reading only one kind of writing (say, SF) and are uncomfortable reading any other (say, "literature"), while for a large number of people the comfort index runs in the other direction. Since these differences are there, since the various categories and practices of writing are carried on by different social groups, are read by people in different social groups, there are going to be differences in language texture. You have to tease apart all these differences; then you have to map them onto other models of textual functioning. This step can either be taken critically and conscientiously, revising the model carefully or trying to come up with a new model that will organize your distinctions—your information—more accurately and more elegantly. (This is frequently called critical, or literary critical, theory.) Or it can be done uncritically, using any model for textual functioning that happens to be lying about in the critic's backbrain. Critical theorists usually refer to this type of criticism as "thematics"; the term is pejorative, because it implies that the critics, as they locate this theme or that, along whatever historical vector, have not sufficiently explored that larger mechanism by which our society recognizes certain collections of signs as a "theme." Such a recognition *always* involves a refusal to grant thematic status to certain other sign collections. Then in light of this model, the various distinctions can be judged significant or superficial.

How did I become aware of the distinctions between SF and literary texts? When I picked some up and read them, I found sentences like "The Marquis went out at five o'clock" in one, while in the other I found sentences like "At o-six hundred our cruiser traversed the monopole magnet mining operations of the outer asteroid belt at Delta Cygni."

How did I begin to intuit that the model controlling the evaluation of the SF text for most academic critics was inadequate? Well, the main thing I did was read their criticism. It was pretty clear.

LM: Until recently most critics have—fruitlessly, it seems to me—tried to define these differences in terms of subject matter: one text deals with outer space and the other deals with the mundane world. But you rely on an essentially semiological argument that the sentences in SF "mean" differently from the sentences in ordinary fiction.

SD: Right. In the phrase "the monopole magnet mining operations of the outer asteroid belt at Delta Cygni" there's a lot of room for misreading by a reader who might not have much difficulty with the five-o'clock Marquis. A lot of people simply do not know what monopole magnets are—or they may think that the mining is done *with* the monopole magnets, rather than *for* the monopole magnets. And there are people who don't know what, or where, an asteroid belt is; or who think that "outer" means the mining is done on the outside of the belt instead of inside it—that is, they don't hear that "outer" means the outer one *of two* belts. Nor do they have a clue that Delta Cygni is a sun in the constellation of Cygnus the Swan.

The same order of problem arises for the student who can't respond to the opening words of Shakespeare's Sonnet 129: "Th'expense of spirit in a waste of shame/ Is lust in action." If you're a modern reader, you may have trouble responding to that because you don't know the Elizabethan meanings of the words—you think "expense" means "cost" rather than, as it does here, "to spill out" or "to pour out." And you think "spirit" means "soul" rather than "alcoholic liquid." You read "waste" as "ineffective use" rather than "desert." And you think that "the cost of the soul" is the referent while "lust in action" is the metaphor for it—when actually it's the other way around. Once you understand the meaning of the words, you realize that the lines mean something like "To act out of lust is to pour out liquor in a desert of shame." *Now* you can go on to the secondary sexual ("spirit" *also* meant "semen") and commercial ("expense" was *also* used with money) meanings that enrich the poem. But if you stall at some non-meaning like

"The cost to the soul in ineffective use of shame is active (or vigorous) lust," you're not really encountering Shakespeare's text. Many readers, perfectly comfortable with the rhetoric of mundane fiction from the eighteenth to the twentieth century, get to the rhetoric of SF and just can't make sense of the sentences. When such readers are academics, it produces the same response toward SF that you get in the philistine students who can't make sense of an eighteenth-century novel. Because they don't understand it as language, they assume it must be meaningless or nonsensical or trivial—so why expend time on it?

LM: Two examples that you've cited in your essays—Heinlein's "The door dilated" and your own creation, "He turned on his left side"— illustrate the kind of confusion you're talking about. A reader unaccustomed to SF might completely misunderstand those sentences.

SD: Exactly. What tends to be metaphorical in the mundane sentence is often literal in SF. The examples you just cited show this. So would the sentence "Her world exploded." In a mundane text that sentence is going to be a metaphor for a female character's emotions, while in the SF text there's a possibility of its referring to a planet, belonging to a woman, which has, in fact, blown up.

The *way* the information is stored, more than any of the individual rhetorical figures, is what really interests me about the texture of SF language. When you start reading an SF story, certain questions immediately arise that are not the same that come up if you're reading a literary text.

SG: Is this true even if the literary text you're reading is a fantasy— say, something by Kafka?

SD: *Especially* if it's a literary fantasy. An example: You have a story in front of you, and you know it's literature because it has all the proper signs—it's in the *Norton Anthology* or whatever—and you read the first sentence: "One morning, waking from uneasy dreams, Gregor Samsa discovered that in the night he'd become a large beetle." Because this is a literary text, the moment we realize we aren't just dealing with an ordinary presentation of "reality," certain questions associated with literature immediately come into play: What does this passage have to say about the character's personality? Are we dealing with some sort of insanity here? If not, What is it telling about the authorial subject— the writer of this text? What is the author saying? One of the first questions a teacher will ask the class is, Who *is* this man, Gregor Samsa? And it's one of the first questions the critical reader must also ask.

Now let's suppose we have an SF text; we know it's SF because it's in an SF magazine and the blurb says the author won a Hugo Award for another story published two years back. You start reading—and it begins with the same sentence! Well, very different questions come to mind, questions that are not about the psychology or the character or the author but about the nature and organization of the fictive world in which that opening sentence was uttered. Is Samsa perhaps some neotenous lifeform that went through some change during the night? Has someone snuck in and done biological surgery? If Samsa *is* insane, what specifically, in the story's world, has precipitated that insanity? If this is an illusion, what specifically, in the story's world, is creating it? In SF, as we encounter more and more abnormal situations, we want to know not only the agent of change (what particular mad scientist brought it about?) but also the condition of possibility (what particular theory has our scientist unearthed?).

In SF, your attention is immediately turned to the organization of the subject; in literature, your attention is immediately turned to the structure of the subject. People talk about this very clumsily by saying that the best SF is social criticism, but it's easy to see the inadequacy of that rhetoric when you try to apply it to a given SF story. Let's go back to our "monopole magnet mining operations in the outer asteroid belt." On the simplest denotative level, that sentence is saying that *mines*, as we know them today, will *change*; they will change their location, their object, and their methodology. And it says this before it says anything about the psychology of any character cruising around between these asteroids. It doesn't say it as propaganda—it doesn't say that mines ought to change or that we would all be better off if they did change. It simply says that they *will* change. To misread the sentence is to miss that critique of the social object—mines in the real world. It's to miss that non-propagandistic critique of the social object (in this case, mining) that SF alone can make, purely through its specific language texture. Now, SF doesn't necessarily ignore the subject, but it makes a statement about the object first. You have to know that, in order to understand its sentences.

SG: There are obvious disadvantages to writing in a genre traditionally associated with hack writing: condescension by the literary world, poor proofreading, lack of hardbound publication, and so on. But there are advantages as well.

SD: All in all, it's probably a tradeoff. SF is a little less constrained at the editorial level, and that's an advantage. But there are more conventional constraints on the writer at the language level. I'd also argue that working in a paraliterary form such as SF can be an advantage for certain types of writers. Any paraliterary form—and this goes for comic books, mysteries, and pornography as much as for SF— is highly stylized and has little to do with *reproducing* the real world. The person who is attracted to a paraliterary field is likely responding to its intertextuality from the beginning. The only way to write an SF story is to read other SF stories and try to write like them. If you want to write comic books, your first teacher is not the real world; it's other comics. The *final* challenge of the paraliterary forms— pornography is the possible exception—is to see how much and how richly you can allegorize the real world within the genre's highly stylized conventions. Whether in comics or SF, the giants are those who are most successful in allegorizing the real. You get people like Neil Adams in comic books; he runs a constant commentary on real urban life, whether he's drawing *Batman* or *Green Lantern*. Similarly, with the best SF writers you can always follow the allegorical presentation of an object world, whether it be Pohl and Kornbluth in *The Space Merchants* or Bester in *The Stars My Destination*. Their distortions are not there to predict the future (even allegory is not the *best* model for the process, so let's throw it out here and try another): they're there to generate a *dialogue* with the world we live in. The best SF is in clear, rich, and subtle dialogue with today.

LM: Have you ever been tempted to try your hand at mundane fiction?

SD: Not since I was a kid. As I once said in an essay, that's like asking a twelve-tone composer to go back and compose diatonic music. It's asking you to give up half your vocabulary. There's little you can do in mundane fiction that you can't also do in SF. But you can do a whole lot of things in SF that are unavailable to the writer of mundane tales. You're not forbidden the subject explorations in SF; but you can relate them to the object explorations. For a certain kind of writer, that's a very exciting freedom.

I might try it as a sort of five-finger exercise. Chances are it wouldn't be terribly good. It would probably, at best, read like a five-finger exercise; and, at worst, come off like Schönberg in one of those Wagnerian pieces—*Pelléas und Mélisande*, or an early unnumbered string quartet. You listen to those pieces and they sound like oatmeal— diatonic oatmeal. Oh, I suppose the *Gurrelieder* are kind of wonderful— still, I doubt any mundane fiction I could write would be very interesting. If I were going to broach another genre, I think I'd prefer nonfiction.

LM: *Tales of Neveryon* and *Neveryona* are obvious departures from your previous books. Instead of being set in some imagined future, both are set in some magical, distant past, just as civilization is being created. Do you consider them SF at all? Is the "subjunctivity level" different? The past seems to be inscribed differently—to be less free— than any future.

SD: They only enter SF via the subgenre of sword-and-sorcery—

SF's despised younger cousin. One thing that must have drawn me to SF in the first place is my natural penchant for working in despised genres. Within SF, you have this odd subgenre, S&S, set in the past. It usually reads as if it were written with a verbal palette knife. Barbarians hack their way through dragons and lascivious priestesses, barely to escape the wizards' spells (beautiful women have an abiding tendency to metamorphose into monsters just at the point of orgasm). The hero staggers off in the end, sadder but wiser, thinking that there are perhaps some Mysteries of the Universe that Man was Not Meant to Know. It's pretty corny—and desperately transparent—stuff. Yet there's something fascinating about it. So these two books are sword-and-sorcery—though the sorcery is at a minimum. Every time there's anything even resembling magic, there's always a question as to whether it happened or was just in the character's mind: Did the heroine merely have too much to drink the previous evening when that dragon crawled up from that underwater city?

Because sword-and-sorcery somehow developed as a subgenre of SF, it shares that paraliterary object priority. This makes it different from the *Anthony Adverse* style of historical fiction, as well as from the Mary Renault *Bull from the Sea* sort of narrative.

LM: Going back to the past, then, becomes a way of examining our lives *today* and is not meant as any actual conjecture about what life was back then.

SD: It's not really going back to speculate on the past, just as SF is not really going off to speculate on the future. In each you're using a purely artificial convention; in sword-and-sorcery the past becomes your convention to establish a dialogue with the present. Because of its paraliterary expectation of a priority of the object, the dialogue can be about some very interesting social-object workings—rather than a portrait of some supposed historically primitive or elemental psychology, as it tends to be with Mary Renault's fiction, say. If Neveryon were based on a true historical past—say, pre-Heraclitian Greece— I'm sure I'd find myself trying to reconstruct all sorts of Ur-human urges. But Ur-human urges don't interest me. I want to talk about the real and objective apparatus that forces us to *create* the subject in a specific way today. I'm curious about what Foucault calls "the techniques of the subject" that give the subject its particular form now. You can't really explore that without looking at the object, the *techne* Pound was interested in in the later *Cantos* (writing, money, weaving, architecture, pottery . . .), and its effect on the subject's view of itself. And you can't explore this if you're limited to a literary re-creation of a specific historical moment.

SG: Were you reading anything that specifically influenced the directions these books take? In addition to the sword-and-sorcery genre, Larry and I were both reminded of Italo Calvino's *Cosmicomics*.

SD: Just more sword-and-sorcery. Particularly, I guess, Joanna Russ's Alyx stories. That's a marvelous series of sword-and-sorcery tales that suddenly, in the middle of the series, becomes SF. Russ grabs up all her opportunities and juggles them marvelously. I'd fooled around with a couple of incomplete fragments of a sword-and-sorcery tale back when I was living in England, but finally I lost the manuscript. Then, when I returned to the States, I was commissioned to write an introduction to Russ's stories, which were coming out in a library edition from Gregg Press. Practically the day after I finished my introduction, I sat down and started writing the Neveryon tales. Russ's stories showed me that you really *could* make the richest and most satisfying art out of sword-and-sorcery. I just had to try it.

SG: The Neveryon stories all seem to deal with power—all kinds of power: sexual, economic, even racial power via the issue of slavery.

SD: Certainly a lot of my interest in slavery comes from the fact that my great-grandparents were slaves; not only that, but my family was always concerned with civil rights and related issues, so the whole galaxy of concerns was something I was steeped in as a kid. There's always been a leftist leaning to my own political sympathies. Power is a highly mystified topic in this country. You can start talking with someone and get into the details of their sexual predilections far faster than you can ask their income. You can kind of sidle up to the former if the conditions—indeed, the power relations between you—are right. But the latter is just *verboten*—unless you want people to really raise an eyebrow. So when you write a decent power analysis, it can be very exciting. It's like stumbling onto your first Foucault historical discussion, or, even onto the simplest Christopher Caudwell analysis of why our culture in the 1920s and '30s was in the shape it was in. I'm very much aware that my analysis in these particular stories is not all that sophisticated. A bright fourteen-year-old might look at it and say, "Wow! I've never thought about things that way before!" But the eighteen-year-old, the twenty-year-old, not to mention the twenty-five-year-old who's gotten around to reading a little Marx, a little Luxemburg, a little Gramsci, is going to know that the view through this particular stained glass window is not all that rich. For these readers, I'm more concerned with presenting whatever view I do present in the most richly textured way I can. In the language itself, rather than in the plot, is where I hope a reader will find the seeds of a real complexity.

LM: What overall plan have you been following in these books?

SD: The basic plan—if you can call it a plan—is just the traditional paraliterary (or specifically SF) series form. And there're many, many of them: Simak's *City*, Heinlein's *Future History*, Le Guin's *Eccumen*, Russ's *Adventures of Alyx*, Asimov's *Foundation* series, Disch's *334*, Varley's *Eight Worlds*, and so on. In each story you start with a problem that's more or less solved by the end. Then the solution from the last story becomes the problem of the next story. You write one story. Then, in a few days, or weeks, or months, when it doesn't seem quite as good as it did, you sit down and try to write a better one.

It's important to remember that a series is not a novel. Its various stories and tales are not simply chapters in some longer, coherent narrative. That self-critical thrust gives the series a set of expectations different from the more unified set of codes that organize the reading experience of the novel. The paraliterary series is much closer, I think, to a prose version of the large-structure serial composition poem— Olson's *Maximus* poems, Wakoski's *Greed*, or Pound's *Cantos*—than to the novel. The SF series is often a lifetime enterprise, in which you can go back to rethink the material again and again, as in those long serial poems.

SG: Since you conceived of the project as a series from the outset, how much mapping did you do in the overall outline?

SD: Some things I knew I'd eventually want to have in future stories. I knew, for example, that in the very first story Gorgik was going to have bad dreams about Noyeed, and that in a later story he would have to reencounter his dream object. But I didn't know what the significance of that encounter would be until I was there in the sixth tale. Mainly it was planned to be an open-ended form where I could go back and rethink. It's a process we all go through in our ordinary lives. That was the most exciting thing about the form when I started out: it embodied this very human and ordinary process in a formal manner. I could rethink—and go on.

SG: Your childhood—growing up in a middle-class black household in Harlem, being somewhat of a child prodigy—has been fairly well documented by now. But there are a few things we'd like you to comment on. The first is being taken from Harlem to Dalton Elementary School in midtown Manhattan. You have described this trip, which you made five times a week during the school year, between the ages of five and thirteen, as follows: "I was subjected to a virtually ballistic trip through a socio-psychological barrier of astonishingly restrained violence."

SD: Of course it affected me. And obviously my white classmates— unlike my few black ones, who were also Harlemites—didn't have the clear visual switch between the kind of neighborhood I grew up in— 132nd Street and Seventh Avenue, with a "Housepaint and Hosiery" store on one side and a small family grocery on the other, and the people I saw daily out in the street—and Park Avenue. I was intensely aware of that twice-a-day transition, but as one is aware of the totally normal. It was a violent transition but it was also my total surroundings. It had to emerge in some form in my writing.

LM: Your father was an undertaker, and when you were a child your family lived above the funeral parlor. Did that leave any lasting, perhaps subliminal, impression? I'm not just thinking of fairly obvious things, like Rydra's visit to the morgue for a needed crew replacement (in *Babel-17*), but, in particular, of the overpowering presence of death in *Dhalgren*.

SD: The first thing that occurs to me is Yeats's comment that the only two topics worthy of the serious mind are sex and death. I went back and forth, many times and with astonishing speed, from being a very silly to a very serious little boy. It's rather hard to be a living creature without being concerned about what death is. If anything, living over a funeral parlor made me easier with some of the overt manifestations of death. I saw corpses almost every day, and they never plagued me with nightmares; that experience may even have gotten certain images out of the way for me. I certainly remember that living where I did gave me an intriguing power over my contemporaries— you know, "Come on into the funeral parlor—ha ha ha! I dare you!" When I was seven or eight, they'd all tiptoe in after me; when we'd get about halfway through the office, I'd laugh ghoulishly. And the four or five of them would shriek and run out. My father did *not* approve of this.

LM: Your presentation of the city in *Dhalgren* seemed very primordial, something out of a childhood nightmare.

SD: Understand, you're talking to a man with a great distrust of the primordial. I find it a very superficial construct. Still, I suppose in one sense *Dhalgren* has largely to do with the fact that the Harlem of my childhood isn't there today. Just as I distrust the primordial, there's a whole concept of nostalgia that I find equally distasteful. I'm not at all interested in presenting a romanticized picture of long-vanished singing and dancing (or sweating and dope-dealing) darkies. They just weren't there, at least not as they're nostalgically pictured. My way of dealing with the obliteration of my landscape is to observe very carefully what's there now. If you travel in Harlem today, you'll see that buildings are now unoccupied, much of it is burned out. Here and there small oases of intense community life are surrounded by blocks of devastation, run through by the most tenuous of public transportation. It's much the same on the Lower East Side, where I spent my next near-decade; and it's much the same in practically a third of every big city in the United States. There are all these ruined urban areas.

Walk through that landscape, and there's a great feeling of death. (Far more than there ever was around my father's funeral parlor. Actually, as such neighborhood businesses go, it was a pretty social spot.) *Dhalgren* rings its changes on those current urban images; that, I think, is what its readers first recognized. It's basically an expression of a very depressed part of the city—and of the kind of life that nevertheless goes on there. These images are what inform the dialogue *Dhalgren* tries to set up with the glass and aluminum and poured concrete of the office buildings and the shopping malls and the other brave new acres of our urban and suburban megalopolis.

LM: You were an undiagnosed dyslexic, which must have caused you all sorts of problems in school. Has this experience indirectly been a source for your conviction that reality and its linguistic expression are fragile and elusive?

SD: I'm sure. Lots of Kid's perceptions of the world, in *Dhalgren*, are simply any dyslexic's perceptions of what goes on. Maybe once a week I used to go down to see my agent in the Village, and I would ride back and forth on the subway. Every few trips, my home subway station would turn up on the other side of the train—some trips it would be on one side, and on others it would be on the other side. I'm forever getting up and going to the wrong door. I've been traveling this route for seven or eight years. Yet, when I pull into the station, it's a toss up—for *me*—which side of the train the station will be on.

That confusion is dramatized by Kid's misremembering distances, misjudging sides of the street, and even watching people changing the street signs as he goes by. That part of *Dhalgren* is a very self-conscious borrowing from my dyslexia. Some things are also taken from my being somewhat ambidextrous—which often goes along with my particular sort of dyslexia. It's a learning disability that, by the way, has many forms.

LM: That process seems related to your hyper-awareness of the difficulties of the language process, your emphasis on the right word, your view of SF as a poetic genre. (I'm reminded of Kid's saying, "I live in the mouth.")

SD: *Possibly* the dyslexic writer is more aware of what he or she does as a craft. But that may be too broad a generalization. I'm not the only dyslexic writer, of course; there's Yeats, Flaubert, probably Virginia Woolf. What dyslexia does, perhaps, is put language at a distance—so that it becomes something to manipulate, however well or badly.

There's an easy and natural relation to written language that the dyslexic just doesn't have. You think of Yeats, with his "fascination for what's difficult." Well, part of the difficulty was that he didn't really learn to read until he was sixteen. (His father read to him constantly well into his adolescence.) You think of Flaubert, *l'idiot de la famille*, in Sartre's phrase, working endlessly on individual sentence after sentence. But it would be silly to speculate on what dyslexia means ultimately for any individual writer.

SG: Was Rydra in *Babel-17* based on your ex-wife, Marilyn Hacker?

SD: Not really. Very rarely do I base characters consciously on real people—though often people, even ones who know me, are sure I do. Marilyn and I had a dear friend, an older gentleman who died just last year, who'd known Marilyn and me since we were teenagers. He was a sometime psychotherapist. He went to his grave convinced that he was the model for Dr. Markus T'mwarba, Rydra's psychiatrist, in *Babel-17*. Markus was a very black African, and Bernie was a very white New Englander. Nor, indeed, had Marilyn ever been his client. But as far as he was concerned, that didn't really matter. I never had the heart to disillusion him.

Rydra and Marilyn are both poets, and here and there I undoubtedly borrowed some of Marilyn's poetic concerns for the book. But I suspect that Rydra is more me than Marilyn—and, indeed, not all that much either of us. Rydra has one speech—on page 16, if you're interested—that I once made, in an attack of post-adolescent grandiosity, *to* Marilyn. But for the rest, it's pretty much invention. Rydra is a twenty-six-year-old Oriental woman from the Outer Satellites who lives two hundred or so years from now. Marilyn was—at least when I wrote the book—twenty-two, Jewish, and from the Bronx. But there are people, some of them rather close friends, who are never going to believe that.

What I try to go through, especially with my major characters, is something like this. On the one hand I want my characters to do things that I've done myself; that's so I'll know what it *feels* like to be in their situation. On the other, I want to have seen at least one other person do the same things; I also want to know what it *looks* like. But to try to associate my major characters with me—or with anyone I know—is a thankless task.

SG: I was very struck by how authentic you make your female characters. This is rare for a male author. What's your secret?

SD: It's hard for me to tell how authentic my characters seem to others. When your're standing inside the balloon, it's hard to see what shape it is from the outside. Many years ago I was thinking about the problem of writing characters of any sort, and I was trying to analyze what seemed to be wrong with the women characters in most modern American fiction. As early as 1959 or '60 I'd noticed that there was something terribly wrong with the female characters in most novels I was reading. Most of the writers (men and women) tended to conceive of their male characters as combinations of purposeful actions, habitual actions, and gratuitous actions. A female character, in contrast, would be all gratuitous action if it was a "good woman," with no purposes and no habits; if it was a "bad woman," she would be all purpose, with no gratuitous actions and no habits. This seemed silly. Very early on I tried to think about women characters in terms of all three— actions purposeful, habitual, and gratuitous. And I tried (I almost want to say "manfully") to make sure that my female characters indulged in all three. When I would try to put this into practice, almost always the "natural workings" of the story seemed to conspire to exclude this diversity of action from the women.

SG: Most stories don't provide a place for the kind of variety you're talking about.

SD: Today we'd say that the basic templates for bourgeois fiction are themselves sexist, patriarchal, and oppressive. Twenty years ago when, in endless dialogue with Marilyn about it all, we were first figuring this out, I just thought they were psychotic.

The standard narrative templates for male characters are richer than those for women, and writers follow them without even thinking. There was a whole twenty years in American fiction when women were *never* portrayed as having any same-sex friends; during the same period the American "buddy novel," from *The Reivers* to *On The Road*, was endemic. Consider the number of women characters who run through American narratives at all levels, from the best novels to the worst films, about whom you never know how they make their money. Once you start asking, "But who's *paying* for all this?" a whole lot of bad narrative falls apart. Making the artistic representation *of* their place so completely unrealistic is an insidiously effective way to keep women *in* their place.

LM: Even your early SF works, *The Jewels of Aptor* and *The Fall of the Towers*, are remarkably sophisticated by most standards. And you had apparently been writing other novels from your early teens onward. What literary interests did you have as a child?

SD: Until I wrote my first SF novel I wasn't particularly interested in SF other than as a reader; I was interested in writing. I'd been trying to write novels since I was fourteen, which isn't *that* odd—some people just know that's what they want to do. During my teens I was omnivorously reading the kind of things any bright, literarily inclined kid would be reading in the '50s—along with a lot of SF.

SG: No writer really stood out as an inspiration or model?

SD: I guess the writer I was most impressed with as a teenager was Theodore Sturgeon—who happened to be an SF writer, but who could do more with a sentence than anyone else I'd ever read. He'd give you the flicker of sunlight through blowing leaves on a bellied-out screen door, in a phrase so vivid that it made you reach to feel the snagged and gritty mesh. He wrote about human emotions as though they were solid objects, with shapes and colors, moving through the body so you could feel their friction. No matter where he set the story, whether in an October suburban schoolroom or in a spaceship cabin between planets or in a village of telepathic aliens under a distantly clouded sun, it was equally sharp and immediate. Later I began to encounter a few other writers who could do somewhat the same thing— Nabokov, Updike, Barth, and—still later—Gass and Gardner; still more recently, Guy Davenport. At least with realistic settings. But Sturgeon was the first and, for a young reader, the most astonishing.

When I was seventeen, Marie Ponsot, an older poet (that is, she was twenty-five or twenty-six at the time), gave me a copy of Djuna Barnes's *Nightwood.* That's got to be the single novel I've reread more than any other—about twenty times at this point. Like everyone else back then, I *loved* Baldwin's essays. I had the traditional '50s awe of Joyce and Eliot and Woolf and Pound. And I always liked Gertrude Stein. So there really wasn't anything too unusual about my interests.

LM: What turned you toward SF when you embarked on your career? Was it mainly the practical matter of Marilyn's being an editor at Ace for Don Wolheim?

SD: It was little more than fortuitous circumstance. Shortly after Marilyn and I were married, I had a series of nightmares. (I suspect they're endemic among people who wed at eighteen and nineteen.) I had lots of difficulty talking about them. Finally I decided to write a book set in their several landscapes, a kind of science fantasy. Marilyn had gotten a job at Ace Books, a paperback house that had first published William Burroughs's *Junky* and where Carl Solomon, of *Howl* fame and nephew of the publisher, worked. Both of us had always been SF readers, so Marilyn was happy to find an editorial position working with a genre she enjoyed reading herself. One thing led to another. I wrote the book, and she took it in, submitting it under the pen name "Bruno Callabro"—we were terribly moral children back then. As it turned out, Donald Wolheim liked it, but he was rather relieved when, at contract time, he found out about the pen name. At his urging, I went back to being Samuel R. Delany.

SG: Your fiction has often been called poetic, and references to poetry and poets abound there. And certain forms of poetry, especially symbolism (à la Rimbaud in *Babel-17*), have affected your concept of the craft of writing. Why haven't you pursued poetry more often yourself?

SD: I've used poetry as a topic in some of my works because making poems is a good metaphor for the language-making process, the art-making process in general. But it can serve as a metaphor for the latrine-digging process or the dry-cleaning process, too. When I was a kid, I wrote a very few, very bad poems. But that doesn't make you a poet. I've watched a few people who are good poets do their work. That was enough to convince me that it just wasn't something for which I had a talent. I'm an enthusiastic poetry reader, and because my temperament lets me enjoy reading it—enjoy it deeply—I'm *very* grateful. But any poem I wrote would, I suspect, be too much *me* in the worst and most uninteresting way.

LM: A number of other "poetic" prose writers have told me that they have remained in fiction because they are interested in "story." Is that true for you as well?

SD: No. Story as it's usually conceived seems to me the most boring thing about fiction. Story is a way of talking about the dullest part of the reading experience. You have the experience of "story" at very few points in the text—often only for a moment or two, sometimes just at the very end. Get back from the writerly canvas and you'll see certain things. One thing that emerges, when you're at a certain distance, is, of course, the "story," so at least it's a real category for *readers* to think about. But for the writer who has to work right up next to the canvas all the time, story dissolves into so many other things that it's almost pointless to think about it directly. From the viewpoint of the writer, I'd say "story" doesn't even exist. It's just not a valid writerly category. Writers face off against the page, put one letter down after another to make a word, one word after another to make a sentence: the sentence has to have a certain shape, a certain melody. Then you have to make another sentence. Then you have to make sure the two of them harmonize—at every level, from sound to semantics. Story vanishes in this process. Move back far enough and, yes, a "story" emerges at a certain point—in the same way that, if you move back even farther, you can see the story's theme; and, if you can get back farther still, you can see its genre. But up close, it's just words and sentences and sounds and syntax, one following another in a variety of patterns, while you try to make those words relate to all the others you've put down in a variety of ways—a very few of which *may* relate to "story."

SG: This sounds a lot like what poets do.

SD: Yes. And if you substitute the idea of "brush stroke" for "word" and "sentence," it sounds much like what painters do. All we're saying, really, is that the construction process in any art tends to follow the same atomic process.

LM: Most critics point to a shift in your work after the popular and widely praised works of the '60s, concluding with *Nova*—a shift that was basically announced with *Dhalgren*. Could you talk a bit about the origins of *Dhalgren*? Did you know from the outset that this was going to be a massive novel, for example?

SD: I certainly knew it was going to be large. It was initially outlined, in 1968, as five separate volumes. Only when I began to work on the first draft, in San Francisco in 1969, and I began to compress and consolidate, did it shrink to its present size.

The really interesting part of your question, you know, is the words you use to ask it: statistically, in terms of sales, *Dhalgren* has been far more popular than any of my earlier books. It's outsold my next most popular SF novel by a factor of three or four, without any extra advertising or push from the publisher. (If anything, it was rather the opposite.) The advance was comparatively small. The editor who bought the book prudently didn't mention its size to anyone in the company. At the first sales conference, after copies showed up in the office, the general feeling was that they had a nine-hundred-page disaster on their hands. It was not *about* anything anyone could grab hold of, much less synopsize commercially in a sentence or a paragraph. "Sell as many copies as you can, then let it sink out of existence; and we'll all try not to do *that* again!" Since they hadn't put much money into the book, they didn't feel obliged to spend any extra on making it back.

Only the orders kept coming in. People began to talk about the novel, and by the time the publication date arrived, they'd actually been through four printings, with a fifth on order. It's continued to sell well ever since, with total sales edging up toward a million. No bestseller, certainly, but it's more than respectable for a serious novel.

The fan letters were also very different for *Dhalgren*. With my SF books, teenagers would sometimes write, "Wow, that was neat!" Or "That was really clever!" Or "That was a lot of fun!" But with *Dhalgren*— and there were many, many *more* letters with *Dhalgren*—people in their twenties and thirties were writing, "Your novel is all about me." "You're writing about my friends." "You're writing about *our* world— and what's more, I've read the book three—or six, or nine—times and given away three copies."

I think what separated *Dhalgren* from an honest to goodness bestseller is that frequently the people to whom these readers gave the copies turned out *not* to like it. Some of them were confused by it. And my readers would write me, "I wonder why? It seemed so clear to *me*." Well, I can't answer that any more than they could.

But now critics began turning back to my earlier books. They saw books that, according to a very standard model of the "average reader," *ought* to have been popular. Some of those books had won awards, and almost all of them had gotten good reviews. Still, the facts are just otherwise. *Dhalgren* was (and is) more popular.

Now, if I were a critic—in the face of information like that—I'd have to revise my model of what is really popular and what is not. I'd have to rethink who the "average reader" really is. But as recently as 1982, a critic writing in the *Philadelphia Inquirer*, reviewing a new book of mine, was explaining how, in 1975, with *Dhalgren*, I "turned away" from my audience to indulge in "abstruse gameplaying and experimentation." Somehow, both the critics who don't like it and the critics who do like it boggle at the notion that *anyone else* might like it. So *Dhalgren* remains "experimental," "difficult," and "hermetic," while my earlier books, which less than a third as many people are interested in reading, are "popular," "exciting," and "accessible."

LM: How did the book actually begin?

SD: Conceptually, I suppose, it started with Mann's notion: "Nothing is truly interesting save the exhaustive." I wanted to write a big, exhaustive book. As far as incident, it began with the present beginning—the woman turning into a tree. Then it stopped for a while, until I had my next structural notion, the idea of building the novel around two parties, the dinner at Mrs. Richards's and the party at Calkins's mansion. I got the idea partly from Jane Austen's notion that "Everything happens at parties." I'll also confess that I was thinking of the two great Proustian parties at the beginning and the end of *Remembrance of Things Past*. Indeed, you can look at the whole *Recherche*, really, as a movement from the dinner party at Madame Verdurin's to the soirée, years later, at the Princesse de Guermantes'.

LM: You mentioned the relevance of Harlem to *Dhalgren*. Your novel portrays the contemporary urban experience—especially the marginal life of poor people and racial minorities.

SD: Urban life is what I know. The motto I chose for the book was from a conversation with the West Coast poet George Stanley, back in 1969 or '70, when he and Marilyn and I were having dinner at the Savoy Tivoli, in North Beach: "You have confused the true and the real." But the motto could just as easily have been "I love New York." I had a lot of cities in mind while I was writing *Dhalgren*—in a sense the city there is Every City, Any City. One person said, with some truth, that *Dhalgren* is a book in which the exteriors are New York and the interiors are San Francisco. Well, a lot of the first draft of *Dhalgren* was written while I was living San Francisco. That's not to say I was transcribing my life during that period, though some of the things that had been going on in the years before—for example, the kind of life I described in my nonfiction book, *Heavenly Breakfast*—certainly resonate throughout the novel. I suppose the central conceit is that what is traditionally socially marginal is re-placed at center stage; there's also an economic distortion at work, and a distortion of the landscape, that allows the marginal to take over. All the "decent people" have left the city, leaving only the marginals, who can then go on leading their lives however they want, without the usual exterior pressures. There's still plenty of interior pressure, though. Another oblique influence was probably Marge Piercy's *Dance the Eagle to Sleep*: the first third seemed so brilliant when I first read it, while the last two-thirds seemed to me . . . well, unrealized.

LM: I felt that *Dhalgren* was, among other things, a very personalized exploration of your own psyche.

SD: I've always hated the idea of art as therapy, yet putting a lot of the confusion and pain and other materials of one's life into a formal pattern *can* make it easier to deal with these things—or at least make them a little less terrifying. I remember when I was twelve or thirteen going into the morgue and discovering a male body laid out on the table and wondering: Should I touch this or not? I ended up just picking up the hand—and found myself with an erection. I was surprised. But my reaction wasn't shock or disgust; it was just, "Boy this is strange!" Kid has a similar response when he picks up the body that's fallen down the elevator shaft. Now although the experience behind what happens to the adult Kid in the book happened to me when I was a child in my father's embalming room, they're really two very different experiences. For the book I tried to retain what was most important about the incident—the response: when it happens to Kid, he's not terrified or shocked or anything. He doesn't pursue it; neither did I. In both cases, it was a real event, something to think about so much—and no more. I'm sure many, many people have had similar "sensational" experiences that, if they're honest, were just not *that* sensational. There's a lot of that in *Dhalgren*—more, perhaps, than people may be used to in most fiction. That may be one reason why so many people have so much difficulty "understanding" it.

I suspect what's shocking—or confusing—about the scene with Kid and the dead boy in the elevator shaft is not that he picks up the body and has a sexual response to it, but that after this happens he just thinks, "Oh, yeah, I'm having a sexual response; but there are other things I have to do—like get this body back to his mother."

It's the same thing we were saying about handling women characters— there are standard fictive models by which we narrate our lives most of the time, so that frequently when we tell about our most realistic experiences we are basically transforming them into something we have read or heard—into some cliché. If you don't do this, it puts a certain kind of reader off—while it draws another kind to you.

LM: You're raising a point that other writers have mentioned: one draws from one's experience when writing, but the effective writer must find a way to transform experience into art. Reality isn't "shapely."

SD: The fiction-making process—and the shape of other stories—can blind you to what's interesting (or, indeed, needed) in life. When I'm teaching a creative writing course, I find this happening time and time again. Precisely when the students think they're really writing about "what happened to them," that's when they are most in the grip of literary clichés and stereotypes. What excited them to write about an incident in the first place was that the reality was already so close to the cliché: that's what made it seem like such good story material. Then all those changes they make so that it will seem more like good fiction manage to take a half-cliché and turn it into a whole one. And once they've got it on paper, they actually can no longer see their own distortions.

The problems of representation are very real. Nobody denies it. You cannot say everything about any situation, and there is no way to verify that any of what's been said or written is true, without a situational context to appeal to. But there is a great rhetorical battery, much of it extant and more of it still inventable, that *can* talk about the world in a recognizable way. To do it takes a great sense of responsibility, some aesthetic sensitivity, and a lot of discipline. But it's also possible that even to have the problem means I'm deluding myself about my own writerly strengths.

SG: When you were writing *Heavenly Breakfast*, your nonfiction essay on urban communes, based so much on your own experience with them, did you find the process fundamentally different from your fiction writing?

SD: No. Some people read *Heavenly Breakfast* as autobiography, you know—though it says right in the introduction that "persons are combined to make" single characters and "atomized to make several" and that dates are shifted and incidents are shuffled between cities. Well, what sort of autobiography is that? But, again, I was trying to maintain the structure of the characteristic incidents.

The difference, I suppose, is that in fiction the process happens against a much finer grid. You take a bushy eyebrow from a subway conductor, the red cheeks from your Uncle Lucius, a snowy November evening from a weekend in Milwaukee a half-dozen years ago, a cornice decoration from a church in Thessalonica you saw a dozen years before that, and a wholly invented stained glass window—though the dirt in the corner is the dirt in the corner of your office window as you're writing. You put them all together into a scene where, one snowy November evening, a bushy-eyed, red-cheeked man stops before a stained glass window outside a church in the outskirts of Secaucus, New Jersey (where you've never been, though you read about some colorful characters in a bar there, once, in somebody's poem), beneath a chipped cornice. Any talk about whether the character is *really* your uncle or a subway conductor is, at this point, silly; so is any discussion about whether the church is really in Greece or New York (or Milwaukee or Secaucus). It's a text. No more—but no less.

In *Heavenly Breakfast* the grid was much coarser. I was trying to take whole incidents, rather than eyebrows and cornice decorations; I was trying to preserve *some* continuity of discourse. That's what makes it nonfiction. Only the continuity of character, or of gross location, and the chronology were fictive. Those fictions didn't seem great enough for me not to call the work nonfiction—not to call it an essay. Yet those continuities—character, place, and time—are so often seen as one with reality by readers who assume all novels are really *romans à clef* (most of D. H. Lawrence's critics, for example).

SG: You have said that writing *Triton* was easier than any book you'd written since you were a teenager, yet Bron was the first unsympathetic central character you've created.

SD: Sometimes it's much easier to write a hate letter than to compose a thoughtful, supportive, positive one. The initial impetus behind *Triton* was to construct a merciless analysis of a monster. It's a kind of monstrosity that many of us share, but it's monstrous nevertheless. Here comes another of those preposterously pretentious declarations: The model for *Triton* was *Madame Bovary*, in the sense, say, that *La Princesse de Cleves* was the model for Radiguet's *Bal du Comte d'Orgel* (rather than in the sense that Bester took the plot of *The Stars My Destination* from *The Count of Monte Cristo*). I wanted to do a psychological analysis of someone with whom you're just not in sympathy, someone whom you watch making all the wrong choices, even though his plight itself is sympathetic. That's the case with Bron. He's constantly taking the easy way out, and finally he destroys himself. He doesn't commit suicide at the end, like Emma, but he's left pretty hopeless. He simply cannot distinguish truth from lies, cliché from reality. It amounts to a kind of madness. Anyway, after five years of writing endless sentences for *Dhalgren* at the head of notebook page after notebook page and revising them, one at a time, down to the bottom margin, then mortaring them back into place—after that, *Triton* seemed to flow very easily. In one sense, *Dhalgren* was a five-year exercise in empathy. *Triton* was a nine-month orgy of antipathy.

LM: You said *Triton* erupted after you had written the "kiss-off" letter Bron reads in Chapter Six—and that the rest of the book evolved around that letter. Is that the way your books have tended to proceed for you—in a nonlinear way?

SD: Usually they proceed in a more orderly fashion. I have to have a pretty good idea of what's going on all through them before I start. Still, I usually begin from the beginning and work through to the end— at least for the first draft. Revisions, of course, come more piecemeal— though even the second draft *usually* proceeds from one end to the other. The third and up? Well, that can happen any old way. Still, in that sense *Triton* was unusual. I wrote out a draft of what you called "the kiss-off letter" first—sitting in Heathrow Airport, waiting with Marilyn for an airplane to Paris—before going back to start with Chapter One.

SG: You mentioned a three-part revision process—I take it that you find rewriting important.

SD: I carry around a notebook and write my first drafts in that. Then I type up a rough draft. Then I do another draft that usually needs to be typed once more. There are lots of revisions in each retyping. And when I got an electronic typewriter, with about ten pages of memory, I found that with the same amount of work I could do *five* drafts! So now I revise even more.

LM: Can you point to anything that tends to begin a work for you— a character, an image, a plot idea, a theme, a metaphor?

SD: Usually the books begin with a character in a landscape. Once a draft of that letter was out of the way for *Triton*, the thing that gave me the beginning of the book was the hope that readers would initially think Bron was just an ordinary guy living in a sterile, depressing, gaudy but ultimately repressive society. Then, as the book goes on, you slowly realize that the society is not so bad—but this *guy* is just *awful!* A switch takes place. I wanted you to end up feeling that Bron is completely hopeless, but that the society is certainly no worse than ours—probably a lot better in some ways. So, again, the book began, as it were, with a character in a place. Then the view of the place— and the character—changes.

LM: Those appendices and reports at the end of *Triton* and the *Neveryon* books actually seem integral—discourses that *open up* what seemed to be the closed system of the novel. What was the inspiration for that approach?

SD: I first found it, of course, in the "Consequential Data," "Notes on the Text," and "workpoints" at the ends of the various volumes of Durrell's *Alexandria Quartet*. That was another spectacularly enjoyable read for me when I was a teenager. Then there were the various journals, fictive and actual, at the end of Gide's *Les Faux Monnayeurs*. Of course, there's a whole tradition in SF novels of having appendices, like those in *Dune* and the glossary in *The Left Hand of Darkness*; so I thought I'd have a go at it. The appendices to the Neveryon books function a bit differently. They're really a kind of scholarly game. All the people cited in the first one are real—except for K. Leslie Steiner. Interestingly enough, I got a call from someone reviewing the book who had just interviewed Schmandt-Besserat, one of the archeologists whose theories are discussed in the appendix to *Tales of Neveryon*. The reviewer was quite sure that if someone that obscure (to most people) was real, then *everyone* in the essay must be real, including Steiner.

One of the things I like in the appendix to *Neveryona* is that there really is a Charles Hoequist, Jr. Not only is he a real linguist and archeologist, then at Yale and currently in Germany, but he actually wrote those letters. Indeed, that particular appendix started because I received a letter from Hoequist, who'd thrown himself into the spirit of Neveryon quite wholeheartedly, and who addressed a letter to Kermit, taking him to task for some of his mistakes in the earlier appendix. So I wrote Kermit's letter back; then Hoequist wrote again. Finally, I wrote, "Dr. Hoequist, would you mind if I published the correspondence between you and 'Prof. Kermit' as an appendix?" He said, "I'd love it." Not only is that true, but the description of his letters as written on the backs of all those strange things is also true. So I'm only responsible for the Kermit side of the correspondence. I thought it was quite in keeping with the flavor of Neveryon to have correspondence between a real person and an imaginary one.

LM: The Ashima Slade figure in the *Triton* appendix could be read as an analogue for Bron Helstrom.

SD: Very much so. Helstrom and Slade come from the same culture—they come from entirely different levels of that culture, yet, in their new home, they go through similar experiences. The basic reason why Bron goes through the sex change is that he comes from a comparatively sexist culture to this different, more open culture, and he can't deal with it. Bron goes through this on a very unsophisticated level, while Slade presumably is much more sophisticated in his reactions; nevertheless, the process is the same. I was hoping it would come as a real social revelation: What seemed a unique story—the main action in *Triton*—is revealed to be not unique at all. Suddenly you see that the situation has wider implications than the personal ones you first saw only through Helstrom's eyes. There are political pressures on all the people from the other planets, and the satellite society as a whole (wonderful as it is) is not set up to help them deal with these pressures. Slade himself is aware of this; perhaps someday Bron will be, too.

LM: Are there any contemporary writers (SF or otherwise) whom you particularly admire?

SD: Like a lot of other people, I find it harder and harder to read fiction. I don't know if that's because of the fiction or because I'm getting older. Probably both. Every once in a while, though, I find a writer who wakes up my appetite for fiction. I've already mentioned Guy Davenport, for example. I find the short stories of John Varley very exciting, though I don't enjoy his novels as much. I like William Gass's criticism a lot. I admire Walter Abish's work: *Alphabetical Africa* is one of the most delightful books I've ever read, and the somewhat more traditional *How German Is It* offers all kinds of challenges. I'm sure there are all sorts of interesting fiction writers out there, but my reading in that area has just fallen off. I'm mainly interested in critics, such as Shoshana Felman, Barbara Johnson, Paul de Man, Jane Gallop.

LM: You were a musician yourself for a while, and musicians and musical analogues appear frequently in your works. It seems to me that you consider the elements of your craft—words, symbols, motifs—somewhat abstractly, as materials to be manipulated, in much the way that musicians do.

SD: I've always felt attracted to Walter Pater's notion, "All art aspires to the condition of music"—a phrase which, when I first ran into it, immediately seemed somehow right.

Many years ago I was a page turner for the rehearsals of a concert of new music at Hunter College. One piece was written for twelve instruments, all of which had to play a different note of the scale—except one, which was left out. The melody was really an absence of that note, which moved up and down, working its way through the composition, a traveling silence through a constant acoustic field of eleven other notes.

When the piece was played in rehearsal in an empty auditorium, the missing note was absolutely audible, hovering and drifting through the cloud of cacophony. But when you heard it in an auditorium full of people, the resonance of the auditorium changed, due to the general noise of people breathing, or shifting in their seats, or the new deployment of mass, or whatever. You could no longer hear the silent note.

That has always struck me as a good analogue for the art of the postmodern artist, who works today in a highly refined field. The writer is concerned with small resonances, phrase to phrase, word to word; such effects sometimes simply vanish before the reality of a statistical audience. But if everyone is very quiet, sometimes you can hear them.

An Interview with

Barry Hannah

The following interview took place in our San Diego home on a warm April afternoon. Barry Hannah arrived looking every bit the Southern gentleman, dressed in a cream-colored suit and carrying a tumbler with the remnants of whiskey and water. We freshened his drink, opened beers for ourselves, and (at Barry's request) turned on the stereo, first playing Elvis Presley's *Sun Session* album and later Bruce Springsteen. As we talked for the next few hours, Barry's attention was often caught by the music; he would lean toward it, his body energized into a bebop rhythm while he continued on, remarking on literature, the South, and his past. At one point when he crossed his legs, a bit of blue pajama peeked out beneath his pants cuff. "I was afraid I might be cold today—you never know about California weather," he explained with aplomb. The incident perhaps points out the cautious side of Barry Hannah, the part that makes him worry about his son's decision to be a rock musician ("It's such a hard, dangerous life"). But prudence, rather like gentlemanly manners, can be set aside in a flash to reveal someone suspiciously like Hannah's crazed narrators: impassioned, wild, funny, ready for action.

Since the publication of his first novel, *Geronimo Rex* (1972), Hannah's reputation has steadily grown, and he has often been cited as the latest in a long and distinguished list of Southern writers. It is true that his fiction often possesses the gothic and haunted power of William Faulkner and Flannery O'Connor. But although Hannah shares certain themes with other Southern writers—the conflict between the civilized and the primitive; the power of the past, both personal and social, to dominate the present; the constant struggles caused by class, race, and sex—his voice is absolutely his own. To begin one of his works with preconceived notions about his slot in a literary tradition is to spoil the party. And Hannah gives grand, wild parties—not the staid gatherings where polite conversation accompanies a few glasses of white wine, but the parties where anything can happen, where ecstasy, communion, humiliation, and violence can all spill out in the celebration of being alive.

Hannah's style has evolved markedly from the long, manic, sprawling fictions of *Geronimo Rex* and *The Nightwatchmen* (1975). In 1978 his collection of short stories, *Airships* (which won the Arnold Gingrich Short Fiction Award), displayed marvels of bizarre perspectives, stunning verbal techniques, and Hannah's typical fusion of sex and violence. By his next novel, *Ray* (1980), he had abandoned the dense, picaresque form of his earlier works in favor of a more compressed, elliptical style. The result is a surreal, brutal presentation of the masculine dilemma, this time in the highly poeticized voice of Ray, a Southern doctor and Vietnam veteran who desires peace and love so much that he's willing to kill for them. In *The Tennis Handsome* (1983) the arena has changed somewhat to include more metaphorical violence and conflict—this time on the tennis court. But here, as well as in Hannah's recent collection of stories, *Captain Maximus* (1985), his central preoccupation remains the same: How do we accommodate our fascination with death, destruction, and power?

Larry McCaffery: What's your reaction when you hear yourself being constantly referred to as a "Southern writer"? I know there's an impressive tradition there, but that sort of pigeonholing must make you feel uneasy as well.

Barry Hannah: Mainly I react with disgust when I hear those kinds of comments. In fact, before we really get started here, could I ask that we avoid all the standard questions about my Southern heritage, at least all the *dumb* ones? I'm not saying this to insult you, but you can't imagine how often I get asked about how Faulkner influenced me and why there's so many good Southern writers and all that shit. Don't get me wrong—I'm from Mississippi and proud to be a Southerner. That's why I've come back to Mississippi to live. I'm buying a home there right now. Mississippi is the poorest, most illiterate state in the Union and it's produced some of our best art: Eudora Welty, Faulkner, Tennessee Williams (I hope you saw my tribute to him in *Rolling Stone*), Elvis, Muddy Waters, B. B. King. I'm proud to share in that heritage.

But I don't like to be called a "Southern writer" any more than somebody likes to be called a "black writer" or a "woman writer" or a
"Southern California professor." That kind of labeling cancels the audience's appreciation for what my books are, gets people to ignore my
books who shouldn't. My writing all comes from inside me, so I'm not
aware of movements or labels at all. As a matter of fact, until I met
Richard Brautigan, I thought he was one of those "lightweight hippies,"
you know, like the singer Donovan. But he's not that at all. He lives
over there in Livingston, Montana, likes to shoot guns, and doesn't
even smoke pot. Shows you how far off labels can be.

Sinda Gregory: Tom Robbins has said something very interesting
about the South (he grew up in North Carolina). He thought that
Southern men were raised with a certain paradoxical attitude about
violence—that although civilized "courtly" behavior is encouraged,
violence is also encouraged or accepted because it is seen as being
manly.

BH: He's right.

SG: I mention that because your characters often seem to have
contradictory responses to violence. They feel guilty about their involvement in violent deeds, but they also feel that violence is one of
the things that makes life exciting or provides a sense of glory. Ray
claims that he wasn't violent before he went to Vietnam, but he also
says, "The only glory I saw is the glory I saw as a jet fighter."

BH: Flying a jet can make you feel all kinds of things. When Ray
was talking about glory there, he wasn't necessarily talking about
violence. He did shoot up people over there; he had to. But the glory
he saw was mainly being in the air, being close to the stars. *Ray*, by
the way, is the only book of mine that I can quote from. For some
damn reason I can never quote the rest of my stuff and don't even
recognize it sometimes when somebody will read something to me that
I've written. Yes, there is a lot of violence in my work, and I've even
sometimes been called the most violent writer in America. But I want
to make this clear: I'm a peaceable man. I'm all for brotherhood, peace,
good marriages, and sitting at my typewriter. I'm not a warrior, I'm a
tennis player. I use violence in my fiction because it puts your back
up against the wall. People tend to lie less in conditions of violent
behavior; they say a lot of interesting things they wouldn't say under
any other circumstance. There's a more straightforward reaction, if you
know what I mean. For instance, I love football, really love it, but I
know there's a lot of people who never go to football games because
football is so violent. Well, *sure* it's violent, but there is something direct
and honest about what's going on out there that I respond to. And I
love the skills involved in football, the conditions under which these

violent actions are played out, especially now that everybody involved is 6'5" and weighs at least 250 pounds. So that's my main interest in violence. I certainly don't advertise it or condone it, and I'm not going to get into a fight if we go out to a bar tonight. But violence is a condition that all of us feel deeply. Just about anyone will admit that there is a violent streak in all of us, something that must be satisfied.

SG: In *The Tennis Handsome* you seem to bring out the idea that people have created these artificial arenas—like football and tennis—where these violent urges and satisfactions can be safely experienced. And inside these arenas the participants and spectators can respond to all sorts of intensified feelings. That's one of the important things about violence, it seems to me: people tend to live these banal, mundane lives, but when violence is involved everything becomes much more intensely felt, more memorable.

BH: You've got it. Intensity is all. I know I live an intense life, even when I'm at peace. I often throw a knife against the wall. And this violent intensity that everyone responds to can come out in tennis, as it does in *The Tennis Handsome.* Tennis is certainly a form of violence. Even though you don't actually kill anybody, you sure try to knock the hell out of the ball and embarrass the other guy. That's violence.

LM: Doesn't Ray say something about it being easy to kill but it's hard to live?

BH: He does, and I think that idea helps balance some of the violence in *Ray*. That recognition that it's hard as hell to live is built into the book in different ways and is supposed to affect our view of Ray. I mean, any asshole can take a gun and shoot somebody; any Navy pilot could take his plane out and use his missiles to blow this house apart. But it's tough to live. Sometimes it's a lot tougher to be at peace than to be at war.

LM: I gather that you're not trying to present violence in some sort of uniquely Southern context so much as describing something that exists in all of us.

BH: Right. Southerners write a lot about violence, but I don't think the Southern mentality is any more violent than any other. The murder rate in Los Angeles is 2000 percent over the national average.

SG: Harry Monroe in *Geronimo Rex* says, "Sex wasn't made for thought, was it? It's only instinct and touch. As intellectual matter it is a swamp from which no man comes back whole. You go into the swamp with your mind—there seems to be so much to contemplate. And you come back, if you get back, with a few pubic hairs in your hand and a shriveled-up backbone." That passage seems to suggest that men can't win at sex—men desperately want sex and they're unhappy when they can't get it; but they're also unhappy when they *do* get it because it wasn't how it was supposed to be. My reaction to these guys is that what they really want from sex is to banish death, or at least the knowledge of death. But again and again they are disappointed in sex because eventually they leave it behind and have to feel death thrust at them once more.

BH: That's it exactly. Yeah, sex does make death go away; at least it drives the thought of death away. But that only lasts for a while. You know, I've never understood why people always ask me why there's so much sex in my books. It is a major part of my writing because sex is a major part of all our lives. People who say they don't want to look at it are liars. I'm not so sure about the philosophy of sex, but I don't know anybody who doesn't enjoy sex in one way or another. Sex is awfully pleasant, it's healthful and helpful. It's fun. It also confirms the feeling that somebody else loves you—and that feeling is very important to all of us; it's one of the reasons why my family is so important to me. So I don't understand why people feel uncomfortable about the sex in my books. I don't write about whores, you understand. I'm not trying to help people masturbate. With a character like Ray, sex is something to be celebrated.

SG: Since your characters seem so involved with death, so sensitive to the fact that everyone around them is dying (slowly or not so slowly), you'd think they would be less likely to kill or involve themselves in violence of any kind. Is this just an inevitable pairing of the fear of death with a fascination for it?

BH: That's part of it. People should keep in mind, though, that as I write I'm always on the lookout for fictional situations that seem like they have certain dramatic possibilities. Situations involving death and violence often contain those possibilities, whereas a lot of other situations don't. But, look, some of my characters are violent and some aren't. Some are extreme pacifists. Not everybody that I write about carries around a howitzer.

SG: But don't all your main characters carry guns?

BH: OK, you may be right about that. You know, personally I can't even shoot a deer. I like sporting chances. But even if he does carry a gun, Ray is against violence very much, so much that when he sees these people come into his office who abuse their children and their wives, he shoots one of them in the stomach with a .30/.30. He knows that shot's not going to kill the guy, and he wants that guy to know what it feels like to be hurt like that. In other words, Ray is against violence. He's a kind of twisted pacifist. He doesn't carry a gun on the street, you notice; he'd rather sit around and write poetry. But he sees this abuse of wives and children and he hurts these guys back because he just wants them to know that it hurts to *be* hurt. He wants to show them that they shouldn't ever hit a woman like they do sometimes. In my second marriage, I once slapped my wife with my left hand— and I feel more guilty about that than almost anything else I've done in my life.

LM: In *The Nightwatchmen*, William Tell says, "Perhaps there it *all* was: fornication is sorrow, trapped by fate into mere motions of the body towards the most accessible female, all the while knowing there is an impossibly distant queen who is yours, a land that is yours alone, but both being worn down by the time it will take to reach them." That quote seems to suggest that same paradoxical attitude about sex that Sinda was talking about a minute ago. Your characters always seem to be pursuing an idealized woman. They chase after sex almost obsessively, but they somehow feel guilty discovering the sweaty, animalistic parts of sex. Maybe this is even exaggerated in the South, with that image of the Southern belle so much a part of the sexual mythology.

BH: I'd certainly agree that Southerners have an idealized vision of women. We tend to put them on pedestals, where they're not too comfortable. I'm not currently married, but I know I'm still looking for the kind of queen that William Tell is talking about, and I have the remorseful sense that I'll never get her. I live in Oxford, Mississippi, where the girls are really sexy but would rather talk to each other about what to wear than about sex. Of course, I don't know what these women actually think about sex. I'm not a philosopher or a sociologist, so it's difficult to answer these questions about sexual attitudes in the abstract. I do know that I'm all for beautiful marriages, for leaving your brother alone, if that's what he wants, or protecting him if he's in danger. And the same goes for your sister.

LM: Let's talk about your interest in J. E. B. Stuart, who appears in a lot of your fiction. Were those stories in *Airships* that involve Jeb originally supposed to be part of a novel?

BH: I was going to write a novel about Jeb, but eventually I cut back and salvaged what I could into stories. I backed off from the novel when I began to see that what I was writing wasn't really a novel— it didn't have the focus of a novel. I began to see that I really wasn't so much interested in Jeb as in the people who reacted to him. I rewrote the book into stories because I thought that the people talking about Jeb were just as interesting as Jeb himself. That original focus had been lost, but I had gained other perspectives.

SG: Like the perspective of that gay soldier who is in love with Jeb in "Knowing He Was Not My Kind"?

BH: Right. That kid had something to say that people don't usually hear. People forget that history is not just a bunch of different folks talking strange languages, the way we usually read about them. There had to be queers in the war, so I just modernized things to make the language maybe a little more accurate. It's really *my* language, of course. So anyway, even though I'm not queer, I thought it would be an interesting story to tell—Corporal Ainsworth in the glass shop. I try that a lot in my fiction—getting inside the heads and voices of people who you know damn well are going to have something interesting to say, some perspective that will make those middle-class jerks out there shudder or smile.

SG: You've only written a few pieces from the female point of view. Are they harder for you to do?

Bh: They sure as hell are. Actually I've just written a piece for Robert Altman called "Power and Light" that's told from the perspective of working-class women. I've tried different points of view, but this is the first time I've ever tried to deal with working-class women. It's tough for a guy to go across that sexual divide. What does Keats call it—negative capability? Which means that you can write from the point of view of someone very different from yourself. Being able to do that, and to get the language right, is what I'm mainly interested in throughout a lot of those stories in *Airships*.

LM: There's something so real about your perspectives, though, that it's often tempting to assume that you are, in some sense, Ray or Harry Monroe.

BH: I am Ray. I was Harry when I wrote *Geronimo Rex*. In a way, I'm all of 'em. In a way I'm those women that I write about in this "novella for the screen," as I'm calling "Power and Light." In that book I try to identify with women, figure out what it must be like to be a woman and work on those lightpoles. Hardhats, real work. I like to cross these borders and try other viewpoints, discover what it must be like to be in these other positions. Take a jet pilot—what music would go through his head?

LM: You must use the traits of people around you as well as your own when you're inventing your characters. From what I've read about your friendship with John Quisenberry, I gather that Ray is almost a combination of you two. And Quisenberry has made guest appearances in your works before, apparently—as Quadberry in "Testimony of a Pilot," for example.

BH: The real Quisenberry was a jet pilot in Vietnam. He's a lawyer up in LA now and he's still my best buddy. I like to say that he and I have a mutual admiration society—I admire him for being able to do the things he's done, and he admires me for being able to write about the things he's gone through. I don't mean to steal his glory or anything. I do a lot of autobiographical fiction drawn straight from my life, but the only theft I commit is from close friends like Quisenberry, people whose stories I can trust. In a way Quisenberry is my alter ego. He came from my hometown, Clinton, Mississippi, which was really just a little hick village. We went different ways. I was the musician, he was the quarterback. I was in the Jackson symphony (I was raised on the classical trumpet), he went away to Vietnam. In Mississippi in those days you were either on the football team or you were maybe queer. I was a musician and never on the football team, and the football coach was always coming up to me saying, "Son, when are you going to *straighten up*!?" Anyway, Ray is partly me and partly Quisenberry and partly other people I've known. It's always a combination with my characters. Quadberry, for example, is a combination of Quisenberry and another good buddy of mine, Will Blackwell, who did in fact play the sax awfully well.

SG: So are all of your characters based on real people?

BH: Most of the time, yes. I usually write about my own life pretty straight on, but I mix up the characters and idiosyncrasies of people I know when I write about them. Sometimes, though, I write them almost literally, as a journalist would. A lot of the people in *Geronimo Rex* were based on real people. Ben Kimpel, my best professor at Arkansas, was the guy Harry shot pool with. He was almost my entire education while I was at graduate school. Ben was someone who took poetry so seriously that he showed me something, made me look at art differently. Now he's dead, and I miss him. I'm a sentimental man, you know, and I just miss him. Oh, I don't think it's sentimentality, really. You just *miss* people.

LM: I know. My mother just died and I still can't get used to the fact that she's so utterly *gone*.

BH: Yeah, people die and then they're gone. And I'm not too sure about what happens afterward. I wish I were a Baptist and believed in the Upper Sky. I believe in spirits and I believe in the power of your good will and Sinda's. I believe that there's strength in our good wishes for each other, which I guess is what you call "psychic energy." But I plead agnosticism on the big issues. I just don't know. So whenever one of my friends goes down, it kills me a little.

LM: Does it ever occur to you that, in writing about people you know, you're making them immortal? Their spirit is part of your work, and in that way they'll always be around.

BH: Yes, that thought has crossed my mind, but it doesn't really decrease the sorrow for me all the time. Sometimes it still hurts. I got real depressed when I lost another friend of mine, a psychiatrist who helped me through a lot of very deep trouble a while back. He once told me, "The only people who can do anything about the past, Barry, are writers and artists. The only people." This was back when I was drinking a bottle and a half of tequila a day, but when he told me that, it picked me up. My fiction is always full of pain—pain is one of the things that makes life what it is—but maybe, like my psychiatrist said, writing about it helps get everything out there in the open.

SG: There's a line that everyone walks that may be especially difficult for writers to negotiate. That's being aware of the past, having these memories and not forgetting anything—having the past be there as something you can respond to and grow from—yet not allowing the past to oppress and dominate you. That's a tension all your main characters seem to have.

BH: They get that tension from me. I know that God (or whoever) blessed me with an almost perfect memory. Everything in this room will never be forgotten. Everything. The reason I can be a writer is that I can see behind me. Even when I was drinking hard, I couldn't forget things. I guess I've just got a different mind than most people, something inside me that doesn't want to give things up.

LM: Is this a blessing or a curse?

BH: It's both at the same time. Sometimes I wish I was a stupid mechanic who could just cut the memories off, cut the dreams off, because I'm a constant dreamer. Sometimes I wish I were dumb and insensitive so I could just move through life straight ahead without responding to it—you know, just *do* it, watch the tube, have a few drinks, and just conk off.

LM: The cliché about Southerners is that they never forget.

BH: There's a lot of truth to that cliché. Southerners do care about the past, we don't forget, we're raised not to. I'm not just talking about academic notions of history, either. If you grow up in Mississippi, your heritage is all around you, there's all those parks and those old busts and those cannons. I know the Civil War like the back of my hand. You know, one of the reasons I'm so interested in the Civil War is that so many people misunderstand the nature of that struggle. A lot of people who fought in that war had no interest in the slavery issue at all. They weren't fighting to protect slavery; they thought it was a war of invasion. Now there are plenty of racists in the South, but there are some out here, too. I've found no harder racists than Los Angeles cops.

SG: Yet you've certainly presented the racial struggles in the South openly. Whitfield Peter in *Geronimo Rex* is one of your most memorable characters.

BH: He's an exaggeration of a lot of vicious segs that I saw while I was growing up. I got over racism very early because I was hit by a car when I was eight years old, and a lot of white people were standing

around saying, "He's dead!" and a black man picked me up and put
me in his pickup truck and took me to the hospital. I was just knocked
out and my thumb was broken, but only that black man cared enough
to help out. My parents never taught me racism, but I'll admit that I
wasn't a civil rights marcher even though I was a liberal. I'd say, though,
that in the South today there is a lot of custom and tradition about
the way blacks should be and should interact with whites, but in a
way there's a closeness between whites and blacks in Oxford, Mississippi, that is missing in places like New York City and Los Angeles.
Anyway, I have never been a racist of any kind. I mean, for godsakes,
everyone who has ever helped me has been Jewish: my agent is a Jew,
Gordon Lish, my editor, is a Jew, the guy who's going to produce my
movie is a Jew. You know, to go back to my interest in Jeb Stuart, Jeb
loved Negroes himself. He was a Presbyterian. One of the things that
first interested me in him was precisely that he was so different from
me in that he didn't drink or smoke. He was also a very arrogant
bastard, very much the show off. But he was terribly good at his job,
which is something I admire. He did a helluva job with what little we
had to fight with in the South. I was interested in Stuart because he
had a kind of puritanical flamboyance that I could respond to. That
kind of complexity is one of the things I look for in my characters.

LM: Could you explain how *The Tennis Handsome* evolved? Obviously
the first thing a reader notices when he picks up the book is that its
first two chapters are revisions of two stories in *Airships*, stories that
had seemed completely unrelated.

BH: *The Tennis Handsome* was originally a 450-page novel, written
six years ago, that nobody wanted in New York. It was contracted for
by Lippincott, but after *The Nightwatchmen* failed so miserably from a
commercial standpoint my fame really hit rock bottom. Later on, with
the help of Gordon Lish, who's one of the best editors in the land, I
redesigned the novel and what came out was *The Tennis Handsome*. It
seems to work the way we've put it together.

SG: *Ray* and *The Tennis Handsome* seem a lot different from your
earlier novels. They're shorter, more elliptical, not as traditionally plotted, more "poetic" in a way.

BH: I was originally trained in poetry and the short story, rather
than in the novel, so maybe that has something to do with the direction
my fiction's been taking. I haven't written a poem, a *real* poem, since
I was eighteen years old, but I grew up on Shelley, Keats, Shakespeare,
Yeats. It was the short story, though, that was really my thing. I've
never been a great plotter, but I love the story, the yarn.

LM: But a lot of your characters want to be poets. Does that suggest
something about you?

BH: Yes. I do wish I could write poetry, and it's been nice when some reviewers have called my books "poetic." But Mama didn't raise a fool. I love poetry, but you can't make a dime out of goddamn poetry.

SG: So were you deliberately aiming for compression in these recent books?

BH: I was. At forty-one, I've finally realized that I don't believe in long novels anymore. I doubt if I'll ever write a long novel like *Geronimo Rex* again. I'm trying to cut back on the sentences, pack as much into 'em as I can, rather than stringing things out like I did in the earlier books. And I think this is the way I'm going to write from now on. I just can't write one of those long books like Nabokov's *Ada*. Sure, I know a lot of things, and I could probably keep working on a book and write about everything I know and then produce another long work. But what would be the point? What I'm after now in my work is to make it short, clean, interesting. I want to let my readers enjoy the book without my having to tie everything together with a conventional plot. I'm not interested in writing beach-reading literature.

LM: Has working on screenplays had anything to do with your new approach to fiction? Ed Doctorow once told me that the cinema had taught a lot of writers about what they could leave out of fiction, that the audience no longer requires all those transitions and other devices that kept the well-plotted novel moving forward.

BH: I've learned a lot by working with Robert Altman and with my friend the sculptor Bill Beckwith, whom I'm going to collaborate with on a *Playboy* article on the Hell's Angels. Both of them have helped me think of the words in my books as materials to be used in certain ways. I've learned to sculpt language now so that it serves the function I want it to—there's no reason to make a fireplace five feet long when you know that three feet is all you need. But I had already written *Ray* before I got out here to California to work on screenplays, and I had already decided that it's dishonest in a way to just fill up your novels with information that nobody needs. For one thing, there's so much information around today that everybody already knows. I don't have to provide that information, and my readers don't want to hear it. Don't get me wrong, I'm not against long books just because they're long. Dostoyevsky is one of my major influences, and look at the size of his books. *Crime and Punishment* and *The Possessed* have possibly been the major influences on my work. And certainly, in a different way, Hemingway has been a much bigger influence on me than Faulkner. I really admire the way that Hemingway packs so much into his sentences. There's so much compression and power there. Of course, Hemingway also wrote some longer books, like *For Whom the Bell Tolls*, but what I like about his writing is that there's so much going on in his sentences. So from now on I'm not going to be gabby and insult the intelligence of my audience. Anybody who is going to read my books—and there's only a few thousand people who read books, really—doesn't need me to fill in the blanks for them, or hear me sermonizing about something they already know.

LM: Your main characters tend to be heavy drinkers and hell-raisers in general. Since you say that you often write about your own life pretty directly, you must have some of this in your own background. There's a quote in *Ray* when his wife notices he's starting to drink again and she says, "There's something about you that wants to set yourself deliberately at peril and in trash." That seems to be something your characters are always doing—deliberately putting themselves "at peril," on the edge.

BH: Perilous situations are almost always more interesting for me to write about. Let me tell you something about me that you can probably apply to my characters. I usually don't drink at all anymore. With my history, I shouldn't drink at all, really. I used to be berserk, but when I was teaching up in Missoula, Montana, I was in a heavy-drinking town (they all are up there, you know), and all my students were drinkers. And since I'm a good pool shooter, I found myself in bars fairly often. Sobriety is fine, it's the thing to do, but there I was, winning at pool while I was drinking White Russians. I knew I had just won a Guggenheim and was going to have a year off just to write—something I've never had, really. Going to those bars got me out. I was getting tired of feeling so remote and clever, I needed to get myself out on that edge. Sometimes you just want to jump in with the other gang, join the human race—

SG: Take up with the people who seem to be doing the living—

BH: Right! So one night I won some money at pool, and another night I got stabbed by some asshole who's locked up now—just a little scar, mind you, nothing serious. Anyway, shooting those pool games felt like living, got me away from those middle-class people with their dull, dead lives. That feeling may be a curse. I guess it's a curse to want to drink, to want a cigarette, to want coffee, to want women. Hell, desire itself may always be a curse. My characters, you'll notice, drink not to escape life but to enter it. They're not trying to get away from anything. That's why it's tough for me to give up drinking completely. Next year's Nobel Prize winner should be the person who invents harmless whiskey.

SG: Your characters are appealing even when they're doing things that are pretty despicable. Sometimes I'm even vaguely bothered by the sense that you're making me like someone I shouldn't. I felt that way about Ray, for example.

BH: Me, too. I don't like Ray all the time and I don't approve of some of his actions, but for godsakes, he's trying. Remember, Ray has been kicked around a lot, he's lost a great deal. And he's tough on himself. He can't forget the bad things he's done—it's my experience that drunks usually relive their sins—and he feels guilty as hell. But the main thing is he's trying, though sometimes hurting others. Just keep giving it your best shot and fire all your guns at once—but don't hurt anybody.

SG: That sounds like a contradiction.

BH: Maybe you're right, but that's the way Ray is.

LM: Ray's combination of likeability and despicability, along with his sense of confusion, seem very "American" to me.

BH: Ray is confused and angry about the same things that a lot of Americans are. Americans are so full of guilt and information and so worried about the economy right now that we really don't get that sense of leisure that the old lady had in White Russia, say, who lived to be a hundred and sixty and drank a pint of vodka every day and ate most of a lamb. There's a lot of anxiety in America, and part of Ray grows out of that anxiety. I mean, look at the situation here in California: people on the freeways worry more about having to change lanes than about any of the big issues that really matter. That's one of Ray's troubles—he knows too much. Samuel Beckett said, "I'm interested in ignorance more than I am in knowledge." Most Americans think too much and spend every waking hour worrying, worrying, worrying. Of course, there is something about America that is very strong and free and wonderful. But at the same time it produces this anxiety that keeps people uptight. Otherwise my buddy the psychiatrist, who helped me so much, wouldn't have had a heart attack at the age of forty-five. Maybe he should have drunk. Like Willie Nelson says, "There's a lot more old drunks than old doctors." But my namesake uncle, who was an alcoholic, only made it to fifty-one, so drinking obviously isn't the solution for everyone. I think worrying kills more people in America than anything else, that and this constant sense of pressure to succeed. And the lack of a sense of humor. My sense of humor has been my savior. That's why I try to write books that are funny, I guess. All life is absurd, but if you keep laughing and smiling, you can make it better.

LM: Could you describe your work habits? Do you have a regular writing routine?

BH: No, I've got very erratic writing habits. Basically I just write any way I can get it down. I scribble things down on pieces of paper if I'm not at a typewriter. I type things out with my left hand if I'm hung over and can't use my right. I write in spurts. Sometimes I'll write for two days straight and then sleep for two days.

LM: Is there any consistent way that your books or stories seem to begin for you? Do you start off with a character, a scene, a plot idea?

BH: All my material comes from inside me, usually from something or somebody that strikes me as interesting. But one thing that's important for me is that I copy from nobody. Usually I start out with an interesting guy or girl and then pull the joystick, see what will happen to them.

LM: So you don't really know where the story is heading?

BH: Right. I care nothing for plot at all, that should be obvious. I think plot is always phony. What I'm interested in is character and language. You put an interesting person into an interesting situation and then you take off on your motorcycle. I do know, in some general sense, what's going to happen, but I can't tell you exactly what that knowledge consists of. I sure as hell don't outline. I just get myself interested enough, obsessed really, in someone—and if something's not worth getting obsessed about, then it's not worth writing about—and then I mess around with 'em, play with 'em.

SG: Sounds like jazz.

BH: It is like jazz because what I do is pure improvisation. It's like Miles Davis (at least I hope it is) in that Miles doesn't really know where he's going, he doesn't know if he's going to play flat or play it straight out or what. The band gets playing and then he just goes ahead. That's the way I write. For me language is always the basic thing. It's that linguistic reverb we were talking about earlier that I'm aiming for, packing as much as I can into the sentences, getting the sounds and rhythms and cadences right.

LM: In *The Nightwatchmen* Thorpe describes the oak trees twisted by the hurricane as having "a grand agony in their beauty." And in "Quo Vadis, Smut?" Reggie John says, "Beauty and death is the same thing. Death is nothing. I love it so much I got to look at it." You seem to return repeatedly to this idea that beauty and pain and death are all interrelated.

BH: I wouldn't necessarily agree with that idea myself, even if it does appear in my fiction. Those quotes all have specific contexts. Remember, Reggie John is a killer. He's a little like that guy Chapman who shot Lennon. I hate him. I hope they fry him slowly. People who don't have any beauty or love want to destroy those who do.

SG: Like Maynard Castro killing Sister in *Ray*.

BH: That's exactly the sort of thing I mean. They're assassins, they're crazy. Some things are so beautiful to them that in some fucked up way they identify with it and also want to kill it. That's why Maynard

Castro kills Sister—she's so beautiful that he can't stand it; he knows he'll never be able to possess her, so he kills her.

SG: Are there any contemporary writers you especially admire?

BH: Ray Carver. Tom McGuane. Richard Brautigan. Jim Harrison. Walker Percy. These are all friends of mine that I really respect. I like people who write short books, not the people who push size and complexity for their own sake. I like Donald Barthelme—he's a "Southern writer," by the way. Kurt Vonnegut. I like what Ann Beattie's been writing. And Samuel Beckett.

LM: In *Ray* you have Charlie DeSoto being told to "cherish" his "adventurous perversity," or Ray himself saying that "it's better with me all messed up," since otherwise he might join "the gruesome tribe of the smug." Somehow this confusion, or adventurous perversity, or whatever you want to call it, seems more honest to me than having your characters' problems artificially resolved at the end.

BH: Life *is* a lot of confusion and pain and death, and the only way to deal with it is to face it with the attitude that there's no place to go but up. "Sabers up, gentlemen!" is the way I end *Ray*. That's all I know. Straight ahead. Hit 'em high. Let's go get 'em again. That's the only solution I know. There's too much depression and confusion and death to allow any *real* hope. We don't have a fucking chance. But "Sabers up!"

Jerry Bauer

An Interview with
Russell Hoban

When Russell Hoban published his first adult novel, *The Lion of Boaz-Jachin and Jachin-Boaz*, in 1973, he left behind two established careers —
one as a freelance illustrator (two of his drawings appeared on the
cover of *Time*, and he did considerable work for *Sports Illustrated*) and
the other as an author of over forty children's novels. Actually his
move to adult fiction could be said to have begun with *The Mouse and
His Child* (1967), a tale of a wind-up mechanical mouse and his son's
search for home, identity, and spiritual awareness. Although marketed
as a young-adult novel, *The Mouse and His Child* focuses on death and
existential issues, echoing Beckett and evoking physics and Eastern
mysticism. It is really a multileveled fantasy that shows off Hoban's
talent for word play and metaphysical speculation.

Hoban's decision to turn to adult fiction was sparked by his relocation
in London following the breakup of his first marriage. After *The Lion
of Boaz-Jachin*, he published two more novels in rapid succession: *Kleinzeit* (1974) and *Turtle Diary* (1975). Although these three novels share
many formal and thematic concerns with Hoban's more recent works —
Riddley Walker (1980) and *Pilgermann* (1983) — they can best be viewed
as apprentice fictions in which Hoban was discovering how to give
full voice to his vision of man's role in the cosmos. Certainly *Riddley
Walker*, whose fractured and corrupted language Hoban spent five years
developing, is an astonishingly rich, demanding, and original work by
any standards. Narrated by Riddley Walker, a plucky teenager who
possesses some of Huck Finn's natural instincts and resourcefulness,

the novel depicts a brutalized post-holocaust society of some almost unimaginably distant future. The plot follows an initiation pattern that leads to man's dual rediscovery of gunpowder and art (creativity and destruction, life and death, beauty and ugliness, ying and yang—these dualities haunt all of Hoban's work). The real triumph here is the way Hoban is able to embody the decay and fall of human society, as well as its insistent yearnings and aspirations, in a debased yet remarkably lyrical and evocative language.

Pilgermann is an equally stunning achievement. Narrated by the disembodied voice of an eleventh-century Jew who is castrated in the novel's opening pages and then embarks on a surreal pilgrimage to the Holy Land, *Pilgermann* is a phantasmagoric rhapsody whose overall effect is probably closest to the horror and beauty that emerge from paintings by Hieronymus Bosch. (Hoban in fact borrows a number of the book's central images directly from Bosch.) Dense with poetic metaphor, highly digressive in structure, *Pilgermann* conjures up an image of man in all his grotesque splendor: we see human skulls hurled over city walls like cannonballs, children being raped and murdered by skeletons; but we also see great art being made, the void being filled with song, poetry, attempts at communion and understanding. The positive and the negative, Hoban constantly suggests, are equally important aspects of existence—their interaction is literally what gives spin to the atom, motion to the universe. Thus, despite the often frightening portrayal of our ability to maim and mutilate, *Pilgermann*, like *Riddley Walker*, remains a strangely affirmative work as its narrator takes us on a journey from castration to transcendence.

We interviewed Russell Hoban at his home in London, where he and his second family have resided for the last several years. As we sat in the combination living room and writing room and struggled to urge our ancient tape recorder into action, Hoban walked to his desk and pulled out a fancy, high-tech recorder from behind his new word processor. Despite these and other electronic gadgets (which included a VCR), there was a homey, cluttered effect to the room that suggested a wide-ranging sensibility. A Vermeer print hung on the wall next to an antique set of Punch and Judy puppets; resting on a stack of video cassettes was a well-thumbed Bible, with dozens of strips of paper marking passages. It seemed the kind of room where nursery rhymes could coexist comfortably with texts on quantum physics, where souls from the past and distant futures could arrive and depart, where a writer could move out of his time and into fiction's space.

Sinda Gregory: You state in the preface to *Riddley Walker* that you began that novel after you had visited Canterbury and seen the St. Eustace mural. Could you discuss what it was about the cathedral and the mural that launched your imagination?

Russell Hoban: All such beginnings involve many things coming together. The night before I saw the painting of the St. Eustace legend I'd been invited to Canterbury to do a talk at the St. Augustine Teacher's Center. As I recall, about three people showed up, of which I was one. (They explained that it was the end of term or there'd been a plague or the wells were poisoned or something.) The next day my host took me to the cathedral to show it to me, and that was when I first saw the painting, which set in motion all sorts of feelings. It's hard to say exactly why this was so, but I was in a state that made me particularly receptive to certain things. I already had Punch and Judy in my mind for no particular reason—I'd simply become preoccupied with Mr. Punch and his unfortunate family for a while, maybe because I'd been having family problems of my own. I'd recently left my wife (and consequently my children), so there was in me a strong feeling of separation and loss, even though by then I was the father of two children and was firmly established in a new family. So the painting of St. Eustace—standing there in the middle of the river, treading water, hoping for the best, while one of his kids is going off with the lion and the other with the wolf—created a lot of strong fellow feelings inside me. I found myself standing there empathizing with this poor fellow in the middle of the river. I also felt that there was something of the general human condition in this, something that referred not just to St. Eustace and to me but to everybody. At the same time, there jumped into my head more of a "given" for a novel than had ever presented itself before; I knew what the whole environment of *Riddley Walker* would be, the time and place and setting, the idea of a desolate landscape long after civilization has been destroyed, a landscape over-run by packs of killer dogs, with the people living in little fenced-in settlements; Christianity is long defunct, and what religion there is is carried from place to place by traveling puppeteers who do a St. Eustace show derived from the Canterbury wall painting. That got me started with much more than I ordinarily have when I begin a novel. Then all I had to do was wait for five and a half years to get it right.

SG: How soon did you make the association between St. Eustace and the United States?

RH: I didn't think of that to start with, but when I saw things written out on paper I saw that that interpretation was a logical one. And it's fair enough because, after all, the atom bomb was developed by the U.S.A. and it was first dropped by the U.S.A.

Larry McCaffery: Did the idea of creating your own language occur to you in that first flash of insight?

RH: A number of things made the language happen. Actually, everybody gives me credit for more invention and knowledge than really came into it. I was already prone to the kind of language play that you find in *Riddley Walker*, partly because I've always liked to play around with sounds. And a long, long time ago I had read a story by Gerald Kersh called "Voices in the Dust of Annan" that's about an archeologist who comes upon the ruins of London in a country that is by then given over pretty much to savagery and primitive tribalism. In the ruins of London he finds little subhumans, only about three feet high or less, who are living underground, herding rats, dressed in ratskins and eating rats, and singing corrupted versions of songs that were familiar to them. They sing "Bless 'Em All" and "Who Killed Cock Robin," but in their versions "Bless 'Em All" becomes "Balasamo" and "Who Killed Cock Robin" becomes "Ookil 'Karabin." Strange, Arabic-sounding verses. Now by the time I started *Riddley Walker* I had long since forgotten not only the title of the story but even its author, but that language distortion had very much beguiled me. Without knowing it, I was waiting to do something like that, although at first *Riddley Walker* was written in fairly straight English. In the very first version, Riddley was a kind of primitive anthropologist or sociologist; out of all of his group he was interested in why the coastal people talked differently from the inland people, that sort of thing. Only after I'd been going a while did the language gradually work itself into something else. I guess this transformation happened when I began to make up a few words, change a few of the old words into variations, so that little by little things crept in. Then, when I saw what was happening—and since I always go backward and forward when I'm writing, rewriting all the time—I simply kept updating as I worked, keeping word lists so that if I said something one way in one place I'd say it the same way in another. I didn't think about the process analytically until later on, and then it became especially pleasing to me that I had *not* planned it analytically. Like an animal, it had just happened by itself.

LM: That's interesting because the language of *Riddley* functions in such a "natural" way. It's obviously much more than realistic ornamentation—that is, it seems to embody some of your themes. It literalizes that culture's loss, its relationship to its past, opening up new insights into the old metaphors.

RH: You're right—at least, I hope so. As I got into the novel it gradually became clear that a real linguistic process was taking place, that language is inevitably an encapsulation of a subculture and a worldview; it has within it fragments of history that aren't even known to the people who speak the words containing those fragments. In this case the language *degrades* the past. The situation they're in is a result of all those clever people before them. Over two or three thousand years they've downgraded all the names, so Herne Bay becomes "Horny Boy" and Dover becomes "Do It Over" and Faversham becomes "Fathers Ham"—they want to show that they don't respect the old names. I also saw, much to my pleasure, that the vernacular I was using worked as a literary device because it slowed the reader down to Riddley's rate of perception. It's really a short book, and there are a lot of things that need to be absorbed slowly. The language prevents the reader from leaping ahead of Riddley, insures that the reader is kept puzzling over the nature of the words.

LM: You said earlier that you've always liked to play around with sounds, and your delight in word play and verbal games is obvious in all your adult novels from *The Mouse and His Child* onward. Could you talk about your interest in this kind of play of language? Is it mainly an unconscious attraction, or do you consciously employ your delight in word play for thematic concerns?

RH: I'd say it's a bit of both. I like to play with language unthinkingly, and I always trust in what I like to do unthinkingly—but this enjoyment has thematic implications, too. Lorna tells Riddley, "Someone is thinking us. It thinks us but it don't think *like* us." Well, it feels to me as if things or forces we don't know of look for utterance through us. Maybe it's nothing that can be explained, or maybe it's frivolity rather than anything heavy, but I find myself walking around the house saying "nuz" or "kruld"—just to hear the sound of these things. With me this sort of thing is occupational and I'm not ashamed to be doing it, so I give myself over to it. But *why* does something want to make those sounds through me? I don't know. Ever since I read a little book by Erwin Schrodinger, the physicist, I've agreed with something he says there— that there's really just one mind, and within this one mind the time is always now. I myself feel not only that the memory of each individual's history is in the individual (not always accessible), but also that the memory of everything in the universe is in all of us. I don't think this memory is consciously accessible, but it can have an effect on us, and it is expressed in one way or another through what we do and feel and say. It's my business to cultivate responsiveness to this expression, whereas it might be someone else's business to repress it, so if I find strange, irrational, even silly noises coming up in me, I'm interested in them. There's something very powerful about sounds. Now that I'm fairly well embarked on my novelistic career, I find that I have urges from time to time to go back and look at the sources of some of the sounds that were in my head—I've already mentioned one of these sources, that Gerald Kersh story, and another is H. P. Lovecraft's "The Call of Cthulhu." "Cthulhu" sounds dire and dark and muddy and primordial, oozy, slimy, and it is all that, of course. Cthulhu is a terrible sort of creature. I've been reading Lovecraft recently, and he makes some marvelous, magic-sounding sentences. I love the opening paragraph to "The Call of Cthulhu": "The most merciful thing in the world, I think, is the inability of the human mind to correlate all its contents. We live on a placid island of ignorance in the midst of black seas of infinity, and it was not meant that we should voyage far. The sciences, each straining in its own direction, have hitherto harmed us little; but some day the piecing together of dissociated knowledge will open up such terrifying vistas of reality, and of our frightful position therein, that we shall either go mad from the revelation or flee from the deadly light into the peace and safety of a new dark age." Then there's this line—Lovecraft is obviously fascinated with the sounds of language—that goes: "Ph-nglui mglw'nafh Cthulhu R'lyeh wgah'nagl fhtagn." ("In his house at R'lyeh dead Cthulhu waits dreaming.") In a couple of things I'm working on now I use language that I might have come to without Lovecraft, but the fact is I read Lovecraft years before I *did* get to it, so he has to be given some credit.

LM: You've mentioned Lovecraft and Kersh as influences, and *Riddley Walker* and *Pilgermann* both have science fictional elements. Do you feel comfortable when critics refer to you as a science fiction writer?

RH: This is not as inappropriate as one might think. I've never won an award for any of my other novels, but I've won two science fiction awards for *Riddley Walker*. And as I look over possible influences, it's obvious that years of reading science fiction have done me all kinds of good. I don't know if I would have thought of the kind of lion I had in *The Lion of Boaz-Jachin and Jachin-Boaz* if I hadn't read *The Place of the Lion* by Charles Williams. And in *Riddley Walker*, when they misinterpret the Eustace legend and think it's a formula for something that would make a big bang, there's a kind of reversal of what happens in *A Canticle for Leibowitz*, where they read electrical diagrams as sacred documents. And there's the Gerald Kersh story, which I've already mentioned. Of course, several major influences are not science fictional—Joseph Conrad, for example, who impressed me with his density and not going straight through a narrative in a linear way. And a lot of other obsessions come into play, like Orpheus and the head of that Vermeer girl in the painting called *Head of a Young Girl*. But I do think that science fiction deserves more credit than it's usually been given by the literary establishment. I haven't been reading science fiction for a long time, although I used to read *Fantasy and Science*

Fiction and *Galaxy*, but one of the things that's always impressed me in science fiction is that it displays a strong element of hope. Running through most modern science fiction, no matter how doomsdayish things get, is the idea that human beings will survive somehow, even when turned loose from all support systems. I remember reading a story in *F&SF* or *Galaxy* about a stranded space traveler who was living in a symbiotic relationship with plants on some planet far beyond the galaxy. He was growing into the plants and they were growing into him and providing oxygen for him, and they were keeping each other alive. And I remember more than one story where a space traveler loses his ship and his spacesuit in one way or another, and he's zooming through the cosmos bare-assed naked, yet he still manages to survive somehow. Usually the idea is that there's something in the human spirit that will find a way through and out of anything, no matter what's coming next. A nice idea.

SG: Several critics have compared your works to such dystopian novels as *A Clockwork Orange*, *Lord of the Flies*, and *A Canticle for Leibowitz*. Despite the violence and the terrible things that the characters do to one another, I wouldn't say your works are *really* pessimistic because of that quality you've just mentioned.

RH: My writing isn't pessimistic, though if you ask me about the prospects for the human race, I couldn't say anything particularly optimistic. I find that however long we're here, and however little of a future we might reasonably expect to have, the action itself is enough reward. It's a lot of fun to be what we are and do the things we do (or at least a lot of them) and have the capabilities we have. We can't reasonably ask for more. And in any case, we know that the sun, after a certain number of billion years, is going to become a red giant and then a white dwarf and then a black hole and the whole thing is going to get all packed in. Then the universe will try something else someplace else, or *another* universe will try something else out somewhere else. You can't really hope for permanence or narrow optimism on a big scale. We have to accept what is.

LM: We visited the Parthenon recently, and as we were standing there staring at one of man's most beautiful creations, we were also intensely aware that man *destroyed* this building through his stupidity and barbarity. We both were reminded of the line in *Pilgermann*, "There is something waiting to leap up and destroy beauty." What impresses me is your presentation of this fundamental duality, the constant opposition that seems literally to create the energy animating the universe. Your fiction frequently points to this duality with that sense of acceptance you've just mentioned.

RH: Yes, and *why not* accept it? But we haven't come very far in recognizing this. We still seem to have to have a public face and a private face. We pretend we don't have evil within us, or that only "bad people" have evil within. But everybody has everything in them. I first began to notice this disparity while reading fiction. For a long time now we've had books in which the antihero sits in his room and picks his nose, masturbates and vomits, eats and shits, and so on—and we know there's nothing grand about this sort of thing. But years before the advent of the antihero, I used to read books about people who *weren't* true to life—young men alone never masturbated in their private rooms, they had no guilt, they immediately had approvable responses to things; if somebody fell down, they picked him up; if somebody was raped, they didn't stand around and watch, but beat the shit out of whoever was doing it and covered the girl up decently and got her to a safe place. Nobody had morbid curiosity and nobody had a furtive, driven, dark inner life. Everything was just the way one thought it ought to be. The presence of these antiheroes in our fiction today is one example of how the self has gradually begun to include these contradictory elements: the sacred and the profane, the clean and the dirty, the dark and the light. It's a healthy sign. Part of the trouble we have being human is that we're not willing to recognize that, when we pick up a paper and read a juicy account of rape and murder, we have a secret delight in these things as well as decently outraged feelings of shock and horror. *Everything is happening within us all the time.* The universe began by exploding, and all these strange gases and precipitations and conversions and explosions are still within us; they define what we are. But a lot of people would still like to think we're just single, not double; simple and straight, rather than complex and dualistic. Because I have an investigative turn of mind and because I try to be honest with myself, I've been forced to see in myself all of the contradictions and dualities. As Riddley says, "You try to be one with something and you come in two." You start out with loyalty and you wind up with betrayal, you promise that you'll never do *that* and the next thing you do is that. Everything, in every way, is always doing that. The nature of the universe is continual change. The only thing you can say with any certainty is that however it is now that's not how it's going to be next. This is a preoccupation of mine, something I'm more and more aware of, but I find that I'm happy with this process.

LM: Pilgermann says, "The pain is the life, the pain is what separates the animate from the inanimate, the human from the stone. What is human may long for the stone of its innocence, the stone of its ease, of no pain; but the pain is the life." That quote, with its suggestion that life not only accepts death but even *longs* for it, reminded me of Freud's notion of *thanatos*, the death instinct.

RH: There is indeed something of that notion in *Pilgermann*. It's been brought up in the studies of Walt Whitman, too, who was writing long before Freud, of course. Edmund Wilson said that when Whitman suggested he wanted to be everybody—the Eskimo, the African, the scientist, the bushman—it was really the same thing as saying that he wanted to be dead, because he wanted to lose completely his individual selfness and be dispersed through everything.

LM: Do you sense some of that longing for death that Pilgermann is talking about?

RH: As I get closer to death than to birth, as the trajectory of my being passes into its descent, I feel myself approaching the source of everything. The way I describe it to myself is that at conception the spark jumps the gap from the reservoir of potential energy to the arena of kinetic energy—we have action. Then, as we get older and pass the peak of our vitality and physical strength, we come closer and closer to the pool of potential energy that we started out from. I don't know that I feel a "longing" for this return so much as a recognition of it. As I get older, I seem to feel close to the primal sources of things. This feeling is not accompanied by a feeling of dread so much as by a sense of recognition. It may well be that this is related to that longing Freud described of the animate to return to the inanimate, to get away from the disturbance that moves us, to return to stillness. These instincts are in everybody, although the world is full of people who don't open their minds to these things. But if a person is developing as a thinker all through life, there'll be a natural progression of recognition along these lines.

SG: Larry and I disagreed about the last scene in *Riddley Walker*, so I wondered if I could get you to comment on it. Larry thought the Punch and Judy show mainly reenacted the violent tendencies—the savagery, cannibalism, sadism—that we find throughout the book. But that ending scene seems to me to suggest that even though gunpowder has been rediscovered and so the whole mess is going to start all over again, still the same analytic spark of imagination has freed the Punch and Judy show from being the propaganda machine it was earlier. Art has been rediscovered, too.

RH: I'd say your view is closer to what I had in mind. Riddley is going away from the establishment and making a free show, a show of his own in which he can explore whatever comes up in front of him. I don't know if I'd say that the artists are trying to save the world while the gunpowder-finders are trying to blow it apart. In this case— and not by accident—they're the same person: Riddley is the one who brought the missing ingredient for the gunpowder, and he's also the new artist. The things that are moving around in the universe find artists to name them. And when the artist puts a name to something, he's just as likely to call up a demon as to describe something beneficent. But, willy-nilly, that's the function of the artist: to name the demons as well as the blessed things.

SG: You say in one of your essays collected in *The Thorny Paradise: Writers on Children's Fiction,* "When we open the door to the artist and say, Go make us perceive again, the artist thanks us and then blows the house up as best he can." Is that your view of the artist—the person who explodes perceptions, who reorganizes the materials around us, even if that process requires some demolition?

RH: Exactly. The artist does anything he can, even calling up the demons if necessary, to find new ways of looking at things, to discover ways of seeing things that haven't been seen before. This can be a scary procedure. But keep in mind that the artist can't really *invent* anything, he can only find new ways of perceiving things that are already there.

SG: But don't you feel that most contemporary fiction evades its responsibility for discovering new ways of seeing things?

RH: I must admit that I avoid most contemporary fiction, so I don't know. Do the kind of books that become bestsellers really reinforce societal values? I'd probably argue that they're just giving us pleasing fantasies—fantasies of sex and action, of personal effectiveness, of immediate gratification of one kind of another. This may be reinforcing social values in a sense; certainly right now consumption seems to be the God of our civilization, and best-selling fiction is usually a fiction of consumption: the women and men consume a lot of one another, and a lot of space, time, action, and goods. But beyond that kind of thing, I'm not sure.

SG: I was really thinking about this issue more from the standpoint of *form.* Most contemporary fiction presents itself so as to reassure readers that things can be explained, that people and events can be understood—that ultimately there is no mystery. I'd say that *Riddley Walker* and *Pilgermann* are unusual from a formal standpoint in that they reaffirm mystery, revel in it.

RH: That's quite true. I'm entirely against the idea that everything can be explained. In fact, I don't think *anything* can be explained.

LM: One thing that strikes me about *Pilgermann* is its peculiar collage-like structure; you break up the linear narrative, you refuse to tell the story. (In fact, the story seems almost to be an excuse for the digressions.) I'm reminded of Pilgermann's statement that "a story is a series of picture cards." What's the rationale for this structural approach?

RH: At the end of 1983, *Fiction* magazine invited a number of people to say something about the best piece of fiction that had come their way that year. I picked a performance by the Impact Theatre Cooperative called *No Weapons for Mourning*. Let me read what I said about the piece: "The distinction of *No Weapons for Mourning* has to do with a perceptual phenomenon of our time. Never before has the human brain been compelled to take in so much and in so many different modes; our minds move in sweeps and scans of words, pictures, noise, emotions, and sensations with flickering speed foreign even to our childhoods, let alone the mental life of those who saw the plays of Shakespeare or Molière or even Strindberg. It is on this acceleration and multiplicity of perception that the Impact Theatre builds its approach. The cinematic archetypes are intensified, and the performance, not realistic but hyperreal, has a syntax of image and sound, speech and movement that is not of the printed page but of the exploding mind. It draws its energy from the same speech and fragmentation, the same lightning circuitry that makes computer technology possible. These young artists effectively demonstrate that the circuitry originates not with computers but with the human mind, and it is there for survival as well as for annihilation." I think the natural way for fiction to develop is for it to move in the direction of this fragmentation and the explosion and scattering of everything, to recognize consciousness *as it is happening*, not to try to define how we think reality or consciousness ought to be or to limit our definitions of it to what's comprehensible. To me, consciousness itself is the biggest mystery. I'm endlessly fascinated by how strange it is simply to be conscious, to have something looking out of the eyeholes in our head and taking in the passing scene. All this probably has to do with the way *Pilgermann* came out.

LM: Lorna tells Riddley, after he admits that he doesn't know the story "Why the Dog Won't Show His Eyes," "That's what happens with peopl on the way down from what they ben—the storys go." It is a commonplace that our society is losing contact with stories because we don't *read* as much today. Are we losing our stories and hence on the way down?

RH: Absolutely not. What's happening is a reenergizing of the mythopoeic capabilities. We see this reenergizing in the lowest common forms—in computer and arcade games, for example, and in other children's games. My oldest son, Jake, got a typewriter for his twelfth birthday because I thought it was time he had one, but what he *asked* for was more books and materials for *Dungeons and Dragons*. And all three of my kids are fascinated with Steve Jackson books and other combat fantasy games. This fascination has to do with storytelling in a very basic way.

LM: I've argued with my colleagues, most of whom are horrified that Johnny is playing these games rather than reading the Hardy Boys or something, that these fantasy games are "do-it-yourself" narratives that may be involving these children's imaginations in more active, sophisticated ways.

RH: Sure, all this has to do with perceiving things in mythic terms, with mythmaking. And it's always necessary for kids to have non-approved modes of thinking. So these games have added value in that they're not approved of by adults.

SG: This business about seeing things mythically, as stories, is relevant to our adult experience as well. Certainly you demonstrate this repeatedly in *Riddley Walker*.

RH: I recently took a trip to Australia and people kept asking me about the mythic versus more objective, literal ways of seeing the world. I found myself saying that the mythopoeic way of seeing things is the natural, the practical, the effectual mode. Suppose you get up one morning and, whatever kind of weather you like, it's not that kind of weather outside. If you like rain, it's hard, bright sunlight; if you like sunlight, it's pissing down with rain. You fall and break your leg going down the stairs, and then when you get yourself out into the street you get run over by a car. You can see it isn't going to be your day. Now if you try to be rational about this, you could say to yourself, Look, probabilities being what they are, it's thoroughly possible that all these bad things could happen to me this morning—it's got nothing to do with me, or anything else, it's just how it is. That kind of response is utterly useless—it doesn't help you to understand what's been happening or to cope with it emotionally. But if you recognize the day as a great shuddering slimy monster who has overwhelmed you and left its repulsive, loathsome track behind it and who is surely going on to deal more destruction and disaster, then you'll be seeing things as they are: this day *is* a loathsome monster. I find myself thinking about where we are right now with weapons. If both the Russians and the Western powers could perceive this situation mythically—if, instead of their seeing us abstractly as the enemy and our seeing them as the enemy, we could both see that at the end of World War II the name of the hideous demon had been spoken and the mushroom-shaped cloud had leapt up, so that now all of us are cowering at its feet like children— *that* would be the correct perception. The Russians aren't *really* our enemies, we're not their enemies. I'm a short-wave freak, and in the middle of the night I listen to enchanting Russian songs from Radio Moscow. And while the Russians are transmitting these wonderful songs, the Voice of America is transmitting *its* wonderful jazz and rock music. The best music of both countries is filling the airwaves with mutual understanding on the nonrational plane; meanwhile, on the rational plane there's mistrust on both sides. What it comes to is that people are pretty trashy at the rational level. When you get world leaders who can only perform and relate to things at the rational level, you have the kind of dangerous, crappy situation we're in now, well over our heads.

SG: Except for *Turtle Diary*, which is basically a realistic novel, your books have developed outside of realistic forms. What has drawn you to fantasy or allegory?

RH: I don't think it was related to my background with children's books. (By the way, I don't write allegories; in my fiction there is no one-to-one relation of representation and meaning.) No, what happened with my immersion in fantasy forms is very complicated. For one thing, I became a published writer through a fluke. I was a freelance illustrator just before I did my first children's book, and I used to go around and make drawings and paintings of construction machinery just for fun. Some friends of mine saw some of these pictures and thought they might make a nice children's book, and a friend of theirs who worked at *Harper's* got me an appointment. So I worked up some roughs and a simple text and sold my first book, which was about construction machinery. I'd done a couple of magazine pieces before that, adult pieces; an essay and a story for *Sports Illustrated* (a science fiction story, by the way), some journalism for *Holiday* magazine, including a piece about Sandy Dennis and another one about an obscure middleweight and his manager. So the first writing I'd sold was adult writing, but then I fell into children's books. It wasn't the children's writing that led me into fantasy and surrealism, because my bent was always that way. Certainly my reading was always along those lines. One of the reasons why I wanted to come to England for a protracted stay was that I have always loved the English supernatural writers: Oliver Onions, Arthur Machen, Algernon Blackwood, Sheridan LeFanu (who is Irish), and M. R. James, one of my favorite writers. I've always been drawn to these other-than-straight-reality writers, who have charmed me and whom I still read just for fun, but this attraction was there long before I knew I was going to become a writer.

A number of other things about fantasy forms appeal to me. For example, ghost stories are really a very reassuring form, even though they're spoken of as being scary, because they suggest that there's something beyond death. Supernatural stories are always comfortable in that their premise is that there is more to things than meets the eye. That feature of fantasy accords with my own experience, at least a little bit. I often feel that there are things whisking by just outside my field of vision, that there are things that might be perceived that are beyond our perceptions. This may seem strange, but I guess I haven't really ever tried to explain my attraction to fantasy to myself. Maybe I don't feel the need to. Basically I suppose I'm just very comfortable with forms that allow for unlimited possibilities.

SG: Did your background as an illustrator have any effect on your work?

RH: I do think of myself as a very visual writer, and I'm sure my background in painting and drawing had a certain effect on my writing. From early childhood I was always very good with words, and I drew very well from the age of five. My parents were Jewish immigrants from Russia and, in the immigrant tradition, they wanted high achievement from their offspring. It was expected that I was going to grow up to become a great painter—an expectation that was more or less laid on me; it belonged more to my parents than to me. That took a lot of the joy out of painting and drawing. I was always said to have a great deal of talent, but that talent didn't really manifest itself. I didn't do very well in art school, and when I got out of the army after the war I painted a bit and didn't do too well with that. Then there was a time in the 1950s when I was working at the advertising agency BBDO as a television art director, and I finally got a grip on myself and said, "All right, you're supposed to have all this talent, so let's see what it's going to be—whether you're going to be an illustrator or a painter or what." I established for myself a working discipline that was the beginning of all the discipline I've had ever since. I had a job from 9 to 5 and I'd come home, take a nap after supper, and then work late into the night, teaching myself to finish pictures that looked as if they were done by the same person. Eventually I became a freelance illustrator and I did some OK things for *Sports Illustrated* and some *Time* covers.

LM: Some painters have specific relevance to your work—Vermeer and Bosch in *Pilgermann*, for example.

RH: Oh, yes. A number of things in that book are lifted directly from Bosch paintings, like the man hanging the bear from the tree (that's in the background of Bosch's St. Christopher painting). And that strange light in the night scene where the barn is burning is in *The Temptation of St. Anthony.*

SG: Did you do the "Hidden Lion" drawing that appears in *Pilgermann*?

RH: Sure, with a compass and straight edge. That's just one of many patterns that will give you six divisions of a circle in which a six-pointed star will appear. I spoke to a friend in America who had taken up quilting, and she told me that that particular pattern is called "Crown of Thorns," which seems pretty interesting.

LM: Do you miss drawing now that you spend most of your time writing?

RH: Not much. When I was a painter and an illustrator, I used to grade myself on a scale from zero to Rembrandt—and that was pretty frustrating. But when I started writing I didn't grade myself on a scale from zero to Shakespeare. I just do whatever it is that I do. When a writer puts together a scene, his job is to *be there*. It's almost like acting. When you become the narrator of a story, you try to let it happen to you—to hear the clang of armor, the rattle of swords, the jingling and snorting; to smell the animals and the trees, feel the breeze coming up. Sometimes I run down a checklist of sensory data. Other times these specifics seem to come in on their own.

LM: Oriental philosophy and recent theoretical physics are two other nonliterary influences that seem increasingly relevant in your works.

RH: My interest in those areas really began when I was in therapy with Leon Redler up in Belsize park. I found he had an intelligent but not intellectual approach that went down very well with me, so I was able to get into a whole lot of areas in some depth with him. He was interested in tai chi, Zen Buddhism, and all sorts of other such things, and he got me interested in them as well. At first I didn't take them seriously, but then I gradually found myself getting involved in Zen and reading a lot of books about it. These hooked up with haiku, which I had always loved, so the haiku and the Zen put themselves together as an approach to things. And some Indian religion came into play during this period. Not much—I've never read *The Bhagavad Gita* or *The Diamond Sutra* straight through—but in bits and pieces. A line like "Form is emptiness and emptiness is form" would suddenly ring very true for me. For quite a while I'd also had a predilection for physics. I'd buy a book of which I might understand only one paragraph, but if that one paragraph really hit me hard . . . I found I just liked holding a book that had all that action in it. I was interested to find out, when I read *The Tao of Physics*, that other people were taking in these lines of intersection in much the same way I was. That is, finding in these patterns of subatomic particles in cloud chambers the design of the universe made manifest. These sorts of things are in the air, and people who are interested in how it is with the universe are tending to think in this direction. I just happen to be one of them.

SG: You've mentioned the effect of the St. Eustace painting and you've given other examples of a specific object or place that helped you begin other works—the toy mouse in *The Mouse and His Child*, the visit to Monfort in Galilee for *Pilgermann*. Is this always the case, or do your works sometimes begin with something more abstract?

RH: Almost always there's something highly specific and concrete, or a group of such things. For example, in the book I'm working on now an olive tree was very important in getting things going. Usually there are personal obsessions that are looking for something to hook up with—like the feelings of loss and disruption that were present just before I began *Riddley Walker*—and the thing that opens up a channel for this material is something specific. With *Kleinzeit* it was a stay in the hospital. With *The Lion of Boaz-Jachin and Jachin-Boaz* it was seeing photographs of that lion hunt relief in King Ashurbanipal's Palace. With *Turtle Diary* it was going to the zoo and seeing the sea turtles. With *Riddley Walker*, as I've said, it was the St. Eustace painting and Punch and Judy. And with *Pilgermann* it was being in the place where *Riddley* had left me, and then seeing the ruins of Montfort opening up a channel for me to establish these feelings into the time and place of their own story.

SG: When you say that *Riddley Walker* had "left you in a place," what "place" are you talking about?

RH: I still had a lot of what I considered to be religious thoughts that hadn't yet found a home. By the time I finished *Riddley Walker* I was thinking of myself as a religious writer. Perhaps I'm not entitled to call myself that, but I couldn't think of any other description for what I was doing. Personally, I think of both *Riddley Walker* and *Pilgermann* as religious books, and I think of my writing in general as a religious act. Making real art is always a religious act. Art that isn't done for commerce or self-display but that comes out hooking up with the thingness of things is bound to be religious.

SG: It's as if you're waiting for something to spark your inner feelings, to get you going. Yet I've also heard that you are a meticulous, almost obsessive rewriter. Isn't it difficult to be an intuitive writer who, in a sense, is staring at the blank page and trusting to luck to get things started, and at the same time to be so meticulous, to be looking for something so particular?

RH: That combination isn't so strange when you remember that I never know precisely what I'm looking for when I start. I even make a point of trying *not* to know. (I never work from an outline, for instance.) I trust luck in the sense that I trust whatever gets me started. After that it's a matter of trying to place myself in a position of active receptivity, you might say, a patient process of trial and error. I'm willing to take whatever time it takes me, go wherever it takes me, go back to page one as many times as necessary. When I'm in my writing routine properly (and I've been *out* of it for a while now) I usually put in about ten hours a day at my desk. That ten hours is not all spent writing, writing, writing; it's being as alert as I can be and doing what I can to bring in whatever it is that's trying to get said through me. That's what I mean by being an "active receptor." It's like tuning a radio, except that the tuning also involves some output. Sometimes the process requires making notes or talking to myself on the tape recorder. Sometimes for weeks on end I might not be able to get anything down on paper that's getting me anywhere, so I'll hope to take myself by surprise by talking to myself on tape. Writing is such a solitary pursuit, I turn myself into a crowd: when I talk to myself on tape, I usually have music in the background; when I play this stuff back, it sounds like a great party—people listening to it would probably say, Gee, I'd love to be where he is! This is just a way of tricking myself into being less alone and, with luck, into saying something I didn't know was on my mind, or hearing something I didn't know was in the words I spoke, and eventually getting this down on paper.

LM: So, to take a specific example, you didn't know at the outset that Pilgermann would never arrive at his destination?

RH: No, when I started *Pilgermann*, even before I had the persona of my narrator and the time and place, I simply had a voice speaking its thoughts. I don't mean I was literally hearing a voice, but I knew I had some kind of narrator whose thoughts were getting themselves down on paper. My first tentative working name for him was Lucifer-Crucifer. But these thoughts weren't specific until that visit to Galilee when the Jewishness in me and the Jewishness in Pilgermann leapt up and became a strong part of that voice. Gradually things began to settle around it.

LM: I've read that you went back and revised the opening page of *Riddley Walker* fourteen times. What sorts of things do you look for in your revision process?

RH: First off, I revised that page more than fourteen times, but there were at least fourteen times when I had to return to page one to start over again, to work my way out again. The first two years of *Riddley Walker*, from 1974 until 1976, I did five hundred pages that eventually were altogether discarded. In making that world real to myself, I had to get together a lot more of the folklore and history to account for a whole lot of things than I could directly use in the final version. For instance, I had a whole chapter in which I described the papermill where they made the cigarette papers and how they all got together one night and made a map there and some of them thought it was a dreadfully unlucky thing to do. I began to see that I had too many characters, too much action, too much space to cover. In a sense, I was compressing things, but I always have the feeling that the thing wants to be *itself* and I have to discover what it wants to be—that's what I'm looking for in my revision. *Riddley Walker* didn't feel right until it pared itself down.

SG: Some of these passages and characters must have been painful to remove.

RH: It's not exactly painful, since I know as I'm removing them that the book is finding what it wants to be, but sometimes these decisions have unforeseen consequences. Every now and then I get a letter from someone who thinks fiction ought to be democratic and who says something like, "What about *women* in your books? Why don't they have more of a role in *Riddley Walker,* for instance?" My reply is: That's just how it was in that story; the story dictated what role women would play. In the case of a primitive society, the older, more powerful men would tend to take over the women or the women would tend to die young, so they're scarcer than men; thus Riddley probably wouldn't have had much of a chance for a woman of his own. Actually, in my first discarded version he *did* have a girlfriend, but introducing her got the book moving astray from what it wanted to be. It became tangled up with things other than the bare, stripped quest that Riddley was pulled into. Let me read you the opening scene of the book as it was first written: "The Eusa man sat outside in the rain and sent his partner in first. The partner was well over six feet tall, he had a bow and a quiver of arrows on his back, a big knife and a rabbit hanging from his belt. He had hands that looked as if they could break anything and squeeze it to death. He poked about with his spear, looked here and there and behind things. He seemed to take in the place with all his senses at once, took in the feel of it, as an animal would. The Eusa man stood with his bundle on his back and leaned on his stick, while the steam came up from his sweating back, and the dog sniffed him. He didn't seem to notice the rain that came down on his little old hat, or the mud he stood in. 'Okay,' said the partner. The Eusa man bent down so his bundle had cleared the opening and came inside. 'Wotcher,' he said."

What happens is that my narrator goes into a lot of explaining about the origins of the Eusa show and the characters in it. I already had that idea of the Eusa show from that first bit of inspiration at Canterbury. What I'm looking for in my successive rewrites is the move from spelling things out to letting it take off on its own. It's an intuitive sense that *that* ain't it and *that* ain't it and *that* ain't it again, until finally, well, *that* looks like it. That's the only way I know how to write.

SG: You took a big leap forward artistically from *Turtle Diary* to *Riddley Walker.* Was this development mainly a matter of the time you put into these books? Your first three all came out within three years, while you spent over five years on *Riddley Walker*.

RH: I'm not sure I agree with your premise. OK, I accept that the others may not be in the class with *Riddley Walker*, but if I had to say which book is closest to my heart, it would be *Kleinzeit*, where I first found what still seems to me to be my most characteristic and comfortable voice. Whether that voice came out as sounding Jewish or, as in *Riddley Walker*, as a kind of post-apocalyptic Cockney or whatever, that *Kleinzeit* voice was the first time my reliable narrator-voice appeared to me. So I treasure that book. When *Kleinzeit* and *The Lion* were recently reissued in America, everybody pissed on them, saying they were nothing, just what I wrote on my way to writing *Riddley Walker*. But I don't feel that way about writers. When I take to a writer, what grabs me is that writer's general approach, so if some things are better than others, I usually don't care—it's the whole output I'm interested in. Of course, with someone like Conrad I may not be able to go much for *The Arrow of Gold* or *Chance*, but when I go for a writer I'm in favor of the whole output.

LM: Those first three novels came out one right after another. Had the dam burst for you, after all those years of not writing adult fiction, or had you been working on those books (or versions of them) earlier?

RH: No, each of them just seemed to take one year to write. I'd written my first novel, *The Mouse and His Child*, from 1963 until 1966. That was a big transition for me: from not writing novels to writing something two hundred pages long, with a narrative and dialogue, and the whole thing situated in a relatively complex fictional world. The next big transition for me was writing adult novels, because until I busted up with my wife and started *The Lion of Boaz-Jachin*, I had never been able to go all the way in a book with everything that was in my head and in my experience, and to write whatever was in me. I started doing that, it was new and exciting. *Lion* and *Kleinzeit* and *Turtle Diary* each got themselves written in pretty much the same pattern: a first draft took me somewhere past the halfway point, maybe two-thirds of the way through; then I got stuck, so I had to go back to page one and work my way forward until I jumped over where the bridge was out and I got all the way to the end of the second draft. Each of those books evolved in exactly that way, and each seemed to get written fairly easily—a first draft, and a second, and that was it, with revisions on each page, of course. But then *Riddley Walker* was a whole new ballgame. I suppose that, in one way or another, *Lion*, *Kleinzeit* and *Turtle Diary* were all "experience books," where my experiences became transmuted into fiction, where a nucleus of my experience was amplified and spread out into a story in a fairly straightforward fashion. But *Riddley Walker* was more of a process of art, where something took hold of me and established a standard and required me to meet that standard. Both in the quality and in the form, something outside me was using me to get itself down on paper, and it was very strict and exacting. I simply gave myself over to it, not caring how long it took. When it let go of me, I knew it was done. That's how it went for me for five and a half years.

LM: I prefer your two more recent books because of the poetic, visionary quality of the *voices* of Riddley and Pilgermann. You found narrators who were sufficiently odd, and in sufficiently odd circumstances, to allow you to give full range to your flights of language and imagination. They are a bit like the fools in Shakespeare's plays, who are brilliant technical devices since they can really say *anything*.

RH: That's an interesting point, and it may indeed have contributed to what I was able to do. There's a pretty weird guy in my current book, another first-person narrator. In one of my physics books (it may have been one by two Chinese physicists who won the Nobel Prize with their theory of the weak interaction) it was suggested that the problem with most conceptions or theories is not that they're too far out, but they're not far out enough, not crazy enough. That's true with my work: when I sense I'm not getting something right, inevitably I'm not being crazy enough. There's such an essential craziness, strangeness, faroutness in things and in the way they put themselves together in our consciousness that whenever I get too straight, too ordinary, I worry about what I'm doing.

LM: Certain images or symbols—your use of animals, and lions in particular, or the motif of biting the wheel—seem to recur in your fiction. Are you self-conscious about this?

RH: Only partly. Mainly I simply like to refer to them. Lions seem very interesting to me; they're powerful symbols. I married a Leo. I suppose animals in general are very important in my books because they represent a mode of being other than ours, a fascinating mode in many ways superior to ours. People can't really hope for the elegance that animals have. Animals don't smoke or drink, are not generally obese, and they seem to be athletic and in good shape right up until the day they die.

SG: You indicated earlier that leaving your first wife and moving to England in a sense freed you to write in new ways. Without going into the particulars, what was going on during that period, and how did it affect your career?

RH: I found that until I left my wife I never felt free to use all my thoughts and feelings and experiences in my own writing. I don't know how to account for this situation, but that's the way it was. At the time when I wrote *The Mouse and His Child*, back in the mid-'60s, I would have been incapable of writing about relationships between men and women, for example. And there were a lot of other things inside me, inside my head, that I simply couldn't use, couldn't explore. It wasn't until after we busted up that I felt free to say anything at all about anything at all, that I was able to get into a truly unlimited exploration of what was inside me. Probably until that breakup I was too concerned with the difference between how things were and how I wanted them to appear. Afterward I didn't care about those differences—I just focused on how things were.

SG: *The Lion of Boaz-Jachin* is concerned with father-son relationships. I suspect that this must have deep-seated resonances in your own background.

RH: Your intuition is certainly right—father-son relationships are very important to me. My father died when I was eleven, and I've been working through that loss ever since. As far as its relationship to the way *The Lion* got written, it's very complicated; when you're living through these things, a lot of different things are coming together. I'd bought that book on Mesopotamian art in Klein's Bookshop in Westport, Connecticut, in 1968, and I accumulated a number of notes for what I hoped would be a supernatural story. I kept accumulating notes, but I wasn't able to get a story together. Then I left my wife, and my three daughters and my son were all angry at me. At that point the story began to put itself together, centering on a son who was angry at the runaway father and who evokes a lion out of his rage. Obviously it's the most autobiographical book I've ever written— having to deal with this encounter of the father-son-father was almost the price of admission for my first adult novel. As to my own relationship to my father, you're right in seeing this working its way into the novel as well. I read somewhere that a high percentage of male suicides had lost their fathers when they were young. Often you don't realize the significance of these family matters until long afterward. I always used to think of myself as an intelligent and perceptive person, but the things I haven't realized about myself in my life, if laid end to end, would go around the moon seven and a half times. Certainly analysis has helped me work through some of these things, perhaps understand them in ways that have been useful to me in my writing. I see these kinds of things all the time now, about my relationship to my parents and about my relationship to my own kids. This struck me when I visited two of my daughters in New York City recently. There are deep and muddy waters between fathers and daughters, and I can see a lot of things now that I couldn't see before. And there's this complex stuff between fathers and sons. Last September I had a very happy visit with my son, who is twenty-eight and now living in Texas; we hadn't seen each other for eight years. I guess a lot of parents and children who live together often don't get to see these sorts of things as clearly as I did. For example, there's obviously a process in which the parent needs validation from the grown-up child and the grown-up child needs validation from the parent. In this case, the son needs the father to say, Yes, you are a worthy man and the father needs the son to say, Yes, you too are worthy. These things are said with all kinds of subtle nuances, but until they *are* said, you can't get no satisfaction.

LM: Were there any other incidents, traumas, or relationships that affected the development of your sensibility? For instance, that you were in the Italian campaign in World War II? Since both *Riddley Walker* and *Pilgermann* have so much to do with a vision of war and the horrible, violent things men do to one another, I wondered if war experiences affected you, the way they obviously affected Vonnegut or Mailer.

RH: I don't know, at least about the literary effects. While I was in the army I used to write fragments of various kinds; my mind already seemed to work in a literary way. Also it's common for young people— I was in the army from 1943, when I was eighteen, until 1945—to feel a bit detached from what's going on around them, to think of themselves in the third person. The bits that I wrote during that time were like that. I was very far from home in situations where I could get killed, and I was in a totally male environment after having grown up with two older sisters. I was in an infantry regiment, but I never fired a gun at anybody, although I was shot at several times by snipers and I was under artillery fire. But I had no big, specific traumas, nothing like Vonnegut experienced.

LM: When you turned to writing adult fiction, were there any particular models?

RH: No, the influences on me have not been stylistic ones. With Conrad you could say the influence was modal rather than stylistic— I was deeply impressed with his use of density, of bafflement, of non-linearity, and also with his moral concerns. Dickens has always been important to me from the standpoint of his word power, his sheer energy. But I've never tried to write like Dickens; I've just internalized a standard of how much power or energy words need in order to make a work succeed on my terms. Words have always got to have action, they need to crackle, be active.

LM: Are there contemporary writers whom you admire?

RH: Borges, of course; I much admire him, but I have avoided him. I remember one time someone had given me a book of his, and I read four or five of his stories while I was waiting in a long queue. Then

I wished I hadn't read them because there was too much of a flavor of my own territory in his explorations. It's baffling to me that he's never won a Nobel Prize—he's done more to advance art in general through literature than so many others. What I'd say is that he has done a lot to advance the art of perception. In a way, I suppose Borges is in a direct line with Kafka; he affects writers of a certain bent in much the way that Proust established a new standard of psychological insight. Borges and Kafka have established a line of reality beyond the limited consciousness, and that's a line that I'm very interested in pursuing. A few years ago John Berger and I exchanged several letters and he gave me a copy of *G.*, which had several bits in it that were real feats of perception. I suspect the world is filled with tremendous writers whom I'm better off not knowing about—which is one reason why I don't read much contemporary fiction.

SG: Did your long career writing children's fiction have any effect on your adult writing?

RH: My picture books are written for four- to eight-year-olds, so obviously they're limited by the fact that they're written for a child's frame of reference. But there are some connections between my children's writing and my adult writing. My picturebook writing freed me in certain ways to do things in my adult books, things other writers might have been hesitant to try. While some novelists would be afraid to write the same word five times in the same sentence or passage, I'm not. If I want to say, "the boy was creeping, the girl was creeping, the night was creeping, the tree was creeping," and so on, I'll be happy to say it as many times as it needs to be said. Other writers might try to find five different ways to say *creeping*, but sometimes there are reasons to play with that sort of thing. Those picturebooks let me have fun with the sound of words, allowed me to pursue writing for the ear, freed me to explore certain obsessions. And the use of little songs and rhymes certainly carries over into my adult books as well.

LM: I think your so-called young adult novel, *The Mouse and His Child*, is one of your best works—and it seems to me to have as much in common with Beckett as it does with children's fiction. Children might enjoy the book, but they wouldn't be able to comprehend what you are implying about death, about identity, about exploring one's potential.

RH: Right. Children can respond to it on a story level, but to get all the juice out of it you have to be grown up. I certainly thought of it as an adult novel; I just didn't try to publish it as such, because I thought an adult novel about two clockwork mice wouldn't have much of a chance.

SG: In an essay you've stated that children today are different—

that they're growing up in a world where they face up to things like mortality and sexuality in ways they didn't used to.

RH: We're not living in an unexpurgated world anymore, and this is very important to realize. Society is very inconsistent about what's right for children. Hardly anyone minds having children watch a James Bond film, where people are killed for laughs, but a lot of respectable middle-aged people still don't want children to know anything about sex. I should think once you're twelve you can read just about anything: *Moby-Dick, War and Peace.* I don't see any limits.

SG: A character tells Jachin-Boaz that all men feel vaguely anxious when they don't have guns; and there is running throughout your fiction a castration anxiety that becomes literalized in *Pilgermann.* These fears seem to be tied up with male violence as well.

RH: I don't think this view is personal to me. Yes, I do have all sorts of castration anxieties, and my experience has proven them valid. (Even paranoiacs have enemies, you know.) I think a lot of male violence is related to the primal fears men have. But aside from that, more and more what I've found myself thinking about (and I hope this will be incorporated into my next novel) is the inability, so far, of the female principle and the male principle to meet correctly. The world's ills are pretty much traceable to this failure. If you think of the female principle and the male principle not just in terms of men and women but as all the aspects of these two complementarities, when you get down to men and women it's obvious that they've just not been able to meet in the right way. The female principle seems to be the earlier, stronger principle. Based on the Big Bang, in which in the first few seconds the explosive womb of things burst open and the universe sprang out of it, it feels to me as if everything has come out of the female. And the first divinity, the first deity, was the mother goddess, the chthonic earth goddess, the female principle of earth; only later did the male sky gods come into prominence. All through human history there has been a succession of males feeling weaker than the female and trying to dominate the female, and so the two have never achieved harmony. As a result, whichever way the pendulum swings—whether it's toward male dominance, with the female barefoot and without a vote, or toward female liberation, where it gets to a point of absurdity so that being a lesbian is the only politically in thing to do—it has never seemed to happen right yet. You can see some of this fear and violence in various ways. It's there in the male film fantasy of the guy who comes to a hotel or motel and peers through the venetian blinds and takes out his black case lined in velvet, and inside is his gun, the instrument, and he puts together this deadly instrument very precisely, click, click; it's a fantasy of this deadly male with the deadly weapon made out of parts; usually he's the unseen killer, the voyeur who kills somebody he doesn't dare look at. You can take this fantasy all the way back to Perseus and Medusa—Medusa, who is the frightful aspect of the mother goddess, and Perseus, who is afraid to look at her, who's like a little boy who can't take in the whole sight of a naked woman, so he's got to look at her in a mirror and then kill her, cut her head off. That's not a very manly way to deal with the female principle.

SG: One thing that struck me in *Riddley Walker* was the impulse of future society to *storify* its experiences. You dramatize how storytelling is one of the fundamental ways in which we relate to both the present and the past.

RH: Writing is the primary art. If the world had to be stripped of all but one of the arts, writing would be the one that would be kept because it communicates all our experience much more than painting or music. It's absolutely the primal art: someone saying, This is what happened to me and I want to tell you about it. We all have an urge to re-present our experience and to gain new understandings of it. Something happens, and then it's gone forever, and so you tell about it, and in telling about it you find something funny about it, or you learn something from it, or suddenly you see the tragedy of it. You have more life and more worldview when you talk about your experience, so that more of its aspects are revealed. There seems to be a human need to do that, to reexamine what has occurred or what might occur. Art is long and life is fleeting, right? Life slips by like shit through a tin horn, so in order to *have* anything of your life in the world, you have to make a story out of it in one way or another, whether you're playing it back in your memory, laying it out as a factual history, or fictionalizing it.

Thomas Victor

An Interview with
William Kennedy

We arrived at William Kennedy's home in Averill Park, New York (just outside Albany) late in the afternoon of August 23, 1983, only three hours after Kennedy and his family had returned from New York City. For the past six weeks Kennedy had been keeping a grueling pace working (sometimes around the clock) with Francis Coppola on the script for *The Cotton Club*, Coppola's latest movie project. It had been a high-powered, high-pressure project, full of impossible deadlines and Coppola's usual theatrics, and we expected to find Kennedy exhausted and drained from the experience, with little energy to entertain questions from strangers. Instead, Kennedy was animated, lively, anxious to talk about books and writing. It was a long interview that began at 5 p.m. and continued through and after dinner; when Kennedy's wife, Dana, excused herself at midnight, we assumed the session was over. But Kennedy danced Dana off to bed (literally: to the strains of Duke Ellington's "Mood Indigo") and came back for more—more talk, more music, more Irish whiskey. We listened to Bix Beiderbecke and Louis Armstrong (an autographed photo of Armstrong is prominently displayed in Kennedy's study), we chatted about Damon Runyon and Francis Coppola, and when Kennedy played his favorite Sinatra song, "New York, New York," he got up and put it back on when it was over ("I played that song twenty-one times a while back at a party," he explained). When we finally said good night at six in the morning, Kennedy was still going strong—flipping through records ("Listen to this one!"), talking about his favorite films, about the wideopen city that Albany used to be, bobbing to the beat of early Miles Davis.

Upstairs, as we lay exhausted in one of the many guest rooms the Kennedys keep ready for friends, we could hear "New York, New York." When the last rich note played out, there was a moment of silence—and then Kennedy and Sinatra rocked on.

William Kennedy was born and raised and has spent most of his adult life in Albany, New York, the locale that has become the inexhaustible context for the fictional universe he inhabits in his imagination. Realizing during one of his rare extended periods away from Albany that his imagination was not energized by other locations, Kennedy has discovered that Albany possesses all the history and politics, local color, clashes of personality, and mythic potential that a writer ever need draw upon. Although his first novel—the highly experimental, surreal *The Ink Truck* (1968)—is set in Albany of the 1960s, it is the wide-open Albany of the 1930s that so far Kennedy has brought to life most memorably in his trilogy of interrelated novels: *Legs* (1976), *Billy Phelan's Greatest Game* (1978), and *Ironweed* (1983). In *O Albany!* (1983) Kennedy illuminates the "reality" of the city he constructs so vividly in his fiction. Part history, part journalism, part personal memoir, *O Albany!* shows Kennedy's fascination for the sprawl of the urban experience as he explores the evolution of neighborhoods and ethnic groups, the machinations of city politics, and the confluence of individual and communal history and psychology.

Launched from this far-ranging understanding of and appreciation for the city of his birth, Kennedy's Albany trilogy is a remarkable fusion of a real landscape—of loud, swinging speakeasies, all-night diners, and hobo jungles—with the landscape of his imagination, where the dead walk side by side with the living, and a bowling alley or a pool hall can become a scene of truly epic proportions. Like the Dublin of Joyce's imagination, Kennedy's Albany is re-created with meticulous attention to detail but is also imbued with a universality that allows us to recognize something of our own fears, guilt, passions, and ambitions. What makes Kennedy's fiction so immediately recognizable and memorable probably has most to do with the more ineffable quality of his prose. When Kennedy's characters talk in his novels—and there is a lot of *talk* in them, plenty of wonderfully extended set pieces of dialogue with a life all their own—they talk about the things that people in desperate, urgent times have always talked about: power, death, love and hate, politics, the glory days now barely remembered, how to keep going, to keep pressing on against the odds. But it's the *way* they talk that arrests our attention, for Kennedy's prose is full of the nuances, idiosyncrasies, humor, and music of the kind of street poetry that only a few other modern writers (Beckett, Damon Runyon, Joyce, Hammett) have captured. And, more than any other writer today,

Kennedy has created a context where America's vernacular can properly *sing*.

Larry McCaffery: The brief biographical end notes in your books state simply that you're a lifelong resident of Albany—implying that this is the most relevant feature of your background. Could you talk a bit about what there is about Albany that has kept you physically rooted to this area and has sustained your literary imagination throughout all your fiction?

William Kennedy: To begin with the physical element—being rooted here—I find that Albany is a most civilized place to live. It's small enough to let people feel they're in control of their lives, and yet it's close to major cities—New York, Montreal, Boston—if you need big-city action. Most of my life I've never needed that action. The day-to-day life was what was really important: a circle of close friends, a private life in a crazy household where you never know what's going to happen in the next ten minutes. That has satisfied me enormously. Living here in this house, close to Albany, provided me with all the things anybody could need to nourish life—except money. Until this year I never made any money to speak of. My condition might have been described as pleasant impecunity. But I was never writing for money anyway. I was writing to say what I wanted to say, to write the kind of books I wanted to write, to do the kind of journalism I wanted to do. What difference did it make if I did it in a Greenwich Village apartment or this Averill Park farmhouse? The end product is all that really matters, and I realized that very early on in my life, long before I aspired to write fiction, I knew I probably wasn't going to become a New York City journalist because I never wanted to live there. There were also a lot of reasons, at one point in my life, *not* to live in Albany, either. When I was a young man, just out of the army, I felt like a displaced person. Before going into the army (this was the Korean war), I had been a sportswriter for three years. Then, instead of being sent to Korea, where we thought we were heading, we went to Europe. We were the first division (the Fourth Infantry Division, which was Hemingway's, by the way) to be sent back to Europe after World War II. I had gotten enough taste of cosmopolitan life in Europe to believe that Albany was a backwater and would stifle me forever.

LM: That sounds like the kind of classic response that a lot of American writers have gone through—they go to Europe, like Hemingway, and then say, "I'm not going back and spend the rest of my life in Oak Park." But you came back . . .

WK: I came back after the army for three and a half years, but then

I took off to Puerto Rico for an extended period. While I was gone I found out some of the answers to the second part of your question, about how Albany sustains my imagination. When I came out of the army I knew I'd had enough sportswriting, even though I'd had a great time with it, and I went to work for the Albany *Times-Union* as a general assignment reporter. That meant I could write about anything, interview anybody—writers, entertainers, politicians, whatever. I covered the police beat early on and I loved it. The fact that so many dimensions of the world were opening up for me kept me here a while. But then I began to feel I was wasting my time in Albany, because I was working under some very limited editors. All young writers and reporters think their editors are limited, or stupid, but in my case it was true. This was confirmed when I took a job in Puerto Rico and had an editor down there who was *not* stupid. It was like night and day. His name is Bill Dorvillier and he and I became great friends and I wound up being assistant managing editor in a matter of a few months. This was a very small, brand-new newspaper, the *Puerto Rico World-Journal*, an adjunct to a big newspaper, *El Mundo*. That work was fun and it was good journalism, but the paper went under because of problems with distribution and advertising. Eventually I met my wife, Dana, married her within a month, went to Miami for about a year, and then moved back to Puerto Rico, where we lived very happily for another six years. In 1959 I wound up being a founder with Dorvillier of another newspaper, the *San Juan Star*. It evolved into significant journalism, vastly different from the kind of thing that had driven me out of Albany. One of my buddies, Andy Viglucci, another of the founders, is still running the paper down there.

Sinda Gregory: This whole experience sounds very positive—so what was it that you discovered about Albany while you were down there that made you eventually return?

WK: While I was in Puerto Rico I started to write about this expatriate life I had chosen for myself. Puerto Rico was certainly exotic enough as a setting. It was a Spanish-language community, full of both hostility and reverence for the United States, with all sorts of politics and beach bums to write about. But while I loved Puerto Rico, I found that I really didn't give a damn about it as a basis for my fiction because I wasn't Puerto Rican. I couldn't identify with the Puerto Rican mind because I couldn't read the language well enough. I felt I'd always be a second-class citizen in Puerto Rico because of the language barrier, that I could never possess the literature, could never possess the intellectual world of the scholars, or the political theorists. I'd written some short stories set in Puerto Rico with the beginnings of political contexts, but they were shallow, and I realized it was because I didn't know very much about the place. Finally I just said to hell with it and started to write about Albany. And the transition was extraordinary. I found myself ranging through sixty years of the history of a family, the Phelan family — Billy and Francis Phelan were part of the characters in that first novel I began down there. I found that by focusing on these people and locations something happened to my imagination that freed me to invent very readily. With Puerto Rico I always felt I was a tourist. But I could understand the psychology of a wino in Albany, or a spinster, or a clandestinely married woman. I didn't know *why* I understood them, but I did. It became magical.

SG: Was this "understanding" a product of your own experience in a direct way?

WK: Certainly the Phelans were not my own family. There may have been paradigms from my family for some of those people, but there was no real transposition of biography into fiction. They were all invented characters and yet I felt very much at home with them. Two or three chapters into the novel I realized that the people were substantial to me. There was some "sand" I could deal with. I was no longer a Yankee trying to use Puerto Rico as an exotic locale, the way so many writers tried to capitalize on Paris after Hemingway — all those people going to the Left Bank in all those boring, boring imitations.

LM: So what became of that book?

WK: I wrote the book, which I called *The Angels and the Sparrows*, three or four times. It went around to maybe twenty publishers and nobody took it on, but nevertheless that was when I decided I was a real writer. Oh, I wasn't a *real* writer — you're never a real writer until you publish something, right? "Writer" is a sacred word. You can't use it until somebody consecrates you by putting you in print. But I was aspiring to something serious, and there were enough people taking me seriously that I felt confirmed that I had written something pretty good. Because Albany fired my imagination, I also felt I should know more about it. Even before we moved back to Albany in 1963 I started taping conversations with my family. Just before he died in 1975 I even taped my father talking about his life, his random, senile craziness — wonderful conversations. He didn't really know what he was talking about, but every once in a while he would be absolutely lucid. Much earlier I had quizzed my mother and my aunts and uncles about their lives and I began to see patterns and structures among families and political relationships and the social dimensions in the gambling world and nighttown and the world of music. I was also coming to know the newspaper world, hanging out with reporters and editors who knew the old days of Albany and understood what it was like to cover all those gangsters in the Prohibition era when Albany was a wide-open city—and Albany *was* wide open for years. This all fertilized my imagination to the point where there were no dimensions of Albany I didn't want to understand.

SG: Could you talk about this "fertilization process" more specifically? How exactly does this kind of research help your imagination?

WK: These random flashings in and out of history create atmospheres. I need the sense of a specific world that is definable, like the Jazz Age, or the Depression, so that if I want to set a book in that time I know the thrust a character will have. I want to understand how an era affects the life of Albany, not in a sociological way—I couldn't give a damn less about that for fiction—but what was happening to people's emotional lives.

SG: So it's the "feel" of the era that gives your fiction its impetus.

WK: That's exactly what I'm talking about. Once I have that, I have everything I need. Then I can begin to shape and cut away things that are not important. By knowing what would be possible in this age, or outlandish in this age, I can make the intuitive leaps you need to make in terms of character psychology—the arbitrary graftings, the sculpting. If you don't have a sense of where somebody comes from, you don't know who they are, imaginatively speaking. If you don't know their roots, or have a feeling for their origins, or their family, then they become characters in a tourist novel, the Left Bank story, or whatever. When I went down to New York City to write the screenplay for *The Cotton Club* with Francis Coppola, I didn't have anything except my sense of the Depression era, I didn't know what I was going to find. All I knew was that the script was going to be about the Cotton Club, and I didn't know much about the place. But I did have the sense of the era and so it was a matter of finding out what was useable from it. So Coppola and I began to create this Dixie Dwyer character, who took shape slowly. By having certain elements of the era to work with we were able to piece together a life on the fringes of music, movies, and the underworld; and by forging that experience into an Irish family situation, we had the basis for something that seemed original.

LM: Could you talk about your family background? I'm especially interested in what your father was like, what your relationship with him was like—some of the most powerful situations in your books revolve around the father-son relationship, and in particular the primal fear of the son being abandoned or betrayed by the father (that's especially important in *Billy Phelan* but also central to *Ironweed*). That fear is presented so forcefully and in so many variations that we sensed it might have deep-seated roots for you, if not in autobiography, then perhaps in some dark corner of your psyche.

WK: As to the fear of being abandoned, I believe it's basic to the unconscious life of a child. We outgrow it, usually, unless there is some trauma, but we don't really forget it. There was certainly never any abandonment of me by my father, in fact there was always a very strong feeling of family as I was growing up. My family was a Catholic working-class family, Irish on all sides. We weren't poor but we never had much money. My mother and father both worked. I had a wonderful relationship with my father; he was one of the main reasons I came back to Albany.

LM: In reading your reminiscences about your Uncle Pete McDonald in *O Albany!* I got the sense that he might have been a model of Billy Phelan.

WK: He was the prototype for Billy. Actually when I was writing *Billy Phelan* what I did was use the circumstances surrounding an actual kidnapping that took place in Albany (Dan O'Connell's nephew) as background music for Billy's story. I knew I wanted to write a novel about politics and in particular about Dan O'Connell, who ran this city for sixty-two years. And I was interested in the dramatic possibilities inherent in the intersection of Albany's nightlife and politics. This fusion of the kidnapping and politics truly did take place during the O'Connell kidnapping. Dan's nephew was kidnapped because the kidnappers assumed the Albany politicians had access to a vast amount of money. They asked O'Connell for a quarter of a million dollars ransom, which he could have paid, but they kept talking until they finally agreed on forty thousand, which *was* paid and then they got the nephew back. But the mechanics of that, the dynamics of it that were unleashed, always fascinated me. I knew there was a great story there but when I started to do it I couldn't place it—I was originally going to use the Jazz Age and examine the beginnings of the O'Connell political machine on up into the present. But then I discovered Legs Diamond and he took over and pushed the politicians aside—there was too much going on in his life for me to deal with them both. When I went back to the material the holdover element was the era in which Diamond functioned and then disappeared. Eventually I found the focus in 1938 that let me tell a political story centered in Albany's nighttown.

SG: So far all your books except *The Ink Truck* are set in the 1930s. What is there about that period that makes it especially interesting to you?

WK: The kind of life that was being lived then. By the time I was in high school and college in the 1940s, Albany was in decline as a hot city. But I had lived through enough of what it had been, still knew the stories, was still listening to people who had really lived through it all. Even as a child I knew it was a unique situation to have this absolutely wide-open city where gambling was condoned by the powers who ran the town. I knew there had been gangsters around but not "around" the way they were in other cities—they could not have stayed here if the boss had decided they should not. That's one of the points I make in *O Albany!*: I think the Machine killed Legs Diamond because he was beginning to get uppity and overstep his boundaries. So what we had in Albany during that period is a unique city, a unique social situation in which power came from the top right down to the gutter, which is what I wanted to show in *Billy Phelan*.

LM: A few reviewers of *Billy Phelan* complained that your involvement with the people and places of Albany and its history got you sidetracked from what they took to be the "main plot" of the book.

WK: The context of the city in that age was one of the points of the novel: the fact that the political machine touched everybody's life; and if it didn't touch you, you knew it could. If you merely voted Republican they could up your taxes by reassessing your house and then you'd have to hire a Democratic lawyer to get it reduced. They could put the word out and somebody like Billy Phelan could be suddenly "marked lousy" to the point that he couldn't even get a drink in his own territory. *That* is real power, and in the kind of controlled environment that Albany was, the individual became a totally subordinate figure whose freedom was very much in question. Everyone kowtowed, everyone had fear, because Dan O'Connell (or Patsy McCall in *Billy Phelan*) owned the city. Everyone used the same taxicabs and the same cigarette machines because the Ryan boys (associates of Dan) had an interest in them. These things were made manifest to the public and the public responded. But Billy didn't understand the way the world worked, even though he thought he did. *Billy Phelan* is about this curious misreading of his own extraordinary moral code that Billy has to deal with, come to grips with. Contrary to what those reviewers apparently thought, I had to reconstruct the city that was, in order to show how Billy was enlightened by its singular power.

SG: You create an equally vivid sense of place in *Ironweed*—but for different purposes, I gather.

WK: Creating this sense of place now seems to be an important part of my function as a writer. I'm bored most of the time with these abstract stories where psychology is everything—and too often nothing. If people don't interact with the place where they live and with the artifacts of their lives, then they are voices in empty rooms. Even in Kafka's *Metamorphosis* there is a fully furnished society—it's about *those* mores in *that* room, with *that* family, *that* food they feed him, and so on. I've heard that people are now taking *Billy Phelan* to downtown Albany to find the places that exist in the story. With *Ironweed* people can go over the same turf and see what the city was through another and older character's eyes.

LM: One thing that links many great writers of Irish decent—Beckett, Joyce, Fitzgerald, and so on— is an ear for the music and sensuousness of language itself. Certainly your own language has these qualities. Do you see yourself working out of a specifically Irish literary tradition?

WK: I really don't. Certainly I love some of the Irish writers. I revere Beckett and I live constantly with Joyce and Yeats. But I don't aspire to be in their tradition any more than I aspire to be in Faulkner's tradition or the tradition of Kafka. As an American writer the useful influences are so varied. The Irish have been an important influence on me, but I don't considered myself an Irish writer. I'm an Irish-*American* writer, which is very different. I value Ireland enormously and I am enthralled by its history, but I could no more live there than I could in Puerto Rico. I don't even consider myself wholly Irish-American, but that's how people are perceiving my work. I believe I write out of a set of influences that extend well beyond Ireland—Grass and Camus and Ellison and Greene and Bellow and Nathanael West, and many more. Critics keep citing the Irish dimension of my work, but I suggest to them that if they look elsewhere they will find a very odd assortment of benefactors.

SG: During the first part of your writing career you were a journalist. When had you settled on that direction?

WK: As soon as I was old enough to fool with one of those tiny toy printing presses. Sixth grade, maybe. I went on to think of a newspaper career without much knowledge of what it would involve—it was a kind of fantasy future that kids grow up with. My high school experiences were minimal, but they confirmed the direction I was taking because I was thinking about writing; I was valuing things like Poe's stories and *Our Town* as a sophomore, and also reading Dashiell Hammett and Raymond Chandler and Damon Runyon, understanding that Runyon was an incomparably comic writer. I was also finding the journalists in the daily paper to be generally valuable citizens. That's where I decided I wanted to go, and I did go into journalism as a serious sideline as soon as I entered Siena College, a small school outside Albany, run by Franciscans. I didn't think much about literature then because it seemed beyond possibility, enormously desirable (in grammar school I used to collect literary classics in comic book form) but somebody else's province.

SG: When did you decide to be serious about fiction?

WK: I was doing it from my last two years in college, and I continued to write it badly in the army, and later when I went to work for the *Times-Union*. I'd work on short stories on my days off, give all afternoon to it, and likewise in the late hours in the city room, when no news was breaking. I produced maybe thirty stories, none of which was ever taken for publication, but which all contributed to both my commitment and my apprenticeship in the use of language. The journalistic experience was a marvelous matrix, but a confusing one.

SG: Was it difficult to make the transition from journalism to fiction? They seem to require different skills, a different use of language and imagination.

WK: I went for maybe six or seven years writing fiction the way a journalist would write it, transcending that now and again but still believing my fiction would be more or less a transcription of life. Philip Rahv has written about the cult of experience in American writing and singles out Hemingway's "bedazzlement by sheer experience." That experience has loomed excessively large for writers of my generation, so much so that if you lacked it, your fiction seemed watery. But that's the journalistic trap of this age; for the writer needs to know that, essential as it may be, experience is only where fiction begins. What sets a good fiction writer apart from the journalistic guppies is that he, or she, understands that the truth comes up from below, that it develops from the perception of the significance of experience, and not from the experience itself.

LM: I've never bought the notion that writers like Hemingway or Crane were great fiction writers because they had "a reporter's eye" or a journalistic background. Crane wrote *The Red Badge of Courage* before he had seen a war; and Hemingway's world is not *really* realistic—it's highly stylized, a world of language. I mean, listen to that dialogue he wrote . . .

WK: You're absolutely right. Hemingway was a reporter and he conveyed ideas of what it's like to be alive and functioning in the real world, but he's telling you in a way that gives you access to a *private* conversation that was not the real world. His dialogue is certainly not that of a reporter; it's novelistic dialogue that gives the illusion of speech the way a Van Gogh painting gives the illusion of life—his private vision of life.

LM: Or the way Damon Runyon gives that same illusion.

WK: That's a very good leap. Runyon was also creating a very private world, and maybe that's why I like both him and Hemingway so well. Both valued language and the internal dialogue. As soon as you put Hemingway's dialogue into the movies it becomes instant caricature, the same way Runyon's does. You can't put in the conversation of Regret, the horse player, or the Lemon Drop Kid, or Nicely-Nicely Johnson, because they were meant to be private eavesdroppings on fantasy worlds. Runyon's dialogue is wonderful, but it's not far from dreams. Faulkner is often the same way with his dialogue. Nobody in his right mind would mistake the dialogue in *Requiem for a Nun* for real people talking. It's absurd, it's so stilted and formalized, so "Faulknerian." It's also fascinating.

LM: And it's that "Faulknerian" quality—or the Kennedy quality of language—that we respond to. It's that highly personalized, distinct *style* that I look for in a writer, more than for what he's writing about.

WK: The great writers I value all create their own language. It's the measure of their supreme originality. Runyon is not very interesting as a writer of substance. He really had very little to say about the world. It wasn't what he said but the way he said it that makes me still able to read him today. That presence of language was there, so he survives even though he wasn't able to do what almost any serious writer is able to do, which is to synthesize experience and make it significant for us. Runyon was working at a silly, gossipy, journalistic level, underworld fairy tales, really. But nobody else used words quite like he did, or gave us the comic, quirky sense of what it meant to be alive through language that way, listening to the world and re-creating it through words alone. Of course, he didn't have access to his own soul. It's a matter of gift, I suppose—not everybody can be Melville or Joyce. But a writer can still be interesting when he or she gets to the point where language alone becomes so important, the way it does with Runyon.

SG: Your first novel, *The Ink Truck*, is so absolutely opposed to any kind of journalistic style that I was wondering if its style grew out of a self-conscious desire to break with "reportage" of any kind.

WK: *The Ink Truck* was a willful leap into surrealism. It grew out of expressionism, out of dream, out of Kafka, Beckett, and Rabelais. I can't remember whom I was valuing when I wrote *The Ink Truck*— certainly all those people and dozens more, including the surrealist painters themselves, whom I love, especially Magritte. I've always wanted to be able to do with language what they do with painting.

SG: Even though *Legs* is probably your most realistic novel, you conclude it with a very dreamlike scene in which Jack awakens momentarily after his death and is then pulled into the void. Larry and I have puzzled over that scene endlessly—it seems to suggest that Jack has, in some sense, failed to make that final leap into transcendence, that he's doomed to be reborn into other incarnations, maybe like the book we're reading. The whole scene seemed very mystical . . .

WK: The whole thrust of that last scene has to do with Legs being reborn into this life as a legend, then a mythic figure, a figure in American history who will be with us for a long time to come because of his inability to purge himself into being one with the "whiteness," however you want to look at that image. You're right about the mystical element. At one point in its trajectory through many, many forms, the novel was going to be structured as a totally surreal work, based in part on *The Tibetan Book of the Dead*, from which that last chapter derives. There is very little left of that original conception except that last chapter. What I wanted to suggest was something very aligned with the sense of transmutation that is one of the most striking things in *The Tibetan Book of the Dead*—the notion that people are born again into this life or they transcend it, cease to exist, enter Nirvana. The principle I was working with—it's an utter metaphor—is that Jack Diamond is still alive. He could not have gone into the great white beyond, Nirvana, having lived the life he had. He was destined to be reborn, maybe in the gutters of Calcutta, or somewhere other than in that whiteness, perpetuated in this society by people like Marcus, and me, who have retold the legends that grew up around him; and not just legends about Diamond alone, but all gangsters. I mean, here I am *still* writing about Dutch Schultz in *The Cotton Club*. Of all the people in the world, I think Schultz is one of the most useless, yet I've spent the last five weeks of my life writing about him. And why? Because men like him have galvanized the imagination of the American people and of people all over the world. People are fascinated by their extremism. That's one of the important things I was driving at in *Legs*, that sense of the gangster as myth, that idea that Legs was moving into mythic status after his life here on earth.

LM: The notion that life is utterly capricious, and the view that life indeed has some sense of plan or design, compete with each other in your fiction, and they coexist there in part because you present an almost mystical view that life is more fluid and interconnected than most people suspect. This view seems to owe more to Oriental philosophy than to Catholicism. Is this a view that evolved out of your own experiences, or does it owe something to your reading in theology or philosophy?

WK: I'm absolutely not interested in either Oriental philosophy or the formalities of the Catholic church. I find I can watch the institution of a bishop and marvel at it or be entertained by it the way I can be by watching the New York City Ballet. But I'm only seriously interested in religions, or anti-religions, to the extent that they suggest something of the mysticism that is at the heart of everyone's life. I believe in the mystical relationship that exists among things. It has surfaced so many times in my life as to confirm my belief that it's worth writing about, thinking about, trying to figure it out. I don't believe in practicing mysticism as a religion, but I do know there are certain affinities and transferences of ideas and confluences of thoughts and interactions that are inexplicable in the ways we usually think or function. In *Ironweed* I'm interested in religion only insofar as I want to present anything you can imagine, including atheism and Catholicism, that would be on a man's mind in extreme situations where he's confronting the deepest part of his own life. And that seems to me to be the *only* thing worth writing about. All the rest is so much gratuitous sociology or out-of-date philosophy or theology.

LM: Your books are about violent times — the Depression era — but you also seem to be suggesting something very much about America itself: our love affair with violence and with the people who perpetuate violence. Do you think that American society has a different relationship to violence from what is found in other countries?

WK: Maybe we're more interested in a certain *kind* of violence — the gangsters and outlaws. But are we really more violent than Latin America, or Turkey, or Germany, or the Soviet Union? Think of the kind of death that García Márquez or Juan Rulfo would write about. Or Grass in *The Tin Drum*. I don't particularly want to write about violence as such, but sometimes it gets in the way of life. That's what's happened with Francis Phelan — he commits these very violent acts almost by accident, due to the situation he finds himself in. There is a time, when you're involved in a strike, for instance, when violence is on the table because your life is in jeopardy. It's a form of war. Francis Phelan throws a rock at somebody and happens to kill him. Later somebody tries to cut his feet off and he retaliates and kills his assailant, because he's the stronger man.

LM: The opening image in *Ironweed*, of the dead relatives speaking to each other, is very striking and immediately demonstrates that *Ironweed* is going to be more magical, less realistic, than the two preceding novels. We were both struck with the similarities to the way Márquez uses ghosts in his fiction as a literalization of the way the past affects the present. Was Márquez a specific influence on *Ironweed*?

WK: Those ghosts probably come from *Our Town* and Dickens rather than from Márquez. I was already fixed in a matrix of influences before I encountered Márquez's fiction. But he's one of the great writers alive and we can all learn from the world of his fiction. I'm sure Márquez has affected me in the same way that any of my contemporaries who depart from the norm have — the way Beckett has, for example. We've all learned from Beckett. Márquez is my age and he comes out of Faulkner and Hemingway and Kafka, it turns out, in much the same way that I did, independently of him. And we both came out of a journalism background, so there are some parallels. But my sense of what my fiction was all about was cast fairly early on, certainly by the time of *The Angel and the Sparrows*, of which all my books, from *The*

Ink Truck to *Ironweed*, are extensions. From the beginning I had this desire for the surreal, the desire for extending the reality of the fiction, the feeling that many writers of my age had that naturalism is dead, that ordinary realism is dead, that the writer can't seriously engage us any longer with that alone. It also seemed to me that if I was going to try to really talk about the deepest problems that everybody has, and the deepest worlds that we inhabit, then I had to move into that world of mysticism I was talking about earlier. In that regard, *The Tibetan Book of the Dead* was obviously a direction for me in *Legs*, as was Martin's foresight in *Billy Phelan*, and going back in time to a mystical Albany in *The Ink Truck*, and the use of the ghosts in *Ironweed* as the reconstitution of Francis's past, which is hardly a new thing— it exists in Joyce, and in films like Fellini's *8½* and Bergman's *Wild Strawberries*. If there was ever an influence on my work it was *8½*, which I think is the greatest movie ever made. And I revere Buñuel even more than Fellini because he did more quality work than Fellini, went deeper into people, wasn't obsessed by imagery alone as Fellini eventually was.

LM: Despite your use of these unconventional devices, every one of your novels (except possibly *The Ink Truck*) seems to re-create the people and places of the era so meticulously that fact and fiction often seem to blur. Certainly this is true of *Legs*, which seems at once utterly mythical yet utterly faithful to Diamond's real life. Did you set out from the beginning with the intent of trying to present the "real" Legs Diamond, or was that not really central to your conception of the book?

WK: When I first started *Legs* I didn't give a damn about the real Jack Diamond because I was inventing everything. The first start was a free-floating ahistorical version in which Legs Diamond was going to be a mythical, generalized gangster whose name was just a designation that people would recognize. In the early version everything was being done as a movie, with a director following Legs everywhere in life to use him as the hero of his film. The only thing left of that version in the book is at the end, where the cameraman is at the courthouse when Legs brushes up against the pillar and dust falls, and the cameraman asks Legs if he'll do that again. But the camera became, as you can imagine, a gimmick that began to interfere with the story. Every time Legs turned around, I had to invent where the hell another cameraman was going to be. This had nothing to do with what I was really interested in—it was just a way of focusing on Legs as mythic hero, who was to be made into a movie hero. But that notion of myth remained with me and became central to the final version of the book: the idea of how myth is created, an act which becomes a public fascination, and then is blown out of all proportion, so that the doer is given legendary status; then the legend is passed on, and becomes one of the defining myths of the age. That notion of myth is what I began with, and because of that I didn't give a damn about facts when I started the book. But the more I went into the book, the more respect I had for facts.

LM: Sounds like a bit of your background as a journalist coming through.

WK: Yes, I suppose I always had the sense of myself as a journalist looking over my shoulder at myself as a novelist, telling myself that you can't *do* this to a historical character. You don't abuse his history for the sake of myth, no matter how good your intentions are. I began to feel that it was very important not to be cavalier about his words and his life, so I wasn't. I then began to accumulate information so I could write that same mythic story, only this time using his particular facts as accurately as possible to build the myth. Once caught up in that desire, I began a period of intensive biographical research, and the farther I went, the more distance there was to go—new information presenting itself to me every day: more books, more magazines and newspapers, more people who knew Legs, or thought they did. And it became an endless process. It also became obsessive and then counter-productive, because I was a novelist; I wasn't supposed to be interested in writing history. But I became so fascinated with the history of the man and the age that I couldn't stop. I became a history junkie, com-pulsively reading still another set of fakey, wrong-headed articles about Diamond, poring through pages 2, 3, 4, 5, 6 and 7 of the *Daily Mirror* and then switching over to the *Daily News* to read 2, 3, 4, 5, 6 and 7 of the same day. I exhausted the files of the *Times*, the *Post*, the *News*. I was having such a great time in the library that I was turning into a mole. I hoarded my notes, was happy only under a microfilm machine.

LM: That sounds a lot like the experience that Bob Coover went through in compiling his research for *The Public Burning*—he couldn't stop, even though he sensed that his research was becoming counter-productive after a while.

WK: The reason my research finally stopped was that I knew it could go on forever. History had become very important to me because I had seen so many renderings of gangsters in so many different contexts—theater, magazines, movies, books, newspapers—that I felt were all wrong. I was convinced that my mission in *Legs* was to write a me-ticulously accurate historical gangster novel. Then I found out that that mission was not possible. There is no such animal. It could never be done because of the conflicting stories of who did what to whom, who paid for it, and who got killed because of it. I became aware that all this information was actually *preventing* me from writing the novel I wanted to write. This goes back to what I said before about the novel coming up from below—your imagination still has to grapple with all this information at gut level. It's never the case that you ingest the information and then create a story *because of* the information. It's got to begin somewhere in your center—which is where Jack Diamond originally began in that first mythic version I wanted to write.

LM: Was there any specific reason you settled on Jack Diamond as your central character, rather than any of the other historical figures associated with Albany?

WK: The Albany connection was the basic thing. He was killed here, he was hanging out here. I grew up reading about him and I knew people who knew him. I even knew his two favorite songs, one of which I've still never heard: "My Extraordinary Gal."

LM: My relatives in Duncanville, Texas, talk about Bonnie and Clyde like that.

WK: You see, *that's* what people talk about—these things and people that are so far afield from their own lives. Talking about them helps them define their own lives in ways they could never arrive at through even-handed reasoning. Through this extreme development of the argument you begin to see things more clearly, see the patterns of what's possible when you take something to its ultimate possibility; and this is what my fiction has been doing, I've discovered. I perceived somewhere along the way that my books had this element in common. In seeing how far the individual will or won't go, we discover things about hierarchies of values.

LM: What was behind your decision to have Diamond's lawyer, Marcus Gorman, narrate the novel? Had you discovered something about the real lawyer that intrigued you, or was it more of a technical matter? Why not have Legs himself narrate, for example?

WK: I didn't want Marcus associated directly with any specific individual, but there was a famous lawyer in Albany who represented Diamond, and who could have been close to him in the way I projected Marcus as being close; I know that Diamond was, in fact, present socially at the lawyer's house, knew his kids. But I created a private life for Marcus that would in no way invade the private life of any lawyer I knew, actually or historically. As far as using Diamond to narrate his own story, I couldn't make that work. I couldn't make him see himself without artificializing him. He was not as interesting a character when he was narrating his own story as he was when others were looking at him.

SG: The parallels with *Gatsby* are obvious, and you even have Marcus refer to Gatsby at one point, but I was wondering how conscious you were of using *Gatsby* as a model?

WK: There's no doubt that *Gatsby* was a conscious model. That's one reason I used that reference. But Nick was different from what I wanted Marcus to be—Nick was a smart but boring presence, as far as I'm concerned. A lot of people have made cases for Nick as an interesting character, but he's not deeply interesting to me, mainly because he rarely *does* anything. His relationship with that golfer, Jordan Baker, is boring, boring. The only time he's interesting is when he gets drunk at that hotel scene and suddenly he's outside himself, almost as if he's no longer the narrator. It's what Percy Lubbock says about James pulling back from the center of consciousness to fall silent except for the description of action; and when the action does take place you discover that the character has become visible in a different way. That's what I sought to do with Marcus—have him act and react, be the person who's subtly and slowly corrupted, into the fallen figure he becomes in addition to being the contemplative narrator who can put Diamond into a social and moral perspective.

SG: At what point did you realize you were going to write a series of books that would be interrelated? *Billy Phelan* and *Ironweed*, for instance, seem much more closely intertwined than *Legs* is with *Billy Phelan*.

WK: Even when I was working on that first book, *The Angels and the Sparrows*, I realized how compelling it was to write books like *The Sound and the Fury*, with the Compson family's saga, and *Portrait of the Artist* and *Ulysses*, with Stephen, and Salinger's Glass family stories—works that carried people, not in any sequential way, through great leaps in time, maturity, and psychological transformation. When you see these people in a later time, having known them at an earlier age, there is this cumulative knowledge that rivets the mind; it makes you believe they did exist in the same way you believe in that uncle or grandfather who, you find, was really visually there—in that old family photograph that just turned up—long after you've heard his legends. And they *are* just as real, you've made them that way. That struck me early on as a thing that was very desirable to do, but I didn't set out consciously to weave a web of novels. You can see that if you compare *The Ink Truck* with *Legs*, for they have little in common except that they are both set in Albany. It's interesting that *The Ink Truck* dips into the 1840s, which is where I am *now*, in 1983, in a new novel. And I'm there probably because I was there then, only now it's vastly different. Even though Albany is never mentioned in *The Ink Truck*, I feel I have the same streets, and the same newspaper as I have in the work in progress, with the same characters running saloons, the same traditional figures existing in the history of this mythic city I'm inhabiting in my imagination. My worlds are interconnected because that's the way life is, and if you can only track the interconnections of any particular family, then the web of coincidences, influences, and prefiguring is extraordinary. That's what I want to represent.

SG: That image of the ink pouring out on the snow is a vivid, constant one throughout *The Ink Truck*. One of the ways it could be interpreted is to see it as the writer pulling out the plug, letting all those inked words go all over the page, a kind of personal liberation. This was the first book you had published—*was* it like pulling the plug?

WK: It was that, and I had that sense of all my previous fiction being dammed up inside me. But, more fundamentally, that image is a metaphor of anything that's obstructed. It was ink because it specifically had to do with a newspaper, but it also represents any letting of blood or bile. But remember, actually only a few drops of ink come out. That struck me as being the nature of what happens; if you get into a fight as a kid and give the guy a bloody nose, that can be traumatic, even if he only bleeds a little bit. And when you try to enter into any world and you achieve something, you usually get at it for only a few seconds where it really matters. But when you turn that petcock and get a drop, that's absolute ecstasy, an orgasm of a kind. It's any achievement, any arrival, the ink being your first story in a newspaper, your first novel, your first entrance into manhood as a macho figure who wins at pool, or love.

LM: *The Ink Truck* deals with union issues, worker oppression by management, strikes, and other highly political issues, and yet its odd, surreal form is certainly not the traditional social-realist presentation we expect from a work that deals with these issues. What's your feeling about the view that many "committed writers" have expressed, that stylistic oddities are a luxury political writers cannot indulge in, that to deal with these issues the writer needs to present things as directly and realistically as possible?

WK: The '30s Communists, led by Granville Hicks as editor of *The New Masses*, probably would not have approved of *The Ink Truck* because it would not have been sufficiently on the realistic mark for them. But that was the '30s. When *I* was writing I was in the middle of the civil rights movement, and it was energy from that movement that informs *The Ink Truck*. There are no significant blacks in the book, but Bailey is really, for all intents and purposes, an isolated nigger. Now I don't believe that Bailey is a black man in the sense that he has had to face the same things that black men have faced, because Bailey is white and has had it better than the blacks. But the civil rights movement definitely contributed to the energy that moves that book, and so did my residual affection for the Wobblies and the other labor organizations of the '30s and '40s. I became disaffected from that, as others did in the age of Hoffa and Fitzsimmons and so on, but I've never entirely lost that sense that the man on the street is still a man who needs to fight for everything he gets because there will be no gifts from on high. As soon as the chance presents itself, the people in power will take it away from you. What I'm describing has never been any clearer than it is right now under the Reagan administration, the retrogression on racial and environmental issues. Reagan is far more a criminal than Jack Diamond ever thought about being because he is affecting the whole society. It's beyond my comprehension that any man in this day and age could allow things like the chemical waste situation not only to prevail but to proliferate. And for what reason? Money and power, pure and simple. He doesn't give a damn about racial or human values; he has this vision of a reign of oligarchs. And this reign must be fought every time you turn around, in every age. *The Ink Truck* is a statement about that, and so is *Ironweed*.

LM: But of course the *form* of those statements is very different from that used by writers of earlier generations, the same way that Godard presents politics from a different aesthetic standpoint than earlier film-makers.

WK: Absolutely, and that opens up another interesting point: Godard certainly *is* different from Odets or Abraham Polansky and all those writers from the Hollywood Ten, and those figures out of the '30s like Dos Passos when he was a leftist. But what those earlier people were involved in seems simultaneously noble and futile today. There was a wonderful commitment, but what did it prevent? What did it change? It galvanized the right wing and led to McCarthy, when so many of those guys had their balls cut off. When I was writing for *Look* magazine Albert Maltz put out a book called *Afternoon in the Jungle*, a collection of stories he'd written back in the '30s and then revised. The title story was about a kid who finds a 50-cent piece down a sewer and then a bum comes along, sees what he's doing, and pushes him aside saying in effect, "I want it." Then the story tells about the fight between the kid and the bum. It's a great realistic story, a classic statement that synthesizes something about the time in the same way that the song "Brother, Can You Spare a Dime?" did. Those pieces are wonderful, but you can't keep doing them over and over. Should we go on making the same statements about social issues in the same old way? If you do that you become boring and tired. The stories fundamentally won't *mean* anything anymore, they won't affect people. We've *been* there already; everyone has heard and absorbed their lessons. If one's politics can be effectively dismissed by William Buckley, what good are they? The writer has to find a way to leap over such people, to make one's own political message transcend both the left and the right. You know that pair on *60 Minutes* that does the "Point-Counterpoint"? They're cartoons. You know exactly what position each will take on every issue. Set up the issue and you already know the opposing elements. They could switch sides and nobody would notice. Or care. Who is convinced? What good is that? That's the kind of approach many so-called political writers take. It's like most newspaper editorials—so many of them are dumb and obvious. If you're a Republican you're going to deplore the welfare state and if you're a Democrat you'll worry about cuts in welfare. That kind of art isn't going to move people.

LM: It's interesting that so many of the best recent political novels— like Márquez's books and Coover's *The Public Burning* and Coetzee's *Waiting for the Barbarians* and Barth's *Letters*—seem to demonstrate exactly what you're talking about. They're trying to create new ways of talking about these things, of forcing people to examine the issues from a different perspective.

WK: That's true, even though a lot of people still haven't realized that we're living in a different world today, a world that requires different ways of talking about it. There was criticism of *The Ink Truck* by certain people on the same grounds that Hicks would have criticized writers in the mid-'30s (Hicks became a neighbor and good friend of mine in the '60s and went out of his way to praise *The Ink Truck*). The old criticism was that writers who aspired to be more than entertainers weren't meeting their obligations if they didn't toe the leftist line, or if they weren't sufficiently realistic so that people could get an easy handle on what was being said. This is the urge for propaganda, Boy-Meets-Tractor-Yet-Again. Now Odets and Dos Passos were enormously important, strong voices during a period when things were really happening politically. But I was writing during a period when a new kind of politics was also happening. *The Ink Truck* is a book that grows out of the late 1960s and it absorbs a lot of the radical atmosphere of the time: the hippie movement, the drug movement, the sexual revolution, the crazy politics, all the death and assassination that was going on with Jack, and Bobby, and Martin Luther King, and so on. My book doesn't reflect these things directly, but they all helped make the book what it is. I think its rebellion is not only in the wild style of writing and storytelling, but in the resistance to the social determinism that the naturalistic writers of the 1930s found so valuable. It seems to me vastly less important to castigate a society, which is easy, than it does to demonstrate how the individual can survive its evils and perils, which is not easy.

SG: Really, all four of your novels can be seen as "political" novels of one type or another; this is very obvious with *The Ink Truck* and *Billy Phelan*, but it's also true in *Ironweed*, which deals with the disenfranchised in a different way. But it's very striking how really *different* all four of your novels are from one another. Could you talk a bit about the evolution of your style, where it's been taking you?

WK: So far I've gone through three stages in my writing. At my first level, *The Ink Truck*, I was trying to talk about the world the way that book does—through surrealism, through expressionism, all those things we talked about earlier. I was trying to leap out of realism because I felt the whole world of Dos Passo and O'Hara, a world I had once revered, was now dead for me. I knew I couldn't do that any longer, couldn't write another realistic line. I was trying to make sense of a new age in which, for me, Kafka was far more of a prophet than anybody with realistic politics.

LM: Even Kafka can be seen as a highly political writer—

WK: Exactly. *The Trial* is an extraordinary piece of political thinking, and so is "In the Penal Colony." When you read these books they react on your soul forever. Anyway, when I finished *The Ink Truck* there were several reasons why I wanted to move into a new kind of statement, a new form, for my next book. In *The Ink Truck* I had been able to say what I wanted to say in a nontraditional way, yet still be true to the impetus for personal achievement in the world, and for political resistance. But I felt I couldn't go on writing this hyperbolic comedy which is always six inches off the ground. I needed to be grounded in reality, yet I didn't want to write a realistic novel. *Legs* is a consequence of that, although, as I've told you, I started off trying to write myth from the beginning. It was a different style from *The Ink Truck* but it wasn't working, it was still too far off the ground. So the next stage for me was to say something at the level of realism, which I'd come to value, but in a different way. I felt that if I didn't have a realistic foundation in *Legs*, I wouldn't have anything. It would have been like William Burroughs's *The Last Words of Dutch Schultz*, which has nothing to do with reality but is a most original reconstruction and invention of society to suit Burroughs's private purposes. That book uses Dutch Schultz and Legs Diamond as names, as mythic signifiers, the same way my original version of *Legs* did. When I first read it I could see that it had nothing to do with what I was trying to do. It reaffirmed my belief that, when you're dealing with historical figures like Schultz or Diamond, realism must be there at the first level; then you can build. So I could not be satisfied with designating my book as mythic. The myth had to grow out of the real, otherwise I wasn't writing from substance but was inventing lifeless metaphors that didn't say anything interesting about gangsters or anything else either. *The Ink Truck* had substantial elements to it: it was about a strike that really did happen, it was about the civil rights movement, and about being a writer and an individual. But to talk about gangsters and deal with them *only* as a myth seemed absurd to me. So what I did was go back down to the documentary level in order to understand the history, and work from some concrete basis on which that reality—which I was about to reinvent and pass on— would have some historical significance. Remember, I was not inventing a gangster. If a writer reinvents Jesse James without knowing what a six-shooter is, he runs a certain risk of inauthenticity. A genius like Kafka can invent an entire cosmos from scratch and we accept it all. But without a historical context for their work, what most writers produce is isolated psychology, poetic music. So I was working for authenticity of a kind in *Legs*, and *Billy Phelan* is an obvious extension of that.

SG: You're leading up to *Ironweed*, which, I agree, has a totally different feel from your other books. It seems both grounded in reality and operating on other levels.

WK: That sense of multiple planes is something I was aiming for. By the time I'd gotten to *Ironweed* my realism was still there, but something else was going on. I'd realized that I didn't want to loosen that hold on reality, didn't want to let the fiction hover six inches off the ground. I still wanted the craziness of *The Ink Truck* but I wanted the craziness to emerge at the level of a more grounded significance. What I wanted to do in *Ironweed* was to take *the reality* of a man and try to move into his *soul*. You might think of Francis Phelan as always being aware of where he is, yet also always aware of all his history. Deeper inside he's aware of the obligations and evasions that go with his existence, and the kinds of conflicts that conscience generates. Then deeper still is his center, and there isn't any way he can *ever* articulate what is in there, and he knows this. That's the center of his soul, the ineffable element of his being. That's what I was trying to suggest— that we're enormously complex beings who can never know everything about ourselves. I know that's true about me. The center of Francis is the place I'd like to go to forever. It seems to me the only thing really worth writing about: the absolute center of somebody. Of course, it's very hard to get there; also to find somebody who has a center worth reaching.

LM: Did you do any sort of research on bums, or model Francis on a real-life prototype?

WK: *Ironweed* wasn't researched, exactly. I hung out with a few winos, and I've been in saloons and watched them. Bums seem to me to have more interesting lives than most businessmen. I did a series of articles on them in Albany during the early '60s and there was one articulate bum whom I got to like. But that bit of journalism was really just an extension of my imagination, since I had already created Francis and the whole Phelan family in that first book I wrote that was never published. Francis of *Ironweed* was not the same character who was in *The Angels and the Sparrows*. The first man wasn't a ballplayer, for example—but he was the basis of Francis.

SG: Despite the depressing nature of the life that Francis and Helen lead, there's a sense that Francis has won at the end, beaten them all. He's alive and has come to terms with certain contradictions about life, and himself, that most people never arrive at.

WK: Well, some people do learn how to save their souls. Not everybody, but it does happen to some people. I decided that Francis probably could. When I began to explore his nature he seemed to be a man of wit and reason, and a pawn of fortune in the sense that he didn't create his own fate. Oh, in a way he did, but he didn't really mean to kill that scab, and certainly not his son. Those deaths, those fated circumstances and events, marked him for life in ways that he grows to understand.

SG: That kind of acceptance you're talking about is not granted to some of the other characters in your fiction that you also feel obvious affection toward, like Francis's son, Billy. What's the essential difference between these two that allows one to develop this wisdom and the other not?

WK: Billy hasn't had the experience Francis had: nothing of the sort. Experience is usually the basic ingredient of a complex character. When I teach writing, my students are always writing poetry about their love affair and its breakup yesterday, and they fill their writing with allusions to *Tristan and Isolde*, or they try to find metaphysical meanings in their valentines. What Faulkner once said is that the problems of children aren't worth writing about. I believe he said that not to disparage children, who can have problems beyond belief, but because in fiction the complexity of life is arrived at through consciousness; children are not fully conscious of what is going on. Billy Phelan does not have anywhere near the conscious awareness his father has. Billy hasn't gone through the valley, has not slept in the weeds, hasn't had to kill people to stay alive, has not been a fugitive unable to come home. Billy has had it relatively easy; he's interesting, I think, and a nice guy, but even his moral complexity, which is the basis of the book, he only intuits, doesn't fully understand.

LM: The sense of play and games is central to the development of *Billy Phelan* and, perhaps more abstractly, it seems relevant to all your writing in various ways. Was Huizinga important in helping you formalize your notions about this?

WK: The sense of play being basic to us all—to even the animal species, that was important; and you're certainly right that *Billy Phelan* is all about games. Just about every form of game you can imagine is being played out in that book. But that notion of play, the way people live life as a game, has always been valuable to me. I feel now I am constantly at play. I've been trying all my life to do nothing except play, and now I'm finally doing it.

LM: Is that what writing is—play?

WK: Absolutely. It's the supreme game. There's nothing I'd rather do tomorrow than go upstairs and play at my typewriter. Writing is the most satisfying game of all for me—you're matching your imagination against everybody else's. Is that a game or isn't it? I've always loved games, always considered myself a gambler—a rotten gambler— at most things. I could never win at craps. I was a pretty good poker player, and a fair pool player. I played bogie golf and got a hole-in-one one day. I was a good bowler—I bowled 299 once, just like Billy. I was a pretty good first baseman. I wasn't bad at any of the games I played. But the real game for me is writing. It's the pleasure principle at work at every imaginable level. What else is as great as creating a world out of nothing? You project yourself out into the beyond, to where you want to go, but you don't know how to get there. And everything after that is a quest for lucidity, a game of light and shadow.

Lisa Kroeber

An Interview with
Ursula Le Guin

Ursula Le Guin is probably as responsible as any other living writer for changing our notions of science fiction and fantasy. Like the works of Italo Calvino, Jorge Luis Borges, Philip K. Dick, and Stanislaw Lem, Le Guin's fictions transcend genres; typically they are a sophisticated blend of myth, fable, political inquiry, and metaphysical parable. Her art takes us on a circular journey to the future and then back again to the world around us now, for not only is she a wonderful spinner of fantastic tales, she also makes us take note of the words and cultural assumptions with which we construct our present. Le Guin creates a world apart and then explores its premise, its prevailing metaphor, to the fullest. After we put down her fiction, we examine with alien eyes our cities, our political and social structures, our commonplace truths.

Le Guin began writing novels and stories during the 1950s, but not until the '60s did she find a publishing home in science fiction. Ever since the appearance of her first novel, *Rocannon's World* (1964), she has been both highly prolific and increasingly influential. Her fourth novel, *The Left Hand of Darkness* (1969), won both the Hugo and Nebula awards (Le Guin is the only writer to have won both of these prestigious awards more than once, having won four Hugos and two Nebulas) and immediately established her as an important writer in the field. Because it examines how sexual roles determine cultural and personal identity and political structures, *The Left Hand of Darkness* also brought Le Guin to the attention of feminists. Her Earthsea trilogy—*A Wizard of Earthsea* (1968), *The Tombs of Atuan* (1971), and *The Farthest Shore*

(1972)—further expanded her audience, winning the Newbery Honor Book Citation (for *The Tombs of Atuan*) and the National Book Award for Children's Literature (for *The Farthest Shore*). *The Dispossessed* (1974), which again won the Hugo and Nebula awards, reflected her increasing understanding of physics and her growing interest in anarchism as a political theory. Like another of her novels, *The Word for World Is Forest* (1972), which used science fiction forms to explore very contemporary issues (colonialism and the Vietnam war), *The Dispossessed* demonstrates Le Guin's ability to create a vivid alien world and sensibility that resonates with our own. In the 1970s Le Guin continued to publish science fiction and fantasy; in addition there were so-called mainstream works of fiction (*The Orsinian Tales* [1976] and *Malafrena*, a novel [1979]), poetry (*Wild Angels* [1975]), and essays (*The Language of the Night* [1979]). Her other major works include *The Lathe of Heaven* (1971), *The Wind's Twelve Quarters* (stories, 1975), *The Eye of Heron* (1978), *The Beginning Place* (1980), *The Compass Rose* (stories, 1983), and *Always Coming Home* (1985).

Even this brief summary should dispel any notion that writing science fiction has limited her work. The freedom of construction offered by the genre's premise has allowed her to build models best adapted to her lines of inquiry: that of the outsider thrust in the midst of a culture where "natural responses" are immediately suspect, where nothing can be taken from granted, and where understanding of the new world brings with it a new awareness of the arbitrary basis of the old. This essentially anthropological approach (her parents, Alfred L. Kroeber and Theodora K. Kroeber, were both well-known anthropologists) is perhaps the most striking feature of Le Guin's fiction.

The cool, detached observer was nowhere in evidence when we met Ursula Le Guin at her home, a beautiful old two-story house with a picture-postcard view of the Columbia River, the many bridges and highways that crisscross it, and the smoky Portland skyline. She was warm, vigorous, open, and tempered her intellect with a generous and humorous spirit. Before we sat down to the interview, she excused herself to get us drinks; from the kitchen we could hear muttering and odd clanking sounds, which prompted us to wander through to see if we could help. There she was, struggling with the pulltabs on three beers: "They're a new-fangled kind," she said, "and I haven't got the hang of it yet." The mysteries and ambiguities of the new age are truly all around us.

Larry McCaffery: As an anthropologist, your father spent a great deal of his professional career trying, in a sense, to re-create other people's cultures. Is that one of the attractions of science fiction for you—that it allows you to reconstruct, imaginatively, other cultures?

Ursula Le Guin: Yes. Science fiction allows me to help people get out of their cultural skins and into the skins of other beings. In that sense science fiction is just a further extension of what the novel has traditionally been. In most fiction the author tries to get into the skin of another person; in science fiction you are often expected to get into the skin of another person from another culture.

Sinda Gregory: You've said that when you turned to science fiction writing in the early 1960s it was partially out of a desire to find a publishing niche—a place that would allow you to publish the unclassifiable things you were writing at that time. But why this particular niche? Why not, say, detective fiction, or historical romances?

UL: The answer to that is simple: science fiction was what bought me. The other genres weren't interested. Whatever it is that I write— this general, odd area which seems hard for others to define, although I know in my own mind what it is—didn't sell until it was given to a science fiction editor. Today my work sells in other areas, because once you get published it is easier to get published again and again and to enlarge that pigeonhole you've been put in. But in all honesty, my entry into the field of science fiction was largely a matter of chance or circumstance. It finally occurred to me that this kind of editor might buy whatever it was that I was writing.

SG: There's a story about your interest in science fiction becoming rekindled about this same time by your being given the works of Cordwainer Smith. Did that really happen?

UL: Yes, I realized that if there was a place for him, there must be a place for me.

SG: What did you find in Smith that got you reinterested in science fiction? I understand you had been an avid science fiction fan as a kid but had given up the field in favor of more traditional forms.

UL: Smith had a highly original imagination expressed in original language. His works were certainly much better than the pulp stuff I had been reading when I quit looking at science fiction back in the '40s. He is not a "literary" writer, but he knew what he was doing as a short story writer—in fact, he was an excellent story writer. And yet here he was, working in the science fiction mode. To me encountering his works was like a door opening. There is one story of his called "Alpha Ralpha Boulevard" that was as important to me as reading Pasternak for the first time and realizing that one could write a novel the way he wrote *Dr. Zhivago*. There are these moments in most writers' careers when you discover that someone else has actually written down some of these things that have been going on in your own head; you realize that this isn't just a private experience.

SG: Could you talk a bit about the effects of your remarkable parents on your writing or your imagination?

UL: I find it almost impossible to analyze the effects my parents and their friends had on me. I wasn't exactly a dumb kid, but I was such an unaware kid. I don't think I was as conscious of things going on around me as other kids might have been. I was a nice serious little Germanic girl, a good girl. I have always liked to work. I was very introverted. And I was the youngest and the only girl. My parents never pushed any of us in any particular direction intellectually. They wanted us to be intelligent, and to be intellectuals if we wanted to be. It was important to them that we be educated people. This was during the war; my three brothers went away to the service, which meant that their education was all fouled up. I was the only one who had a normal progress through school. But my parents made absolutely no distinction between the boys and the girl. It never occurred to me that because I was a girl I was expected to do less or do other than my brothers. That was enormously important to my whole attitude. The intellectual milieu I grew up with was, of course, high powered in a kind of easygoing way. A kid doesn't recognize how unique the situation is, because a kid doesn't have anything to compare it to. I thought that every kid lived that way and had these impassioned, intellectual conversations around the table. To me that was just how it was, I didn't question it, it didn't seem strange. It was a very articulate family—my brothers and I were always encouraged to talk a lot— and there were books all over the place. It was no holds barred, as far as what we could read or talk about. There were also a lot of refugees around the house, and academic friends of my father. One Indian who always came and stayed with us every summer, Juan Dolores, was like a member of the family. As I look back on it, I suppose that was the kind of thing that must have influenced me later on. It's not every child who is lucky enough to have a Papago uncle!

LM: I've heard the suggestion that the Napa Valley country place where your family spent its summers must have been one of the sources for your later wilderness settings. Did you and your brothers ever invent fantasy worlds while you were there, like the Brontë children?

UL: Nothing so elaborate as that. We were a close-knit family and we did what most kids do when they play together. When, for example, my nearest brother was doing *Julius Caesar* in junior high, we'd do our own version at home. We did build some forts, and I had to be the Germans attacking. So we basically played the kind of imaginative games all kids play. When my brothers were off in the war, there were several summers when I was there more or less alone. This was a different experience, since I had the woods to myself. Entirely to myself.

LM: When you said that you had the run of the house as far as books were concerned, it occurred to me that you must have run across a lot of mythology because your works so often seem fascinated with the myth-making process. And *Rocannon's World*, your first novel, was directly based on Norse mythology. That doesn't seem like a coincidence.

UL: No, it certainly wasn't. My mother was the mythology book collector in my family, partly because she liked mythology and partly because she liked it for us. So by the time I came along (I was the fourth kid), there was a lot of mythology around, mostly in kids' versions, but what's the difference? Beautiful big books with lots of illustrations. I plunged around in those books and in everything else; the Norse myths were my favorite. Sometime in here I also came across Dunsany's *Dreamer's Tales*, which proved to be another revelation. Dunsany was important to me because he was the first writer I had come across who wrote what I would call "pure fantasy." Today his works probably seem old fashioned—I know my kids didn't take to him at all. He wrote in a biblical-grand-Irish-romantic language, a very mannered style. But as a kid in the 1930s, I wasn't so far from that early twentieth-century mannerism. What I saw in Dunsany were these absolutely pure invented fantasies: a mythology that one person had made up. The idea that people could invent their own myths, use their imaginations to the limit, was a wonderful discovery.

LM: So it wasn't just the mythic quality of the work but the fact that it was completely made up, not handed down but invented on the spot, that intrigued you.

UL: That was the magical quality. After all, that's the basis of our modern notions of the difference between myth and fantasy: in myth story is handed down, while in fantasy one person is inventing things on his own. This can be quite a revelation for kids. They use their imaginations a lot this way—as with the stories they tell themselves or tell each other before they go to sleep—but they may not realize that adults engage in this fantasy-making activity and are willing to share it. Of course, nowadays fantasy and children's books have become an enormously bigger industry than they were in the '30s and '40s, so probably children often make this discovery a lot earlier than I did; it probably doesn't hit kids with quite the air of glorious revelation that it did me, an introverted kid who needed an *outlet* for a strong imagination.

SG: When I first read *Rocannon's World* I didn't realize that it was so elaborately based on Norse mythology. When you were conceiving the book, were you using these mythic parallels more or less unconsciously, or were you more systematic about it?

UL: Oh, quite systematic. I was still fairly young when I wrote that novel and rather uncertain of what I was doing—I thought it was science fiction I was writing, but now I'd say it's more a fantasy. I initially plotted it myself, but somewhere in the building I began to see the parallels with Odin's adventures. So I thought, All right, I'll just use these parallels more systematically. Then I went back and read Padraic Colum's Norse legends, *The Children of Odin*, and I stole various things like the episode where Odin is standing in the fire—only I put him in that stupid impermasuit . . . I was a beginner, and *Rocannon's World* is really a beginner's piece. With the charms and many of the limitations of a beginner's piece.

SG: I can't recall any of your other works using specific myths like this.

UL: I never consciously borrowed in that way again, although obviously unconscious residues appear. I must admit that I'm made uncomfortable when a fiction writer systematically uses myth. Oh, Joyce's borrowing—one major writer to another—is all right; but when writers base a fantasy or science fiction piece directly on some myth, there is often an intellectualization that trivializes both the myth and the novel. I have tried to avoid that and get down far enough inside my own head, where I can at least believe I'm creating while I'm writing. Later on, a critic may get a look at what I've come up with and point out some parallels and explanations, and I say, Oh, *that's* what I was doing . . .

SG: Rumor has it that you wrote your first story at the age of nine and had it rejected by John Campbell's *Astounding*. That's a pretty early start.

UL: Writing was never a hobby for me. Writing has always been what I've done. Actually, I was so pleased to be getting the same kind of rejection slip that grownups did that I wasn't cast down at all.

SG: Did you take creative writing classes in college?

UL: I took one at Radcliffe out of curiosity and a sense of duty. I'd said to myself, Look here, you consider yourself to be a writer, now take a class in writing. But the class was a disaster. I got an A and all that, but I didn't belong there. I was also very arrogant. Nobody could teach me nuttin'.

LM: I was intrigued with your reply to the special issue of *Science Fiction Studies* that scholars might do well to go back and check some of your critical work in college which dealt with Renaissance literature.

UL: I was being facetious. I doubt there's anything of interest in the critical work I did in college. I was training myself to make a living and I knew I couldn't do it writing, at least not for a long time.

LM: What I found interesting about that comment, facetious or not, was that a number of recent writers, including Barth and Coover, have said that they went back to Renaissance literature and studied it when they were starting out as writers. Both say that they found this area interesting for formal reasons—these pre-novelistic, pre-realistic forms opened up all sorts of possibilities for them. The other thing that occurred to me is that Renaissance literature is filled with fantastic voyages, landscapes that fuse inner and outer states, and several other motifs that have found their way into your works. Did your immersion in that area have much of an effect on your work?

UL: Undoubtedly it did because it was such a long and loving immersion. I found that I had an affinity with writers like Ariosto and Tasso, at least to the extent of loving their poetry. But my motivation was basically the opposite of Barth's. I knew I had to earn a living but I didn't want to try and earn it by writing because I wanted to write what I wanted to write—not what some editor wanted. What I was most suited to earn a living by was scholarly work in literature, and so far as I was concerned it had *not* to be English literature, because I didn't want my studies to get near what I was doing with my writing. So I focused on literature in a foreign language from the relatively distant past. One of my hangups before I left graduate school was that I was going to have to take my orals in twentieth-century French literature and I didn't want to do that reading; I wanted to read only the contemporaries I wanted to read, not be forced to read anybody. In retrospect I can see that I was protecting my own integrity, my selfhood as a writer, against contemporary writers who might threaten me because they were doing what I knew I couldn't do, or confuse me by excellence into an effort to imitate. I was also trying to protect myself against an intellectualization of what I did. Being an intellectual, I'm extremely aware of the dangers of that. So what I did in school was turn back, in a sense, to an area of literature that seemed safely remote.

SG: So you weren't looking for pre-novelistic sources for your own works.

UL: Exactly. But of course what happens is that you do find sources, only you distance them enough so they don't overwhelm you. It is a matter of respect for yourself and for the older artists. At twenty-one or twenty-two, both my arrogance and my modesty as an artist led me to work with stuff written in a different language by people who had been dead for four hundred years.

LM: I haven't found much information about Jehan Le Maire de Belges, the subject of your unfinished Ph.D. thesis. Who was he?

UL: He was a fifteenth-century Frenchman. Just before the Renaissance. A little after Villon, who was totally medieval, and just before the Pleiade, the great court poets who flowered during the Renaissance. You can tell by his work that he knows something's coming, but he doesn't know what. I found him a touching figure in literary history— there's this young imagination trapped in the outmoded armor of medieval imagery and allegorical forms. Pivotal people are always rather touching. I think any artist will identify with someone struggling to get out of a cocoon. Of course, he never made it—he's a thoroughly and deservedly unknown figure.

LM: Those allegories of Ariosto and Tasso were in some ways very futuristic with those fantastic voyages—they were almost like science fiction without the science.

UL: Of course they didn't really have science to use. But they had a similarly disciplined imagination.

SG: Even in your early works that preceded your entry into science fiction—like the 1950s pieces that would later be incorporated into *The Orsinian Tales*—you were doing something quite different from the fairly narrow brand of social realism that most writers were pursuing back then.

UL: That's maybe why I didn't get published during that period. When it comes to writing I do not think in abstract terms, such as, "Am I going to write a traditional or a non-traditional work?" I was in college when I started the pieces that eventually became *The Orsinian Tales*. I was trying to write fiction rather than poetry, which is what I was mainly doing up to that point, and I was stuck in that old formula that everyone always tells you to write about what you know, what you've experienced. This is a terrible thing to tell an eighteen-year-old. What does an eighteen-year-old know? I remember thinking finally, "To hell with it, I'll just make up a country." And since most of what I knew came out of books at that point—I'd read a lot more than I'd done—I made up a place that was like the places in books I liked to read. But as soon as I began work in Orsinia, I realized I didn't have to imitate Tolstoy. I had created a place I could write about in my own terms; I could make up just enough of the rules to free my imagination and my observations. This was a big breakthrough for me—to say, "All right, I don't give a shit whether I get published or not, I'm not going to write for anybody but myself; I'm going to make these stories good by standards I set for myself." It was a step out of the trap of feeling that I had to get published right away. It was a step inward that finally led me out.

LM: *The Orsinian Tales* seem very "literary" in an almost nineteenth-century European sense.

UL: They had a literary origin, as I said. I was soaked in the Russian novels from the age of fourteen on. I read and reread Tolstoy and Dostoyevsky, and it's obvious to anyone who's familiar with their work that I've been tremendously influenced by them. Another thing important to Orsinia's development was that I became aware politically. The first thing I really noticed and took personally, from a political standpoint, was the invasion of Czechoslovakia in 1947 by the Russians. That's when I came of age and realized I had a stake in this world. And of course if there's any country Orsinia is like, it's Czechoslovakia. It's puzzled me that everyone says Orsinia is like Hungary, but nobody mentions Czechoslovakia. Writing about Orsinia allowed me to talk about a situation that had touched my heart, yet I could distance it, which was very important at that time. This was during the McCarthy period, and you can't imagine what the McCarthy era was like. Well, maybe you can, these days, because we seem to be trying hard to bring it back. But in a political climate like that, one's imagination begins to look for ways to say things indirectly, to avoid the polemic, the soapbox. You have to decide whether you're going to be a preacher or a novelist.

SG: Was *Malafrena* written during this same period?

UL: I got the original idea for that book in the early 1950s but for a long time it never worked itself out. I would occasionally find myself doing a bash at it, but it wasn't right and I'd put it away again. I had eventually put it away in despair when some editor asked for something, and so I thought I might as well have another look at it. I had to rewrite it almost totally. This time it seemed to work.

LM: It's amusing that so many reviewers kept saying things like, "With *Malafrena* Le Guin has at last decided to work her way into the literary mainstream."

UL: I was surprised and amused as well. There are whole paragraphs and passages which are very old and hadn't been changed at all. But there were things I needed to rethink entirely. Getting the women characters right. Itale was always OK, the men's story was easy, but I had a terrible time with the women. I didn't understand them. I especially didn't understand what was happening to Piera, the heroine. I know now why: I needed to become a conscious feminist to understand why my women were acting this way and what was happening in their relationships. Without the teaching of the movement of the '70s, I would never have got the book unstuck. So although the general conception of the book was twenty years old and bits and pieces of it remain intact, I can't say *Malafrena* was like one of those books found in the bottom of a trunk; it kept coming out of the trunk and being worked on, and then hurled back in despair. Until I finally grew up enough to write it.

SG: In one of the science fiction journals, you list literary influences, but the only science fiction writers included were Philip K. Dick and Italo Calvino.

UL: That's why I'll refuse to give you a list—there are so many people I'd be sure to leave out. Wasn't Borges on that list? How could I have left him out? What I've started to do when people ask who influenced me or who I like is to say whom I *don't* like. That list is much shorter.

SG: Well, whom *don't* you like?

UL: I don't like Nabokov. I'm told I have to read *Ada* because it's a science fiction novel, but I can't read it. Boring.

SG: The reason I brought up that list of influences was to see if you'd say that your main literary influences were from outside science fiction.

UL: I wouldn't say that. It would be silly. Obviously I have been influenced by science fiction writers in my science fiction books. If you're going to write science fiction, within even a moderately narrow definition of the term, you must have read it. If you haven't, you're wasting your time and everybody else's. There are several mainstream writers who have happily launched themselves into the sea of science fiction because they see what a glorious field it is; and since they haven't read any science fiction, they do things that were done forty years ago and have been done a hundred times since. A situation embarrassing for everybody. I've read a lot of science fiction and enjoyed a lot of it, been influenced by it. I'm an omnivorous reader, except for mysteries, which I can't seem to get anything out of; I can enjoy a Harlequin romance. And, of course, only snobbery or ignorance apologizes for liking science fiction anymore, with writers like Philip K. Dick and Gene Wolfe around.

LM: *The Lathe of Heaven* obviously owes something to Dick.

UL: Of course. You could almost call it "Homage à Dick." I was openly, I trust, acknowledging the influence. My approach was like saying, "This is one great way to write a novel, invented by Philip K. Dick." That's one thing about science fiction: writers in the genres are less uptight about imitation and emulation than "mainstream" people. Writing should be really more like music, with its healthy spirit of borrowing—as in the period of Bach, as in all healthy artistic periods. Everybody borrowing from each others' tunes and ideas like crazy and nobody worrying. There's plenty of music to go around.

LM: After you listed your literary influences, you mentioned that music may have had as much to do with affecting your works as fiction.

Music occurs in your works in many ways, both directly and, I think, structurally. Could you talk a bit about the way music may have affected your literary sensibility?

UL: I made that comment partially because when people ask you for "influences," they almost inevitably mean literary ones. How silly. It's very probable that listening to Beethoven might influence a writer far more deeply than anything read, but only musicians are asked about Beethoven. The same thing is true, of course, with painting. We really ought to run the arts together more.

LM: We talked with several writers who have made much the same point—that various media, like painting, music, television, the cinema, affect the way they think about fiction.

UL: Right. These other media shape your aesthetic sensibility, your intellectual perception of things. Most of my cognition is via art. I think as an artist. I don't think as a thinker. Very often I don't think in words at all. Cognition often comes to me visually or is heard. The trouble is that we don't have a vocabulary for talking about these things. But except for the very purest types of art, these various inputs are bound to have an effect on the creative process.

SG: Let's talk about the specific creative process that allows you to invent whole universes over time and space. For example, when you began the Hainish cycle, did you have a grand vision in mind? Or did you just invent as you went along and not worry about consistencies, linking things up, until later on?

UL: The so-called Hainish cycle wasn't conceived as a cycle at all: it is the result of a pure economy of imagination. I'd gone to the trouble of creating all these planets in that insane universe ("insane" because nothing alive can go faster than light), and had discovered that it's a lot of work to invent a universe. I certainly didn't want to do that work all over again; it would probably have come out pretty much the same since it's all out of the same head. So each succeeding book was placed in a different time but in the same universe.

LM: So you never sat down and charted things out precisely, the way we assume Asimov or Heinlein did with their macro-histories?

UL: No. My history is really pretty scroungy. I'm certainly not like Asimov, who I've heard has an office full of charts. Of course, when I'm writing a novel I'm very careful about that world. *The Left Hand of Darkness* and *The Dispossessed* both took a year or so of research and planning. I work out the details of the individual world very carefully beforehand. But I'm not very careful about the connections between the different novels. Those connections have never struck me as important; it's merely entertaining for people to have a reference here or there to other books. On the other hand, I created a very detailed map of Orsinia for myself, with all the distances; I had to know, for instance, how long it would take a coach-and-four to get from one place to another. That sort of internal consistency is, I think, important to most novelists. When you build a world, you are responsible for it. You don't want a coach traveling too far in one day. I want these details to be right. They have to be.

SG: Was the map the first thing created for *The Earthsea Trilogy*?

UL: Yes. At first the map could be adjusted to fit the story. This is the beauty of fantasy—your invention alters at need, at least at first. If I didn't want it to take two weeks, say, to get from one island to another, I could simply move the islands closer. But once you've decided that the islands *are* that far apart, that's it. The map is drawn. You have to adjust to it as if it were a reality. And it is.

LM: Obviously you must have had to think about the geography of the universe in your Hainish works very differently from the more limited world of *The Orsinian Tales* or *The Earthsea Trilogy*.

UL: Actually there's no geography at all between the worlds in those books; there's only time. The only thing that's interesting is when each book happened, whether events are taking place before or after other books. Time moves closer and closer to now, after starting way in the future. A critic was the first person to point this out to me. I hadn't seen it, nor do I have the faintest idea why I've been developing the books in that way.

LM: One critic suggests that you deliberately don't set things too close to the here-and-now to distance yourself and your readers from painful subjects. But your two novels, *The Lathe of Heaven* and *The New Atlantis*, and quite a few of your stories, are set right here in Portland—and take place not too far in the future. Is there any conscious reason why you might choose to use a real rather than an invented setting?

UL: First off, that critic was on the wrong track. One thing I've noticed about my settings is that when I have something I really don't want to say but which insists on being said I tend to set it in Portland. *The Lathe of Heaven* and *The New Atlantis* are among the saddest things I've written, the nearest to not being hopeful, and they're both set right here. I don't know the reason for this.

SG: In your National Book Award acceptance speech, you said, "I think that perhaps the categories are changing like the times. Sophisticated readers are accepting the fact that an improbable and unimaginable world is going to produce an improbable and hypothetical art. At this point, realism is perhaps the least adequate means of understanding or portraying the incredible realities of our existence." Are you dissatisfied with realism because you feel the world is itself, in a sense, less "realistic," more fantastic? Or does this view have more to do with the formal restrictions that realism imposes on writers?

UL: That statement is several years old. I made my comments aggressive to combat the patronization suffered by the fantastic arts and the critics' tendency to undervalue or brush them aside. My comments were therefore deliberately provocative—science fiction has been spat upon a great deal—and I was getting back at an attitude I deplore. Anybody who loves Tolstoy as much as I do obviously has a strong respect for realistic fiction. Let me pursue your question, since it's an important one. I do indeed think that at this point the world is in a degree of flux, is more fantastic than the world of the great nineteenth-century realistic novel. Consequently the description of what's right here in front of us can end up reading more fantastic than any fantasy. That's surely what García Márquez is doing: simply describing what's happened. So in the National Book Award acceptance I was also trying to say, "Don't worry about categories, they're becoming irrelevant, or maybe have always been irrelevant."

SG: One other quote I'd like you to respond to: "Science fiction has inherent limitations which may keep it always on the fringe of the greatest potentialities of the novel." What did you have in mind there about "inherent limitations"?

UL: That quote goes even further back. I was thinking of science fiction in a fairly narrow definition, the way it was conceived about 1967 or '68. I wasn't talking about fantasy in general. What I was driving at was simply that science fiction has certain inherent limitations because no genre is going to break all the barriers the way absolutely unlimited art forms can. But I no longer believe first-rate science fiction can be categorized as genre fiction at all. Take Gene Wolfe's *Book of the New Sun*. He calls it "science fantasy." Is it science fiction? Is it fantasy? Who cares? It is a great novel.

LM: But when you're at work on a novel, isn't it useful for you to make distinctions between science fiction and fantasy? *Some* sort of definition would seem to be necessary for the artist to know what the boundaries are, what can be done and what can't.

UL: Yes, I've found that I have to make certain distinctions of this sort for myself. When I failed to do this, as with *Rocannon's World*, I wound up with an uncomfortable hybrid between fantasy and science fiction. Later on I discovered that I personally do much better when I clearly separate straight science fiction, like *The Left Hand of Darkness*, from straight fantasy, like *The Earthsea Trilogy*. But that's not true for all writers, many of whom work very comfortably within hybrid forms. And as far as critics are concerned, even Darko Suvin's very intelligent attempts to create a classification system for science fiction and fantasy don't seem very useful.

SG: While we're on the subject of the ambiguity of labels, the importance of true names runs throughout *The Earthsea Trilogy*. This insistence seems a further extension of the idea in your other works that words are slippery and misleading, and that they can lock people into modes of thought that often are removed from the essence of experience. This view of language, which may have some connection with your familiarity with anthropology, must occasionally strike you as paradoxical since as a writer you must try to have language serve your purposes as precisely as possible.

UL: I'm constantly struck with the paradox you're talking about. George Steiner says that language is for lying. What language is for is not merely to say that what I'm sitting on here is a chair—if that's all we did with language, what the hell good would it do us? Language is for saying what might be, what we want to be, or what we wish wasn't. Language is for saying what isn't. This is paraphrasing Steiner rather boldly, but I think it's a marvelous approach to the use of words. As for what it is that fiction writers do: I tell lies for a living.

LM: You've said that *The Left Hand of Darkness* began for you with an image of Genly and Estraven pulling a sled.

UL: No, it wasn't as particularized as that. It was just an image of two people (I don't know what sex they were) pulling a sled over a wasteland of ice. I saw them at a great distance. That image came to me while I was fiddling around at my desk the way all writers do.

SG: At what point in your planning of *The Left Hand of Darkness* did you realize that the inhabitants of Winter were androgynous? They weren't that way in "Winter's King," the story on which you based the novel.

UL: I didn't realize their androgyny until early on in the planning of the novel, long after I'd written that short story. At that point I was trying to figure out what exactly this novel was going to be about, what was going on, who these people were, and so on. I had a vision or mental plan and I was beginning to think about the history of the countries, that sort of thing. As I was going through this planning process, I realized there was something strange about the people on this planet—were they all men? At that point, I said to myself, "These aren't all men; they're neither men nor women. And both. What a lovely idea . . ."

LM: Have most of your books and stories begun with the kind of visual image that began *The Left Hand of Darkness*?

UL: They've all begun differently. That image from *The Left Hand of Darkness* is a good one to talk about, though, because it's so clear.

Angus Wilson says in *Wild Garden* that most of his books begin with a visual image; one of them began when he saw these two people arguing and he had to find out what they were arguing about, who they were. That fits in beautifully with the kind of visual image that started *The Left Hand of Darkness*. But the others have come to me totally otherwise: I get a character, I get a place, sometimes I get a relationship and have to figure out who it is that's being related.

SG: The sexual implications of *The Left Hand of Darkness* seem to have a lot in common with what feminists have been writing about. Were you much aware of these writings while you were developing your conception of what you wanted to do with that book?

UL: This was back in the '60s before I'd read any of the feminists, except for Virginia Woolf. *The Second Sex* was out, but I hadn't read it yet, and the rest of the American feminists were just writing their books. *The Left Hand of Darkness* served as my entry into these issues— issues that all we proto-feminists seemed to be thinking about at the same time. Of course, if I wrote that novel today I'd do some things differently, perhaps handle certain issues more effectively and dramatically. But that's no big deal. I did it as best I could at the time.

SG: A number of feminist critics, including Joanna Russ, criticized *The Left Hand of Darkness* for being too "masculine" in its presentation. How do you respond to that sort of criticism?

UL: As I said, I was writing that novel back in 1967 and 1968, and we've all moved on a long, long way since then. When I'm at work on a novel I'm not trying to satisfy anybody who has a specific program they want propaganda for. I dissatisfy a lot of my gay friends and I dissatisfy a lot of my feminist friends, because I don't go as far as they would like.

LM: You've mentioned in several places that you don't so much plan your books consciously as "find them" in your subconscious. Could you talk about what you mean by this?

UL: I'm given something like a seed, a beginning. After that the planning, the intellectualizing, and the plotting take place. Let me try and make this process a bit clearer by going back to that vision that started *The Left Hand of Darkness* because it's fairly easy to talk about. I had this vision of the two people with a sled on the ice—that was the generating seed. Well, I already had found out a lot about the Antarctic by years of reading journals from the Scott and Shackleton expeditions; so first I had to figure out if that vision was occurring in that Antarctic. I realized it wasn't the Antarctic, so I had to find out where they were. And I had to find out who they were. As I began to find that out, I began to think, What exactly am I talking about here? Is this a novel? A short story? A novel starts relating to everything and getting bigger and bigger; if it's a story then it's self-limited and intense, it comes as a whole, so that I have to write it all down as fast as possible.

LM: One of the impressive things about your writing is the way you work out the full implications of the premises of your fictions. I mean, if you have a world in which there are tiny people living in forests— as in *The Word for World Is Forest*—then you carefully work out what the implications would be about these people's language, culture, mythologies, and so on. How do you proceed in developing these details?

UL: It's fiddle, fiddle, fiddle, trying to get all the pieces to fit together. It's an enjoyable process, but one you can't work with very fast. What does it really imply that beings exist in a forest? Are they going to clear it? Cut it? Eat it? When I'm developing a novel, which may take two years of planning, everything's a constant jiggling and resorting and figuring out. This means a lot of note-taking for me, because I forget details easily. I also lose notes.

SG: What kinds of "fiddling" were required in *The Dispossessed*?

UL: That book took me the longest. It began as a crappy short story, one of the worst I've ever written. But I sensed that buried in that ten pages of garbage there was a good idea. I can't even remember now what the story was, but the beginning of the character of Shevek was in it; he was a man on a sort of prison planet. This was before I had done any reading of the anarchists; but somehow that failed story led me to them. I read Goodman and Kropotkin and Emma and the rest, and finally found a politic I liked. But then I had to integrate these political ideas, which I'd formulated over a good year's reading, into a novel, a utopia. The whole process took quite a while, as you might imagine, and there were hundreds of little details that never found their way into the novel.

LM: *The Dispossessed* seems different from your other books in that it presents a vision of society that you seem to want your readers to consider as an actual possibility. Can anarchism work on this planet?

UL: First off, I don't agree with the distinction you're making—I'm completely in earnest in *The Left Hand* and others in the same way that I am in *The Dispossessed*. But in terms of anarchism, the problem is how to get there. As Darko Suvin has pointed out, all utopias tend to be circular and isolated. They tried an anarchist utopia in Spain in the 1930s, and look what happened there. The only trouble with an anarchist country is going to come from its neighbors. Anarchism is like Christianity—it's never really been practiced—so you can't say it's a practical proposal. Still, it's a necessary idea. We have followed the state far enough—too far, in fact. The state is leading us to World War III. The whole idea of the state has got to be rethought from the beginning and then dismantled. One way to do this is to propose the most extreme solution imaginable: you don't proceed little by little, you go to the extreme and say Let's have no government, no state at all. Then you try to figure out what you have without it, which is essentially what I was trying to do in *The Dispossessed*. This kind of thinking is not idealistic, it's a practical necessity these days. We must begin to think in different terms, because if we just continue to follow the state, we've had it. So, yes, *The Dispossessed* is very much in earnest about trying to rethink our assumptions about the relationships between human beings.

LM: You chose to set your utopian society, Anarres, in a bleak, harsh landscape. Were you trying to suggest that any utopian society is going to have to abandon the dream of luxury and abundance that we take for granted here in America?

UL: The way I created Anarres was probably an unconscious economy of means: these people are going to be leading a very barren life, so I gave them a barren landscape. Anarres is a metaphor for the austere life, but I wasn't trying to make a general proposal that a utopia has to be that way.

SG: Your use of names has intrigued me ever since I saw your comment that to know the *name* of a person or a place is to "know" that person or that place. Could you talk about the process that's involved in selecting these names? Obviously with a name like Genly Ai there must be a lot of conscious decision-making going on.

UL: Genly's name is *Henry*, evolved in time. What happened to the "h" is what the Russians do, and then the "r" became "l." He first came to me as "Genly Ao," but I thought that sounded too much like "ow"—as when pinched—so I decided this isn't right. This selection process sounds mysterious, but it isn't really. One listens. You listen until you hear it, until it sounds right. You go: Eye, I, Aye, Ai . . . and "ai" is *love* in Japanese. What more could you ask for in a name? When something like that comes together, you grab it. But it's not really as if I chose it in a truly volitional, deliberate, intentional sense. It's more as if I opened something and then waited until something came out. A box. Pandora and her box?

LM: You've gone on record a number of times suggesting that the specific "meaning" or significance of the specific episodes in your works is unconsciously produced. Yet when one looks closely at your books, they usually seem extremely carefully put together—for instance, the mythology or background sections in *The Left Hand* seem to have been created with specific intentions in mind. When you're at work on something, are you really not conscious of the specific implications you're developing?

UL: The tricky bit in answering that question is what you mean by *unconscious*. What I mean when I say that I'm not conscious of certain elements or implications of my work is that I don't have an intellectual, analytic understanding of what I'm doing while I'm doing it. This doesn't mean that I don't know what I'm doing: it does mean that there are different modes of knowing, and the analytic mode is inappropriate to the process of making. As the old song says, "I know where I'm going . . ." I've got a good intellect, and it was fairly highly trained, long ago. But the intellect has to be kept in its place. As the emotions and the ethical sense and intuition have to be kept in theirs. For me, personally, the intellect plays its major part in *revising*. And also at the very beginning, in disallowing an idea which is inherently stupid or self-contradictory. But once it's served there, the analytic mind must serve other functions during the first draft of a piece of fiction; it cannot be the controlling function. If I were thinking while I wrote of whatever it is the Antarctic means to me, let's say, all those snowy wastes that this California kid is always dragging her readers through, if I were thinking of it as a symbol of something else, let's say Snow is Loneliness or whatever — zonk, I might as well drop it and go garden. And once I know what Antarctica means to me, I won't need it any longer and will have to find a new metaphor. I'm not saying that self-knowledge destroys creation. I'm saying that, for me, self-*consciousness* vitiates creation. A writer like John Barth deliberately plays with self-consciousness; I doubt that Barth thinks much of my writing, and I don't take pleasure in his, but I know he knows what he's doing and I respect him for it. But I don't work that way. My mode is not to intellectualize about what I'm doing until I have done it. And when it's done, I don't want to, because it's done and I want to get on with the new work, with what has to be done next.

SG: I'm among those who feel that *The Earthsea Trilogy* is your best work to date, despite being aimed at a young-adult readership. Did you approach these works differently, in any fundamental sense, from your adult novels?

UL: *Earthsea* is the neatest of all my works. In purely aesthetic terms, it seems to me the best put together. When I started out I said to myself that I didn't see why this kind of book had to be different from any other, except for the commonplace that the protagonist had to be young, or there had to be a young viewpoint character. This viewpoint is simply standard for books slanted for the juvenile, but it wasn't hard at all for someone like me, who can drop back into adolescence without noticing it. After an initial self-consciousness, as soon as I began to see the characters and the plot, I wrote the same way I always had done. I don't know of anything you "do" for kids that is different than you do for adults; there's maybe a couple of things you don't do. There are certain types of violence, for example, that you leave out, and there's a certain type of hopelessness that I just can't dump on kids. On grown-ups sometimes; but as a person with kids, who likes kids, who remembers what being a kid is like, I find there are things I can't inflict on them. There's a moral boundary, in this sense, that I'm aware of in writing a book for young adults. But that's really the only difference, as far as my feeling goes.

SG: One of the things that surprised me about *Earthsea* was the way you explore the function of death in human life—I guess I'd assumed I wouldn't find that subject in a young adults' novel. And your exploration of death is done in what seemed such a sensible, reassuring manner. Was that the artist talking? Are you personally that accepting of death?

UL: Not at every moment. Not many critics have been willing to notice that the view presented of life and death in *Earthsea* is not only non-Christian but anti-Christian. This can't be as reassuring as any view of death that includes a real personal immortality. But, sure, that view was written out of personal conviction. Sometimes the idea of becoming grass is pleasant, sometimes it's not. We all have our night terrors. Those night terrors are one of the things you can't dump on a kid. You can share them—if you're able to—not dump them. Kids want to talk about death. They are often more willing to talk and think about it than adults.

LM: And of course a lot of fairy tales deal with death and violence, although usually in disguised forms.

UL: Disguising things, presenting things metaphorically, is the way you generally do it. You don't force, you don't scream. You don't treat kids that way. The metaphor is the means and the end in one. By metaphor we may evade dishonesty.

SG: At what point in your life did you become interested in Taoism, whose influence seems everywhere apparent in your work?

UL: The old Paul Carus translation of the *Tao Te Ching* was always on the downstairs bookshelf when I was a kid, and I saw it in my father's hands a lot. He was an anthropologist and an atheist; I think this book satisfied what other people would call his religious beliefs. He clearly got a great lifelong pleasure out of this book, and when you notice a parent doing something like this it's bound to have some effect on you. So when I was twelve years old I had a look at the thing and I reacted the same way my father had—I loved it. By the time I was in my teens I had thought about it quite a lot. I was never in the position of most kids in having to break with any church. My father was quite strongly anti-religious—his generation of anthropologists more or less had to be. He was respectful toward all religious people, but he counted religions as essentially superstitious. There was a certain feeling among intellectuals of my dad's generation that the human race was done with religion, that religions belonged to the past. That, of course, has not proved to be true.

LM: Despite your disavowal of propaganda, your works can often be seen as responses to specific political and social concerns—the elaborate critiques of current political and sexual attitudes in *The Dispossessed* and *The Left Hand*, the satire of the arrogance of many scientists and politicians in *The Lathe of Heaven*, the Vietnam analogies established in *The Word for World Is Forest*.

UL: Sure, I care about what's going on, and my books reflect these concerns. I just hope my ax-grinding doesn't intrude too much. Haber in *The Lathe of Heaven* is an almost allegorical figure of what I most detest in my own culture: people who want to control everything and to exploit for profit in the largest, most general sense of exploit and profit. He's the ultimate, controlling man. And Vietnam was very central to *The Word for World Is Forest*, obviously. I was living in London when I wrote that novel. I couldn't march so I wrote. I prefer, though, to keep my activism out of my art; if I can march downtown with a banner, it seems a lot more direct than blithering about it in a novel. When I was in London I couldn't do anything and I had an anger building up inside me, which came out when I was writing that novel. It may have hurt that book from an artistic standpoint.

SG: So you feel there's a contradiction between aesthetic aims and moral ones?

UL: No. Art is action. The way I live my life to its highest degree is by writing, the practice of art. Any practice, any art, has moral resonances: it's going to be good, bad, or indifferent. That's the only way I can conceive of writing—by assuming it's going to affect other people in a moral sense. As any act will do.

LM: How does your worry about "ax-grinding" fit in here?

UL: That's different. By that I mean that I don't want to get on hobbyhorses in my fiction, saying that this is "good" in my works and that is "bad." That kind of moralizing is a bad habit and, yes, I wish I were free of it forever. Such approaches are always simplistic and are usually uncharitable. Taken as a whole, overt moralizing is not an admirable quality in a work of art, and is usually self-defeating.

SG: Science fiction seems to appeal to a lot of Americans who are concerned about the things you write about, who feel that something drastic needs to be done before we blow ourselves up or completely destroy our environment.

UL: We have to thank Reagan and friends for this mood, maybe.

They've scared us. Poor Jimmy Carter, who was perfectly aware of what World War III would be like, couldn't get through to the public. We let him do the worrying for us and then blamed him for our problems.

SG: What happened to Carter seems to reinforce the point you make in *The Dispossessed* that even idealistically oriented programs will inevitably become contaminated by the same power structures they're fighting against.

UL: That's what history, unfortunately, seems to teach us. An anarchistic society inhabited by real people. The imaginary garden inhabited by real toads. As soon as you get real people involved in something, no matter how idealistically motivated they are, everything is eventually going to get mucked up. With people, nothing pure ever works quite right. We're awful monkeys.

LM: Is that why all utopias are, as the subtitle to *The Dispossessed* suggests, inevitably "ambiguous"?

UL: I think so. Besides, I'm rather afraid of purity in any guise. Purity doesn't seem quite human. I'd rather have things a little dirty and messy. Mixed up. Mucky.

Paul Dix

An Interview with

Thomas McGuane

The themes that run through Tom McGuane's fiction are strongly traditional: the nature and sources of masculine rivalries, a despair at
seeing our Republic corrupted by materialism, the struggle to keep alive
a free and spontaneous spirit in an increasingly homogenized society.
As his male protagonists combat their own obsessions and find a way
to let themselves be loved, they are both victims and culprits who
suffer from what was done to them by the past even as they perpetuate
the crimes of their fathers (who lurk everywhere, sometimes real, sometimes ghostly, but always about to step into the room). Self-conscious
and self-flagellating, McGuane's sad, funny heroes are hard on others
but even harder on themselves — "I have the soul of a lab rat," says
Lucien in *Something to Be Desired*. Thus they flounder in the world,
unable to protect, or even to retain the respect of, the headstrong
women they love. In McGuane's violent, excessive world extreme measures are often required to test one's worth. Blowing up a rival's fishing
boat (as Skelton does in *Ninety-two in the Shade*) or nailing one's hand
to a lover's front door (Pomeroy in *Panama*) is a desperate measure
taken by a man willing to do anything for the values he believes in
or the people he loves — anything, that is, except change the kind of
man he is.

Given the commitment of McGuane's heroes to self-reliance and to
the development of a proper code of behavior, one might assume that
reading his works would be a solemn affair; but McGuane's vision is
also essentially comic (the inevitable comparisons with Hemingway

have been misleading), and his fiction is infused with a distinctive humor that energizes language, action, and character. There is always an element of surprise, and even though these surprises may involve rejection, fisticuffs, or disaster, McGuane's heroes revel in the possibilities of the next moment. This zest and curiosity, a sort of animal good spirit, keeps them going and occasionally permits them to confront the (often self-generated) havoc around them. McGuane's ability to present the pathos and humor of this confrontation is perfectly illustrated in a passage from *Something to Be Desired*, in which Lucien rationalizes his abandonment of his wife and child for another woman: "If I'm so bad, he thought, they are better off without me and I have done them a good turn. With that, his spirits began to rise minutely. Sexually speaking, he thought, haven't I been a real success? I've spent thousands of hours with my ass flying and sweat spraying off me. In almost every case my partner pumped and sprayed with comparable ardor, sometimes when paid to do so. I've been the real article. He looked around himself with fear, confusion, and dismay: God almighty!"

McGuane's fiction projects a volatile, highly personalized mixture of power, vulnerability, and humor that has made him a controversial and (for some) nearly irresistible figure. His first three novels—*The Sporting Club* (1969), *The Bushwhacked Piano* (1971), and *Ninety-two in the Shade* (1973)—while never achieving mass-market appeal, earned McGuane considerable critical attention. *Bushwhacked* won the Rosenthal Award, *Ninety-two* was nominated for the National Book Award, and all three works were widely and favorably reviewed. McGuane was also writing screenplays: *The Missouri Breaks, Rancho Deluxe, Ninety-two in the Shade, Tom Horn*. During this period in the mid-'70s McGuane's tempestuous personal life (a lot of drinking, some drugs, two divorces) won him the nickname "Captain Berserko." McGuane's response was to write his fourth and pivotal novel, *Panama* (1978), his most surreal and nakedly autobiographical work to date. *Panama*'s Chester Pomeroy is an exhausted, artistically depleted, emotionally wrecked figure who has reached such a low point in his life that he has nothing to lose and so decides to come clean with himself and the world, to work for the first time "without a net." The critical response to *Panama* was overwhelmingly negative, lacerating not merely the novel but also the promising young novelist "gone Hollywood." Although McGuane continued to believe *Panama* his best work, he was affected by the vehemence of the criticism and his next novel did not appear for five years. *Nobody's Angel* (1983), *Something to Be Desired* (1985), and *To Skin a Cat* (1986) reveal changes in McGuane's craft; less rambunctious in their humor and with a tighter control of language and more subtle textures of characterization, these works indicate a maturation and an attempt at a quiet, more evocative kind of verbal power.

McGuane and his wife, Laurie, live just outside Livingston, Montana, where their ranch has been a focal point for a burgeoning artistic community. People like Richard Brautigan, William Hjortsberg, and Peter Fonda have made the western town into an enclave of diverse talents. Yet the McGuanes are not merely celebrity residents enjoying the seclusion and magnificent scenery of Montana; theirs is a working ranch, and both are justifiably proud of the spread where they raise and train cutting horses, some to be sold for ranch work, the best to be used in rodeo competition. Tall, muscular, rugged, McGuane has been the Montana cutting-horse champion three years in a row and, at forty-six, exudes a powerful physical presence. He is the kind of man who knows how to do things, who studies how things work, who can talk with equal assurance and knowledge about guns, horses, books, boats, and hot peppers from Sonora. As he took us on a tour of his ranch and we talked about water problems, fishing, and his fiction, we acquired a sense of McGuane's approach to things: when you find something you want to do, you work at it systematically, whether it's learning to tie casting flies or to write a novel. That you'd want to do it well, and that you'd be willing to make whatever sacrifices are necessary to that end, goes without saying—championships don't come to those who only want something halfway. As we sat together over coffee with the busy, cheerful household buzzing around us, McGuane seemed a man at peace, emerged hale and whole from a difficult period of personal and professional upheaval. It was to this period of turmoil that we addressed our first question.

Larry McCaffery: Has the personal storm really passed?

Thomas McGuane: The storm has passed in the sense that my steering linkage has been restored. A storm system is still in effect, though, and in fact if it weren't I'd want to change my life because you can get to a point where the risk factor has been overregulated. That's an alarming condition for me, a ghastly thing.

LM: Without going into all the particulars, could you talk a bit about what you feel, in retrospect, was going on in the mid-'70s—the period of stumbling down the yellow line, when you were known as "Captain Berserko"?

TM: During the early part of that time I had been successful in creating for myself a sheltered situation in which to function in this very narrow way I felt I wanted to function, which was to be a literary person who was not bothered very much by the outside world. My twenties were entirely taken up with literature. Entirely. My nickname during that period was "The White Knight," which suggests a certain level of overkill in my judgment of those around me.

Sinda Gregory: What sorts of things had led you to develop this White Knight image?

TM: Fear of failure. I was afflicted with whatever it takes to get people fanatically devoted to what they're doing. I was a pain in the ass. But I desperately wanted to be a good writer. My friends seem to think that an hour and a half effort a day is all they need to bring to the altar to make things work for them. I couldn't do that. I thought that if you didn't work at least as hard as the guy who runs a gas station then you had no right to hope for achievement. You certainly had to work all day, every day. I thought that was the deal. I *still* think that's the deal.

SG: I've heard that you had a brush with death in a car accident that shook you up pretty badly. The usual, maybe simpleminded, explanation is that you suddenly realized that you could have died there without ever having given yourself a chance to live.

TM: That explanation is not so simpleminded. I still don't know exactly what it meant to me at the time. I do know that I lost the power of speech for a while. And I had something like that realization going through my mind. It was outside Dalhart, Texas. I was driving fast, one hundred and forty miles an hour, and there was this freezing rain on the road that you couldn't see, so when I pulled out to pass, suddenly life was either over or it wasn't. I thought it was over. The guy I was driving with said, "This is it," and all of a sudden it did appear that it was the end: there were collisions and fenceposts flying and pieces of car body going by my ears. It would have been as arbitrary an end as what's happening to a friend of ours who's now dying in a hospital of cancer, or our friend who has an awful neurological disease, or a kid who chases the baseball out in the street. You believe all this stuff, but then suddenly you're standing in the middle of it with the chance to choose and it seems like a miracle or a warning that you've been spared this time but you'd better get your life together. I remember thinking along these lines, but my thoughts were so overpowering that I couldn't speak for a week, even to ask for something to eat.

LM: Pomeroy says at the beginning of *Panama* that he's going to be "working without a net." It's tempting to read that novel as *your* attempt to work through some of your own turmoils from that period. If you were up there, taking the risk to expose yourself, the highly negative, even personally vicious, reviews of *Panama* must have hurt a lot.

TM: The whole *Panama* episode really jarred me in terms of my writing because that was one time I had consciously decided to reveal certain things about myself. I was stunned by the bad reception of *Panama*, it was a painful and punishing experience. The lesson that I got from the reviewers was, Don't ever try to do that again. And it was odd to watch reviewers incorrectly summarize the story, then attack their own summaries. It was like watching blind men being attacked by their seeing-eye dogs. But then, I look back at when John Cheever published *Bullet Park*, which was the advent of the good Cheever as far as I'm concerned, and the critics and public crucified him over that book. Afterward he went into an alcoholic spiral. People don't understand how much influence they can actually have on a writer, how much a writer's feelings can be hurt, how much they can deflect his course when they raise their voices like they did over highly personal books like *Panama* or *Bullet Park*.

SG: If it's any consolation, I feel *Panama* is your best book.

TM: I think it may be my best, too. In the middle of all this outcry, I'd get the book out and read stuff to myself and say, "I can't *do* any better than this!" I really do love *Panama*. But I'd also have to admit that right now, if I were driven to write another novel like that, I wouldn't even try to find a publisher for it. It simply wouldn't be published. I'd be writing it to put in my closet upstairs.

SG: So what effect did the *Panama* experience have on your work?

TM: Its first effect was to confirm my desire to write a book that was, in a traditional way, more shapely than anything I had done before. Actually, I'd been wanting to do that for a long time. That at least partially explains the architecture of *Nobody's Angel*. The novel I'm working on now picks up from *Panama* more than from any other point. Importantly it's not a book in the first person, which made *Panama* completely different from anything else I've ever done, so it doesn't sound and look like *Panama*. But *Panama* is still the last piece of growing tissue that I've been grafting from.

LM: In terms of its flights of poetic language, its surrealism, and other formal features, *Panama* is probably your most extreme novel to date. Yet these features seem entirely appropriate in capturing the sensibility of its crazed narrator, Pomeroy. Was creating this voice and perspective especially difficult for you or did your identification with him make things easier, in a way?

TM: It was very difficult. I invented a word once a long time ago and I was always going to write a book that could be described with this word. The word was *joco-splenetic*. *Panama* was to be my first joco-splenetic novel. What was especially difficult about that book was that I knew that in certain parts I wanted Pomeroy to be absolutely lugubrious. I saw him as somebody who would live quite happily in a

Gogol novel, a laughter-through-tears guy. I knew that his emotions are frequently "unearned," that the kind of hangover quality in which he lives produced fits of uncontrolled weeping. I'm not saying that the book isn't sentimental in that technical sense, but I also felt that this tissue of distance that I created between myself and Chester was adequate for people to understand this and to see the book for what it is. For people who don't like the book, when poor Pomeroy goes off into one of his spirals, they think, "What right does he have to this?" The point is that he *has* no right—that's what's interesting about him.

SG: This sounds like the same sense of moral indignation that seemed to be directed at you during the mid-'70s—the sense that here's this talented person who has everything going for him, yet here he is taking all these drugs and doing all these bizarre, self-destructive things.

TM: There are those who question the right of a wealthy person to commit suicide. A person who doesn't have enough to eat has the right to commit suicide, but not a person whose income is over fifty thousand dollars a year. It's as if wealthy or talented people have no right to be miserable. So in this age of cocaine we just expand this principle and say, "My God, look at all that Chester's got" (half of which is made up: his automobile, his house, they don't even exist). The idea that he's so miserable that he can't name his dog and can't get his true love back, that doesn't count in this strangely economic-based view that only certain people are entitled to their unhappiness.

SG: I gather that in some ways you transformed some of your real-life feelings for your wife into the figure of Catherine.

TM: Yes, in many ways Catherine became Laurie. I saw Pomeroy going downhill in various ways and, being madly in love with Laurie at the time, the most miserable thing I could imagine for him (or me) was to lose this person he loved so much. That's one of the reasons I think there's a specific emotional power in that ending, because I was going through Pomeroy's loss, imaginatively, as I wrote it. I felt that the coda to all the pain in that book had to be that loss, but it was so absolutely agonizing that, unlaminated to something better, it was nihilistic. And I'm not a nihilist and didn't want this book to be nihilistic.

LM: Is that why you have that last scene with the father, where Chester finally seems to acknowledge him and you write, "There was more to be said and time to say it"?

TM: Partly, although this business about what he's going to do about his father is present throughout the book. At that point in the end, when he's hit absolute rock bottom, the question becomes, Does he bounce, or does he flatten out and lie there? In my opinion he bounced. Slightly.

SG: All five of your books seem to have distinctive stylistic features.

Nobody's Angel seems to be almost understated in comparison with your earlier books. Could you talk about the specific evolutions your prose has undergone?

TM: I started my career distinctly and singlemindedly with the idea that I wanted to be a comic novelist. I had studied comic literature from *Lazarillo de Tormes* to the present. The twentieth-century history of comic writing had prepared me to write in the arch, fascist style that I used in *The Sporting Club*. Then the picaresque approach was something I tried to express in *The Bushwhacked Piano*, although I've now come to feel that the picaresque form is no longer that appropriate for writing; writers are looking for structures other than that episodic, not particularly accumulative form; at least I am. *Ninety-two in the Shade* was the first of the books in which I felt I brought my personal sense of epochal crisis to my interest in literature. It's there that you find this crackpot cross between traditional male literature and "The Sid Caesar Show" and the preoccupation with process and mechanics and "doingness" that has been a part of American literature from the beginning — it's part of *Moby-Dick*. The best version of it, for my money, is *Life on the Mississippi*, which is probably the book I most wish I'd written in American literature. When I got to *Ninety-two* I was tired of being amusing; I like my first two books a lot, but I tried to put something like a personal philosophy in *Ninety-two in the Shade*. That book also marked the downward progress of my instincts as a comic novelist. Starting with *Ninety-two* I felt that to go on writing with as much flash as I had tried to do previously was to betray some of the serious things I had been trying to say. That conflict became one that I tried to work out in different ways subsequently. The most drastic attempt was in *Panama*, which I wrote in the first person in this sort of blazing confessional style. In terms of feeling my shoulder to the wheel and my mouth to the reader's ear, I have never been so satisfied as when I was writing that book. I didn't feel that schizophrenia that most writers have when they're at work. That schizophrenia was *in* the book, instead of between me and the book.

LM: You don't seem to have lost your comic instincts, but I sensed in *Panama* a change in the *kind* of humor you were creating: a move away from satire, which characterized your earlier books, toward something deeper, more painful. There's a line in *Panama* that seems relevant here, where Chester describes "the sense of humor that is the mirror of pain, the perfect mirror, not the mirror of satirists."

TM: I now agree with that Broadway producer who said that satire is what closes on Saturday night.

SG: Patrick in *Nobody's Angel* and Pomeroy both lose the woman in the end, but that loss somehow seemed more inevitable in *Panama* than in *Nobody's Angel*, where you appeared to give Patrick the chance to learn and change. I was a bit surprised that you didn't devise a happy ending for Patrick.

TM: There's a difference in those two losses. In Pomeroy's case, it is a little bit as though there has simply been too much water under the bridge for him to ever get Catherine back. There is a momentum that has become so black that current conduct can't turn things around. With Patrick the ending has more to do with this notion of the outsider or stranger, which has fascinated me for a long time and is reflected in the book. Patrick's situation is the modern situation: the adhesion of people to place has been lost. This can be just ruinous. The result can truly be, as in *Wuthering Heights*, the ill wind that blows across the heath, a thing you can't beat—you either get out and do something else or the conditions will destroy you. I didn't think Patrick could win his war because his basics are fouled up, so he had to accept himself as an *isolato*. This isn't a very happy ending, certainly not one I would wish upon a dog, but it was the one that I felt had inevitability.

LM: Does this fascination with the figure of the outsider and the adhesion of family identity to place derive from your own family background, which, like Patrick's, is Irish?

TM: The outsider-stranger-bystander has always intrigued me in regard to my own family history. My family were all Irish immigrants originally and so I became interested in Irish history and traveled a lot in Ireland, which brought things even closer to home. People in Ireland feel like outsiders in their own country because the English have owned things for so long that the Irish consider themselves as living in a massive servants' quarters for the British Isles. When they immigrated to the East Coast (my family went to Massachusetts), they saw themselves as an enclave of outsiders in a Yankee Protestant world. My parents moved to the Midwest, and I can assure you that, whatever we thought we were, we did not consider ourselves to be Midwesterners. We saw ourselves as Catholics surrounded by Protestant Midwesterners, and when we wanted to feel close to something, we went back to our old world in Massachusetts. When I moved to Montana in my twenties, I felt myself to be an outsider in still another world. The only thing that seems reassuring is that most Montanans feel the same way—they're mostly from somewhere else, and their history is so recent that to be one of the migrants is really to be one of the boys. You can see this same feeling developing in F. Scott Fitzgerald. I'm sure that no one in his family felt like they were "from" Minnesota, which is one reason why he was drawn to the East Coast and why so much of the magic of his fiction is his famous method of "looking through the window." And yet that mental quality, the glassy distance, is behind his craziness and his alcoholism. The vantage point of most authentic modern fiction is dislocation.

LM: Your first three novels are all extraordinarily ambitious works in that each of them links the heroes and action with a vision of America at large. But in both *Panama* and *Nobody's Angel* the move seems to be more inward, more personal. Was this a conscious shift?

TM: *The Sporting Club* was really the last genuinely political book I've ever done, at least political in an overt way. It was meant to be a kind of anarchist tract. I was reading a lot of political writers at the time, especially Kropotkin, and I was very self-conscious about using the situation of the novel as a political paradigm.

LM: Isn't *Ninety-two in the Shade* overtly political? You seem to be using Skelton there to suggest a deeper crisis in America that is signaled in the very opening line of the book: "Nobody knows, from sea to shining sea . . ."

TM: " . . . why we are having all this trouble with our republic." Yes, I was using Skelton very deliberately in the way you're suggesting, but I was more interested in the inner, personal dynamics than in the larger political implications. There's another line from the book that seems very appropriate to the political issue you're raising: "It was the age of uneasy alliances." But we're not in that age anymore, which is one reason my fiction has shifted its focus. We're currently in the age of *no* alliances. We're in the age of, shake hands with the Lebanese and give their neighbors a bomber so they can blow their asses off the planet. We're in the age of the most sordid possible political cynicism. We're in the age of foreign aid to death squads.

SG: I would assume that these sorts of attitudes make moving inward, away from the larger political arena, more attractive.

TM: Right, and that's one of the reasons why *Ninety-two in the Shade* is such a strangely public book compared to my last two. It was a kind of New Age book that reflected my sense that I was caught up in some huge cultural change that was taking place in this country. It was a book about private survival. You have your skins and your mate and your place, and you're aloof from an obviously suicidal society. The chief metaphor for the book should have been bomb shelters, with people storing water and tinned food. My father and I had very much of an adversarial relationship that is unresolved to this very day. I remember going to see a bomb shelter with him back in the '50s; one of our neighbors had built one of them. It was a very elegant bomb shelter and we walked around and looked at it; my father was a very direct guy, so when we came up he was filled with thoughts about this thing—the main thought being, Should I build one for my family?— and he pondered this, and I was very interested in what he was going to say. Finally he said, "I think we'll just stay up on the ground and take our lumps." Boy oh boy, did *that* ever become a model for future reflections on my part! It was a key point in our dialogue.

LM: Skelton obviously doesn't follow your father's advice—he wants to find a shelter, a personal survival module.

TM: Right, which made *Ninety-two in the Shade* a rebellious book for me to write, because I'd built this novel about a guy who obviously wasn't thinking in terms of staying above ground and taking his lumps. He's at the fork in the road and he chooses to construct a place where he can be safe. Right now, though, the progress of my fiction is toward my father's point of view, to *not* build a shelter, to just stay up here and fight it out.

SG: The father-son relationship is constantly a major issue in your fiction. Is some of the tension of these fictional relationships autobiographically based?

TM: This is plainly so. If you'd been around me while I was growing up, you'd have clearly seen that my relationship with my father was going to be a major issue in my life. My father was a kid who grew up rather poor (his father had worked for the railroad) and who had a gift for English; he wound up being a scholar-athlete who went to Harvard, where he learned some of the skills that would enable him to go on and become a prosperous businessman, but where he also learned to hate wealth. My father hated people with money and yet he became one of those people. And he was not only an alcoholic but a workaholic, a man who never missed a day of work in his life. He was a passionate man who wanted a close relationship with his family, but he was a child of the Depression and was severely scarred by that, to the point where he really drove himself and didn't have much time for us. So while he prepared us to believe that parents and children were very important, he just never delivered. And we were all shattered by that: my sister died of a drug overdose in her middle twenties; my brother has been a custodial case since he was thirty; as soon as my mother was given the full reins of her own life, after my dad died, she drank herself to death in thirty-six months. I'm really the only one still walking around, and I came pretty close to being not still walking around. It all goes back to that situation where people are very traditional in their attitudes about the family, a family that was very close (we had this wonderful warm place in Massachusetts where my grandfather umpired baseball games and played checkers at the fire station), but then they move off to the bloody Midwest where they all go crazy. I've tried to work some of this out in my writing, and my younger sister tried to work it out in mental institutions. She was the smartest one of us all, an absolute beauty. She died in her twenties.

LM: There's an interesting structural relationship between *Nobody's Angel* and *Ninety-two in the Shade* that seems relevant here. In *Angel*, Patrick's father is dead, preserved within that Montana ice floe. In *Ninety-two*, Skelton lives in a fuselage, and the father figure is preserved, offstage, as part of his internal life. Was this a consciously designed motif?

TM: Let me answer that one as candidly as I can. When I started *Nobody's Angel* I was so tired of the pain of the father-and-son issue that I didn't want it to infuse yet another book. But for it not to be present at all would have falsified it. So I did what religion does: I simply canonized one of the characters and got him the hell out of the book.

SG: Your characters at times seem to be trying to build a better model of society within their families than they find out in the society at large.

TM: The way I see it now is that you either make a little nation and solve its historical and personnel problems within the format of your own household—accepting all the mistakes that you've made, all the ones your parents have made, all that your children make, and all the mistakes your country has made—and you win that one, or you lose the only war worth fighting. That's what I'm trying to do; I'm trying to study this problem in my writing, intensifying it for the purposes of art, and in my own life. Moreover, as soon as you step out of this personally constructed world and, say, drive into town or stand out on I-90 and watch our nation cycle through these placeless arteries, it's there that you confront the true horror of the other option. The America you see in public is the monster who crawls up to the door in the middle of the night and must be driven back to the end of the driveway. That's the thing that scares me to death. We've all seen these nameless, faceless people out there, and when we track one of them back to wherever they came from we sometimes find that this is the one person who can pull a breechbirth calf without ever killing the mother cow, or the guy who goes over the hill and does beautiful fencing even though nobody is watching, the valued neighbor who will get up in the middle of the night to help you get your water turned back on. But for some reason, in this country, at a certain point this man turns into this absolute human flotsam whom we make fun of when we see him standing in front of Old Faithful. This syndrome is scary to me because I'm not sure which team is going to win. Are we really just going to rinse, like the third cycle in a washing machine, from the Atlantic to the Pacific? If so, why don't we get into *The Whole Earth Catalogue* mentality, really save some energy, and just shoot ourselves? I had that sense of family security with my grandparents, and then I saw the results in my own family of deciding that all that was worthless. My dad had no use for it, felt that people who valued it were just dragging their heels.

SG: You've talked a lot about your father and his family. What about your mother's side of the family?

TM: Actually, I derive myself matrilineally, and all the photographs you see around here are of my mother's family. There are two kinds of Irish people—one is the kind that doesn't say anything, and the other is the kind that talks all the time. Well, my mother's family were talkers and my father's were the silent types. My father's father was a fine old railroad Irishman, and my father couldn't wait to get away from him. So we saw very little of my father's father. In fact—this is something I've slowly been reconstructing—my grandmother died fairly young and then my grandfather married a woman from Prince Edward Island; she just loved the old man, and when he died she more or less didn't invite my family to the funeral. My feeling is that she went back up to Prince Edward Island and turned down my father's offer to buy her a house or something. Firmly. She felt that the way my father did things and the way he had treated his own father were pretty shabby. So he died, she buried him, and she split.

SG: Did you derive some of your own instincts for storytelling from your mother's fast-talking Irish relatives?

TM: Very much so. My maternal grandmother's house was always full of people who valued wisecracks and uncanny stories. And we had a real history there. I'm more homesick for that than for anything that ever happened to us in Michigan. My mother was so attached to her family that the moment we got out of school she'd pack us off back to Massachusetts until school started in the fall, and my father resented that tremendously.

SG: Was it your father who got you interested in hunting and fishing?

TM: He set those out as great ideals, but generally when it came time to go out and do them, he never showed up. We went out enough so that I wished we'd do it more, but then there'd be some other grown-up who *really* wanted to go, and my father wouldn't like that because he felt he should be doing that but didn't have time. So he'd say, "Well, if he had his nose to the grindstone, like he should have, he wouldn't have time to take off and go fishing on Lake Erie with you." But one way or another, I was tremendously involved in hunting and fishing all the time. I had a .22 and I was gone every chance I could get, out in the woods or on the lake or, if the lake froze over, I'd be out on the ice miles from shore. That *was* my childhood.

LM: What is there about developing sporting skills that seems so satisfying to you?

TM: I'm not sure I fully know. When I'm involved in these things myself, I feel like I'm being asked a lot of questions. Tools of elegance and order, developed and proven in the sporting life, are everywhere useful. Right now, for the first time in my life, I feel like there's something wrong about doing sports just for recreation—if it's just that, I don't want to do them. Their purpose is more than getting away from the pressures of work. Also, part of my interest in developing specific skills is surely to counter the sense of fragmentation and regret that crops up. With horses, I feel I've discovered some ancient connection, as though in some earlier life horses were something that mattered to me. The close study of all animals teaches us that we're not the solitary owners of this planet. As my horses procreate, and as they search for food and companionship and try to grow up and face one another's death, we see these things and it's very moving. You can't be around it to the degree that Laurie and I are and just say, "We'll synthesize our food and we'll get rid of these other species because they take up a lot of land." I don't know what that has to do with how we own the earth and own the universe, but in a way I feel religious about it. It's not an accident that there are these sentient creatures other than human beings out there. And we're not supposed to populate the universe without them. We're seriously and dangerously deprived every time we lose one of these animals.

LM: Nicholas Payne in *The Bushwhacked Piano* says, "I've made silliness a way of life." Was "pranksterism" part of your own life as a kid?

TM: Yes, it was, but there's more to it than that. We have chances for turning the kaleidoscope in a very arbitrary way. I wanted to be a military pilot at one time and came that close to joining the Naval Air Corps until I got into Yale, which I didn't expect to happen. One of the practical things they teach combat flyers is that you can only reason through so much, and therefore in a combat situation if at a certain point you feel you can't reason through a situation, then the thing you must do is *anything*, so long as you do something. Even in the navy, with its expensive equipment and its highly predicated forms of action, you are told to just splash something off and do it! Doing something arbitrary or unexpected is probably the only way you're going to survive in a combat situation. Game theoreticians have made this an important factor. The first strike is really very close to pranksterism. Pranks, the inexplicability of comedy, and lateral moves at the line of scrimmage can sometimes be the only way you can move forward. In silliness and pranks, there is something very great. It's in that scene I created in *Panama*—the decision to jump off the diving board not knowing if there's water in the pool. Sometimes that's not a dopey thing to do, but a very smart thing. It's the first strike.

SG: In your more recent books, your central characters are more likely to avoid confrontation.

TM: I hope it's a maturity on the author's part. The growing awareness of consequences is something *Nobody's Angel* reflects, and it also reflects what is appropriate to Patrick's stage in life. There were things that Billy the Kid was able to do by the age of twenty-one that would not have been appropriate to Pat Garrett at the age of forty-one. And as we will our way through the world, we begin by laying about ourselves with a heavy sword. It's one thing to jump off a diving board into a possibly empty pool at a certain stage in your life, but that same person with three children is not doing something good. A man with three young children who dives into a pool not knowing if there's water in it is someone to be despised. Patrick has moved into another part of his life, and he's dealt with some inadequacies in his life—maybe he shouldn't have been diving into pools when his sister was falling apart, for example, and maybe he's reviewing that. I wanted to suggest that there's remorse in him.

LM: You said just a minute ago that you wanted to be a navy pilot. Hadn't you decided that you wanted to be a writer by the time you were in college?

TM: I knew from very early on that I wanted to be a writer, but I also knew that that was not a very practical idea. So I was constantly trying to think of a profession I could pursue and still write. As a kid I had always associated being a writer with leading an adventurous life. I used to read William Beebe, Ernest Thompson Seton, W. H. Hudson, writers like that. That's really a key thing for me: I associated a life of action and a life of thought as being the writer's life. But I didn't do much writing when I was a kid. I wanted to *be* a writer before I wanted to do any writing. Then when I went away to boarding school there was a good friend of mine who was very strange and marvelous, and who became a kind of literary guide for me—Edmund White, a fine writer actually beyond category. Interestingly enough, back in school we all knew he was gay, and remember, this was the benighted '50s. A lot of his friends were athletes and I was this macho punk, but we were all friends and nobody cared. Ed was not only a good writer at that time but he was also a scholar. He had read Proust by the age of twelve, and he used to give me reading lists. A lot of my early readings were things he had me read, mainly the decadent works: Baudelaire, Rimbaud, Huysmans, Lautréamont, Wilde, Proust. When I got to college, I kept reading, but I was also trying to figure out what I could do. I tried everything: I was a premed student at one time, and a prelaw student, though I was mostly an English major. But I didn't really know *what* I was going to do to survive.

SG: As a graduate student, you studied playwriting at Yale Drama School. How did this contribute to your ear for dialogue?

TM: That's when Off Broadway was very wild, interesting, exciting. There were all those good young playwrights and the theater-of-the-absurd was a true force. Reading those European and American playwrights and seeing their stuff, to the extent that it was possible, had a lot of effect on the way I eventually wrote fiction. Dialogue is very important to me because I've always loved it in novels. Lots of people read novels racing from dialogue to dialogue. In fact, I would like to really compress the prose in a novel, without getting too arch about it. Some people, like Manuel Puig, have written novels almost entirely in dialogue, but it gets to be a little too much sometimes since readers need to know where they are a bit. At any rate, writing dialogue is probably the best thing I do, and I'm always trying to work up an aesthetic for my fiction that will acknowledge that fact. Of course, Hemingway was really a great dialogue writer; it's one of the reasons we read him. Dialogue is a very useful tool to reveal things about people, and novels are about people and about what they do to each other. That's what novels are for. They're not pure texts for deconstructionists. One day, that will be clear again.

SG: Could you talk a bit about the background of your first two books?

TM: I went from Yale to Europe to live in Spain, and while I was over there I worked on an early version of *The Bushwhacked Piano*, which was really my apprentice work. I was always working on novels at Yale and there were parts of that book that I had worked on for years. I sent it off to Stanford, on the basis of which I won a Stegner fellowship. *The Sporting Club* was really my fourth or fifth novel. By the time it came out I had actually been writing for ten years, with most of my material going right into the wastebasket, where it belonged.

SG: In addition to the playwrights, who were the writers you were reading during that period who had some influence on the direction your work was taking?

TM: I remember that Malcolm Lowry's *Under the Volcano* just floored me. Incidentally, I consider that to be quite a funny book; a lot of it isn't funny, of course, but its perverted energy is obviously akin to comedy. Fielding, Sterne, Joyce, Gogol and Twain were heroes. So were Machado de Assis, Thomas Love Peacock, George Borrow. There had never been a period when I was not reading Shakespeare. I loved Paul Bowles when I was just starting to write, and I loved Walter van Tilburg Clark. Stephen Crane seemed to me a fabulous writer, especially the stories. Knut Hamsun, Evelyn Waugh, Anthony Powell, Muriel Spark, Henry Green, William Eastlake, Walker Percy. You know, Barry Hannah and I were talking, and we agreed that *The Moviegoer* is one of those books that, for a lot of writers, was looked at like *The Sun Also Rises* was by writers back in the '20s.

LM: In what sense?

TM: Percy's insouciance. He seemed to retain passion, gentlemanliness, and this cheerfully remote quality about the things going on. It was exciting, like brand-new life. I still think just as much of that book today as when I first read it. It seems like one of the real groundbreaking books of the last thirty years. *Huck Finn* continues to be a book whose range of sadness and funniness, whose pure narrative momentum, is hard to get around. Unfortunately, it's become canonized and emasculated. Hemingway's stories. I don't know anyone who can honestly read *In Our Time* and say that there's not something wonderful in it or not be tremendously moved by that incantatory style. *A Farewell to Arms* is a tremendous novel. And I remember that *Henderson the Rain King* was another book that floored me when I first read it. The same for the Snopes trilogy.

LM: Writers like Pynchon and Barth are conspicuously absent from your list . . .

TM: Actually I like their work, but if you compare them to Bellow or Mailer you start discovering their deficiencies. Barth and Pynchon are clearly *brilliant* writers, but that quality of what the Spanish would call "caste"—I'm not sure it's in those two guys. I guess I'm basically simpleminded as a reader. For example, I have no interest whatsoever in Borges. He just doesn't do anything for me, even though I would concur with the most positive statements that people make about his writing. He's just not for me. Neither is Cortázar.

SG: What about Márquez?

TM: Márquez is unbelievably good. I just read *The Autumn of the Patriarch* and, God, it's fabulous stuff—I almost prefer it to *One Hundred Years of Solitude*. Márquez is breathtaking because you feel that, down to the little harsh details, he's right on. Márquez and Günter Grass both present this tremendous congestion of life as well as more abstract issues. Márquez and Grass are two of the few writers who can engage their whole monstrous personalities in the projected world of their novels. Faulkner could do it. Melville did it. Mark Twain did it. They make the New England Renaissance look like an aviary. I am fascinated by this ability, and in fact I hope to get some of it into my own work. My biggest problem with the novel is whether or not I'm producing a sturdy enough tissue for that tension, since it's so miserably low in its lows and in its highs it approaches goofiness. I'm trying to find a way to avoid trivializing the serious stuff without undermining the comedy of it.

SG: Are there any contemporary American writers you especially admire or feel affinities with?

TM: Nobody very surprising, I suspect: I like Barry Hannah, Raymond Carver, Harry Crews, Don Carpenter, Don DeLillo, Jim Harrison, Joan Didion. DeLillo has categorized a certain kind of fiction in a way that seems absolutely definitive: "around-the-house-and-in-the-yard fiction." There are a lot of good writers who belong to that group—a lot of recent women writers are in that school, for example, and many of them are tremendously good. At the same time, writers with broad streaks of fancifulness or writers who have trained themselves on Joyce or Gogol, as I did, may feel a little reproached when we compare ourselves to these writers who write about the bitter, grim, domestic aspects of living. You feel, Gee, I'm pretty frivolous compared to these serious people. Sometimes this can be a misleading reproach because you may decide that you need to change your subject matter if you're going to be a serious writer.

LM: Have comparisons to Hemingway been an albatross for you?

TM: There's a lot I like about Hemingway's writing, so when people say there are Hemingwayesque aspects to my writing, what am I supposed to say? Within the last year, writers as disparate as Cheever, Malamud, and Carver have been accused of Hemingwayism. When people say that, they're attacking you. Hemingway lived a kind of life that I would like to have lived, although I've never identified with him closely. I see Hemingway as being a real American Tory, the sort of guy I couldn't have gotten along with, and I see a cruelty and heaviness in his personality. When I was growing up, I was very much in rebellion against the Midwestern Protestant values he represents to me, so a lot of these Hemingway comparisons have seemed a mile off. His worldview was much more bleak than mine, more austere, and his insistence on his metaphysical closed system was very deterministic, fanatically expressed. Still, I have to say that there was a time when I would read his stuff and it seemed wonderful. I read books of his today that I still love. But when I look at a lot of writing now I come across that clipped Hemingway rhythm, and it can have an appalling, scriptural feeling to it. At his best he was a fabulous writer. I just read an interview with Heinrich Böll and he acknowledged that Hemingway's surface was a carpentry that you just couldn't walk by without acknowledging. Any writer who says he has walked by without noticing it is a liar.

SG: Your presentation of female characters seems to have changed distinctly for the better over the years.

TM: First of all, I would like to concur with Malcolm Lowry in saying that a writer is under no obligation to create great characters. Nevertheless, part of the explanation for my portrayal of women in my earlier works has to do with my trying to find my way through a problem that a lot of men from my generation have: that attitude that you weren't even *supposed* to know anything about women, that they were frightening or something to be made fun of. When I went back to my high school's twenty-fifth reunion recently, I noticed that the men immediately went right back into the adversarial business that we had shared back in the '50s. When I was growing up, men and women were raised in the atmosphere of what used to be called "the war of the sexes." One of the macho-comic aspects of *The Bushwhacked Piano* was to deal ruthlessly with the women in the novel, using satire as a purgative. I hope, though, that I'm coming closer to an authentic presentation of women in my recent books, a vision that maybe has something to do with me casting off some of my own ignorance about women. I'd say that a big part of my education about women has come from having three daughters. I wonder what type of place I'm helping to prepare for them, what societal vices I'm perpetuating for them. These are the kind of moral issues I want to deal with in my writing. I don't sit around worrying about what nations are invading other nations; I don't understand those issues.

SG: Working here at the ranch must make your writing habits a lot different from those of most writers. What kind of routine do you have?

TM: Let me give you what my dream day would be, if I could stick to it. It would be to get up early, get all the horses and cattle fed so that wouldn't be hanging over our heads, eat a bowl of cereal and make some coffee, and then go to some really comfortable place and just read for three or four hours. Most of my morning reading for the past ten years has been some form of remedial reading, my personal list of things I feel I should have read, all those books that make me feel less than prepared when I sit down as a writer. For example, this last year during the winter—a season when I have lots of time to read here—I read the King James Old Testament. I'd never read it. I've known for thirty years that I was supposed to have read it, but I never did. All this type of reading is a steady scrubbing away of the possibilities of guilt, of the fear of pulling my punches when I sit down to write because I feel inadequate in my education. I think you should expect a writer to be a true man of literature—he should know what the hell he's talking about; he should be a professional. So this kind of preparation is one thing I'm trying to get covered, knowing, of course, it's a lifetime project. Anyway, after I read I spend three or four hours in the afternoon writing, and then I go back working on the horses until dinnertime comes, eat dinner, and then spend the evening reading things I just want to read until it's time to go to sleep. Of course, lots of things go wrong with that schedule. Part of it depends on the season, and there's days you've promised to do things with the children, or days you'd rather go fishing or hunting, or days when there's a problem with a horse and it takes four hours to get it straightened out. But that's the pattern I strive for.

LM: What comes first when you begin new work?

TM: I hate to keep speaking in analogies—Charles Olson said that the Sumerian word for "like" meant both "like" and "corpse," and that the death of a good sentence is an analogue—but with some things you just have to use them. When I start something it's like being a bird dog getting a smell; it's a matter of running it down in prose and then trying to figure out what the thing is that's out there. Sometimes it might be a picture. This morning when I was writing I was chasing down one of those images. It was just a minute thing that happened to me while I was recently down in Alabama. We had rented a little cottage on the edge of Mobile Bay, and at one point there was stormy weather out on the bay; I wandered out to see what kind of weather it was and the door blew closed and locked me out of the cottage. I thought about getting back inside and I sat down and there was one of those semitropical warm summer rains starting to come down like buckshot. Somehow the image of stepping outside to see what's going on and having the wind blow the door shut has stuck in my head. I don't know what the image *is* exactly, or what it means, but I know that ever since I came home I've been trying to pursue that image in language, find out what it is. That image begins to ionize the prose and narrative particles around it so that words are drawn in, people and language begin to appear. That's when things are going well. When that's happening, any reader will recognize that flame-edge of discovery, that excitement of proceeding on the page that is shared between the reader, the writer, and the page. You're feeling that gathering energy as it burns through the page. And it's not a made-up thing that you've laid on the page, it's an edge that you feel going through it. To me, it has always come in narrative form. Sometimes the process draws in these adversarial relationships, as with these rivalries, which are not a conscious thing on my part.

LM: Once this "ionization process" begins to occur, do you know in advance where these relationships are going to be taking you? Or is it a process of discovery for you?

TM: The latter. I begin to feel where the fiction is going on its own, and then I begin to guess at what the consequences of certain things would be. Let's say that you're riding your bicycle on a warm October day down the old road in front of the ranch here, and you're three miles from the house and you begin to think, What if it starts to snow? That's the kind of question I begin to ask while I'm writing. I may only have written about the bicycle ride and then I start thinking about the snow, positing the things that could happen. It's a cloud chamber: you have these clouds first and then you drive electrical charges through it and things begin to take shape. That's how I write—with a lot of "what if's?" Procedurally what I do before I start is to make a deal with myself that I am willing to revise to any degree that is necessary. I have to make that deal in a very sincere way: I assume I have all the time in the world to finish a book, because I know it may take many revisions before I get it right. *Ninety-two in the Shade* took six or seven complete drafts. Once I've made that deal with myself, I'm free, because as I'm writing I can try any kind of expansions of the armature of the novel as it goes, knowing that if it doesn't work, that's OK, I can try something else. I'm not going to say, "God, there's fifty pages I've just wasted." I don't let myself think in those terms. I'll also admit that I've outlined every book I've ever written before I've started it. Then I've thrown out every outline relatively early on. It continues to seem important to make those outlines because their wrongness energizes what I finally find, whereas that doesn't seem to happen if I simply start and roll on. But if I begin by trying to live up to the outline and then find forceful reasons not to use it, then I'm getting somewhere.

SG: Could you talk about how you decide to leave things *out* of a book? In *Nobody's Angel*, for example, you chose to leave out the scene where Patrick discovers that his sister is dead.

TM: Whether or not that was a good idea I can't comment on, but here's the way I arrived at it: I decided that the situation had been prepared for to the degree that the reader's version of it would be better than the writer's. I also thought there was a grave danger of having almost *anything* that was said seem to be a trivialization of it. So I decided to say nothing. That was a tough choice, and it wasn't a choice where I did it and immediately knew it was exactly the right thing; it was just my best judgment under the circumstances. I'm very interested in what's left out in fiction and in the stops a writer imposes on his material. Montaigne said that there's no better way that the power of a horse can be seen as in a neat and clean *stop*. There are great cutting horses who can run and run continuously, making all kinds of moves back and forth, but they're limited horses because they don't know when and where to stop. A *great* horse, though, like that roan out in back, will make a tremendous move and then *stop*: he knows that the cow is held, even though the cow is in a complete state of confusion, and he'll hold that position until he is threatened again by a cow trying to return to the herd, and then *crack*, he'll start again and then *stop*. This is so much more powerful a thing for an animal to do than simply roaring back and forth in front of the herd to prevent that cow from returning by sheer athletics.

LM: You lay your plots out for readers differently in each of your books.

TM: Sure. Imagine a good gambler who is playing an important poker hand: the way he lays his cards down makes all the difference. With a certain number of cards, a certain number of the enemy are falling off their chairs, so the sequence of the cards can often determine who wins the hands. A writer needs to play his hand very carefully; he doesn't need to play fifty-two card pickup with the reader and throw the whole deck in his face just because he's got control of the deck. That's not playing cards at all.

SG: One suspects that you've probably identified with all your main characters fairly strongly. Is that identification essential to your creative processes, or could you write a book from a perspective that is utterly foreign to you?

TM: Writing a book from that kind of a perspective is one of the things I love to plan to do, but I wonder if I could ever do it. I was trained on protagonist-centered fiction, and the first way I learned to write was to view the world from a single perspective—the protagonist's. I often wonder, given how much work it is, whether or not I could go the distance in a full-length novel in a point of view which is utterly alien to my own. I wonder how inventive I would be with that form. Nabokov obviously could do it, but he's so detached. And he is far more boring than it is proper to admit. The game-level is much higher in his kind of work, just as it is with Robert Coover, or Borges, or any of those other systems writers. But for some reason I've never been drawn to that kind of fiction.

SG: You've said that you've never been interested in the movies and don't really know much about them. Didn't that make the move from writing fiction to writing screenplays seem especially difficult?

TM: No, it didn't seem difficult. It's a bit harder if you've been writing screenplays to go back to writing fiction. Especially after you've seen some movies made from screenplays, you know there's no sense in your doing a lot of interior decorating because somebody else is going to be building the sets. So you just write "Interior, the First Security Bank," in your script and that's all the evocation of atmosphere that you need to supply. Then you write the dialogue. Once you've written screenplays and you go back to writing fiction, you realize the weight of being the full production company for the novel.

LM: Has your involvement with screenplays affected your notion of fiction writing?

TM: It's made me rethink the role of a lot of the mnemonic things that most novelists leave in their books. The worst about these things is probably Faulkner, who frequently had his shit detector dialed down to zero. We all read Faulkner in a similar way: we move through these muddy bogs until we hit these wonderful streaks, and then we're back in the bogs again, right? Everyone agrees that Faulkner produced the greatest streaks in American literature from 1929 until 1935 but, depending on how you feel about this, you either admit that there's a lot of dead air in his works or you don't. After you've written screenplays for a while, you're not as willing to leave these warmups in there, those pencil sharpenings and refillings of the whiskey glasses and those sorts of trivialities. You're more conscious of dead time. Playwrights are even tougher on themselves in this regard. Twenty mediocre pages hardly hurt even a short novel, but ten dead minutes will insure that a play won't get out of New Haven. Movies are like that: people just can't sit there, elbow to elbow with each other and stand ten boring minutes in a movie. Oh, they will to a degree if they're prepared enough about the historical moment, if they're watching *Gandhi* or something, but not usually. At any rate, I think I go more for blood now, scene by scene in my writing, than maybe I would if I had never had that movie training. But basically it would be more appropriate to ask me if having to do my own grocery shopping has affected my writing. According to reviewers, I've spent the last ten years of my life in Hollywood, but to tell the truth I have logged less than thirty days in Los Angeles. Total. I do have one level of interest in movies, and that's that I like to read screenplays. They're little books. If I hear there's a wonderful new movie out and I can get my hands on the screenplay, I'll read that rather than to go see the movie itself. I enjoy shooting the movie in my mind. I love to read plays for the same reason.

LM: You once said, "Contrary to what people think, the cinema has enormously to do with language." Do you mean that the cinema relies on dialogue?

TM: There's only one thing that you can't be without when you set about putting together a movie deal: you can't do without a script, the "material." This material is always some kind of bundle of language, it's a book or a screenplay. You can't take any director in the world and go to a financing entity (like a studio or a bank) and make a deal without that bundle of language. Producers always come back to the same point: Who's got the book, or who's got the best hundred and twenty pages of writing? Yet that point is often disguised. Screenwriters are not particularly prized members of the moviemaking community, and as soon as things get rolling suddenly it's the director who's the star, or an actor. But when that movie is over and they're ready to go back and make another one, suddenly they're desperate for a writer or a book. That's the irreducible element in the moviemaking business. And in most movies you go to, the characters are continually talking. You get the impression in reading from the *auteur*-theory days of cinematic criticism that there's no conversation in films, that they're all silent movies. And yet if a Martian were to come down and analyze what's happening in films, he'd say, "These humans never shut up. They have pictures of humans and they're talking all the time. They get in machines and they talk in the machines and then they lean out of the window of one machine and talk into the window of another machine."

LM: One of the legends that grew out of your work on *The Missouri Breaks* was that you wrote the script and then Marlon Brando showed up wanting to change everything. Supposedly you two holed up for a week in a motel to thrash things out. Any truth to that story?

TM: None. The closest thing there was to that story is that Brando did have ways he wanted to do that film: he wanted to be an Indian and he had two pet wolves that he wanted to be in the movie; moreover, he wanted these wolves to kill the girl's father, wanted them to jump up on the girl's father's horse and eat him. So I was told to go out to Los Angeles and see Brando and get the wolf stuff stopped. I went out there and Brando was at home and I spent a couple of days with him. I had a wonderful time but we never talked about the movie at all. We just talked about literature. You know, he's a very erudite guy and really smart, a kind of crazy-connections smart. At the time he was reading a history of the Jesuits in Minnesota and a book about Louis Leakey's skulls and the prehominids in Africa. He'd get up in the morning and dress, gather all of his books together, and then get back in bed with his clothes on and read all day. He's on the verge of being downright scholarly. So that's what we did there, and when he eventually went off and did the movie he wasn't an Indian. I still don't know *what* he was. He was this kind of tubby Irish killer. I know many people hated that goofy, wild humor he injected into the movie, but I appreciated it.

LM: What about your involvement with movie directing? I would imagine that directing *Ninety-two in the Shade* must have been a difficult task for various reasons: it was your first film, it was based on your own novel, you were unfamiliar with the technical aspects of moviemaking . . .

TM: The technical aspects of moviemaking aren't that complex, and anyone who's ever directed would say that. There are technical components of the movies that are very complicated but no director knows them. Maybe Hal Ashby or Nick Roeg and a few other guys know the editing process, which is impossibly difficult to figure out, but I don't know of any director who really understands what the state-of-the-art sound or camera equipment is. For that kind of technical knowhow you have to rely on your cameraman or sound man to give you what you want to see and hear, or on your editor to give you the narrative sequentiality you want. A director has to rely on the people around him. I had never directed before, and I'm not particularly delighted with the job I did, but at the same time it became clear pretty fast that this was just another typewriter and I had to sit there and write as good a tale as I could.

LM: Instead of having Skelton killed at the end, you changed the conclusion of the movie and gave it a kind of wacky, funny ending. Given the kind of relationship that was developing between Skelton and Nichol, I could believe the new ending, but I wondered what your own thoughts were in making that change.

TM: First of all, unless you have a lot of money in your budget, you're forced to shoot out of sequence. So as I started doing the film I began wondering about the relationships of all the different parts, and I wound up shooting the ending both ways. You just happened to see a version of the movie with the happy ending; other people see it and it has the other ending. It was released with both endings and they tried to find the one that would play best. That's called not having the final cut.

SG: Which ending do you think works best?

TM: The ending as it was in the book is probably the better of the two, but the happy ending was fun and I thought it was amusing with Warren Oates reading that crazy letter and his angler going off into that surrealist Zululand, wading ashore with his trophy.

SG: Are you interested in directing other movies?

TM: I don't think so. Strangely enough, I was offered the directorship of *A Star Is Born*. Cute, huh? But while I was making *Ninety-two in the Shade*, I remember thinking what a pale experience it was compared to writing fiction. At first it was rather frightening, with all these people around and a lot of equipment and a lot of power-tripping going on, but then soon it had become as if I were trying to say something with this extremely ungainly typewriter. I kept thinking over and over, This is so much less good than writing fiction, because I'd get an idea and then I'd have to move all this junk around to shoot it, and then by the time I did that, inertia had set in again. That's why movies have to be so well planned, because that's the last chance you have to be really inventive; there's not much room for invention at the process level. At any rate, I don't think I'd want to direct again.

LM: Does writing about Montana, or about the West in general, present some special challenges for a writer?

TM: Part of the difficulty for me has to do with the lack of attachment between people and place that I was talking about earlier. So an aspect of this crisis lode that I'm trying to mine as a fiction writer is that I have to make some kind of ligature of connection between people and place. That has to happen, but it doesn't happen here in the West, as has often been thought, by simply stationing human beings in this grand landscape. There's actually something much stronger than that going on between people and places out here. It's more numinous in the sense that "place" for my little daughter Annie is that tree which keeps the heat off her while she's on the swing set. That's what place is for her for much of the day, and that's what place is for anybody else, even though the *nature* of that place is different for someone from Montana than it is for someone from New Jersey, somehow. It's not different simply in the calendaresque way, but it's hard to pin down how place really affects people. Somebody said that nobody is born a southern writer—Poe is not a "Southern writer"—it's something you elect to be; you let place influence you or you decide it doesn't. I know people from Texas or Montana who are absolutely urbane. Do we think of Donald Barthelme as being a Southern writer? Or Tom Wolfe? But I know people from Cairo, Illinois, who consider themselves to be deeply southern.

LM: You're obviously one of those writers who has chosen to be influenced by place.

TM: I want to find a way to profit from having spent half my life out here, particularly the half of my life that has been superimposed on a really fragmented upbringing. I've struggled to have a sense of place; as a kid I was always saying, "When I grow up I'm going to go and live at Uncle Bill's house in Sakonnet and work on a lobster boat." But very early on I decided that as soon as I could I was going to go out West. I did, at fifteen, when I went out and worked on a ranch, so my fantasy life became my real life. Today, even though that fantasy is one of the most banal elements of my life, I'm still excited about it. I certainly don't want to become one of those regional writers who collect funny phrases, but I do think you can use nature to charge a fictional landscape with powerful results. I have no interest in replicating Montana or rendering landscapes in a recognizable way, but I do know there is something forceful about these landscapes that should turn up in language.

SG: Is the myth about men and women being freer out here in the West really true?

TM: The air of the fresh start is alive here. People are willing to accept the idea that you can pull your life out of the fire and turn it around completely. It's an echo of gold mining days.

LM: Or the story of some Midwestern kid who comes out here, becomes a famous writer, and winds up being Montana's cutting-horse champion for three straight years.

TM: Sounds improbable, doesn't it? As time goes by, I feel closer to Ring Lardner, Sherwood Anderson, Scott Fitzgerald—drifters from the Midwest. You fetch up somewhere. It just happens.

Matt Brown

An Interview with

Tom Robbins

Some writers make piles of money, others are canonized by the literary establishment, but very few are as beloved by their audience as Tom Robbins. His fans embrace his books with a devotion and fervor that writing these days rarely elicits. The source of this adoration comes mainly from the philosophy that permeates his fiction, a philosophy that celebrates the power of human consciousness to find laughter, transcendence, and something of interest in everything we come in contact with. Robbins's philosophy is unabashedly exuberant and joyful, full of play and the sense that the universe is filled with all sorts of mysterious harmonies and passions that Western rationalism— with its emphasis on consistency and logic—trivializes and distorts.

Although this effervescent quality has led some critics to dismiss his novels as pop fare for adolescents, Robbins's work is deceptively sophisticated both in terms of its central thematic concerns and in its relentless drive to develop an aesthetic appropriate to its vision. All of Robbins's novels can be shown to explore many of the most basic issues that define our existence: What is the nature of sexuality, and what is the relationship between the male and female aspects we all share? How can people break free of the systems (political, spiritual, social) that repress our natural passions and sense of play, that rigidify belief into dogma, that encourage us to stop personal exploration? Robbins's method of presenting these issues—with its nonstop verbal pyrotechnics, its digressive structure, its authorial intrusions, and its general refusal to "contain" events within the usual framework of causality and linearity—*is* playful and full of surprises; but such methods emerge naturally from Robbins's conviction that the real enemy facing most people today is the threat of standardization and manipulation. "We all have the same enemy," as one character puts it in *Even Cowgirls Get the Blues*. "The enemy is the tyranny of the dull mind."

Despite a generally positive critical reception, Robbins's first novel, *Another Roadside Attraction* (1971), was only a modest success until the paperback edition gradually found its audience (primarily among college students). The book's outlandish plot—the mummified body of Christ is discovered in the basement of the Vatican and is subsequently sent into the stratosphere in a hot-air balloon piloted by the philosopher/proprietor of a roadside hot dog stand—contains myriad digressions and diversions. But here, as in later work, the plot itself is of secondary importance to its manner of presentation. One of Robbins's characters explains this emphasis on style by noting, "Those folks who are concerned with freedom, real freedom . . . must use style to alter content. If our style is masterful, if it is fluid and at the same time complete, then we can re-create ourselves, or rather, we can re-create the Infinite Goof within us. We can live *on top* of content, float above the predictable responses, social programming and hereditary circuitry."

Even Cowgirls Get the Blues (1976) found a much larger audience at once, partially due to the irresistible appeal of its protagonist, Sissy Hankshaw, a young woman with a monstrously large thumb and a taste for the open road and high adventure. As she hitchhikes the country looking for intellectual and sexual enlightenment, she conveys the spirit of spontaneity and the willingness to explore the eccentric that characterizes the maverick hero and heroine of Robbins's next novel, *Still Life with Woodpecker* (1980), a book about redheads, pyramid power, and the boundless mystery inherent in the most ordinary objects. In all three of these novels, as well as in *Jitterbug Perfume* (1984)— which takes as its modest theme the search for immortality—there is a fascination with the infinite variety of shapes into which reality is constantly transforming itself. Robbins offers his readers a vision of life as a glorious but ultimately mysterious adventure—"Mystery is part of nature's style," says a character in *Another Roadside Attraction*. "Behind everything in life is a process that is *beyond* meaning. Not beyond understanding, mind you, but beyond meaning." Life, then, is a short but exciting trip, especially rewarding for those willing to take the metaphysical outlaw's pledge to "stand for uncertainty, surprise, disorder, unlawfulness, bad taste, fun and things that go boom in the night."

Because his fiction is so full of acrobatic, slaphappy energy, we were expecting Robbins himself to be a pretty wild character. When we met him at his home in a small fishing village outside Seattle in June, 1982, we found a reflective, soft-spoken individual, still possessing a trace of a North Carolina accent he acquired as a boy. While we admired the artwork in his living room (Andy Warhol prints of Mao and of Marilyn Monroe, along with several of his own paintings) and bathroom (a framed cover of the *National Enquirer* featuring the headline "Vatican Considers Sainthood for Elvis"), Tom finished taping some Beatles music for an upcoming trip to Mexico, concluded a conversation with two young visiting writers, opened us all some beers, and generally puttered about, probably giving himself a few minutes to get a feel for us. It wasn't an easy conversation for him or for us at first, but after we exchanged some pleasantries about his beloved Seattle Sonics, our beloved San Diego Padres, and our mutual passion for rock and roll, we were ready for literary topics and a delicious salmon dinner at the local seafood restaurant. Gradually it became clear that, beneath the shy, boyish demeanor, Tom Robbins *is* a wild character ever ready to take off on whatever adventures the Infinite Goof has in store for him.

Larry McCaffery: What's a successful popular writer like you doing living in a remote fishing village up here in the Northwest?

Tom Robbins: I suppose I could live anywhere in the world and do what I do, so apparently I live here by choice. Here's one reason: In the summer, during the relatively warm months, I can work until 4:30 or 5 in the afternoon, get my sleeping bag and a quart of ale and some bread and cheese, go out walking across the fields until I come to what used to be an island—it's landlocked now—and walk into the woods and work my way up across the crown of this island; eventually I come out on the other side on a grassy cliff and spread my sleeping bag down in the soft grass overlooking a deep-water slough. When the moon rises, I can watch beavers playing in the moonlight, slapping their tails in the water; minks frolicking and large salmon jumping. There's a great blue heron that roosts on a dead tree spar almost above my head. Nobody's around, it's like wilderness, and yet it has only taken me twenty or twenty-five minutes to walk to this spot. And the next morning, in the same amount of time, I can be back at my desk writing; or I can drive to Seattle and within an hour and a half be going to galleries, eating in fine restaurants, seeing first-run movies, shoplifting lingerie or objets d'art, girl-watching, kicking the gong around, whatever. It's the best of both worlds.

Sinda Gregory: The rainy season doesn't get you depressed?

TR: Great weather for ducks? No, contrary to popular opinion, ducks don't like rain, but it's ideal for writers. It reduces temptation. During the rainy months you're forced to stay indoors. You turn inward. It's a cozy feeling, very comfortable and introspective. In life as in literature, I prefer wet to dry. And, of course, living out here in Monsoon Central, I can be as secluded as I need to be.

LM: Do you feel you need this sense of seclusion to write?

TR: Yes, very much so. I think it's important to live far from the centers of ambition, to keep away from literary politics and the sort of social contacts that can put the wrong emphasis on one's work.

SG: Do you mean emphasis on the commercial aspects of writing?

TR: Maybe "commercial" is not the right word. I don't object to commercialism unless it compromises a writer's personal truth or native style. Trevanian's *Shibumi* is an absolutely delicious novel and it's commercial to its core. Have you ever noticed that nothing upsets an intellectual as much as discovering that a plumber is enjoying the same book he or she is? The literati are too insecure to ever admit liking a book that isn't inaccessible or esoteric. At any rate, I'm not talking about commercialism so much as egoism, the pathetic desire to be more highly regarded than one's peers, the neurotic need to be lionized at cocktail parties and favorably reviewed in the correct periodicals. When we are trapped in the ego, our finest energy goes into these foolish competitive things instead of into our work, or, more importantly, into the development of our higher consciousness. When a writer is more interested in the reaction to his words than in the words themselves, he's a victim of misplaced emphasis.

LM: It's surely no coincidence that so many West Coast writers— you, Ursula Le Guin, Gary Snyder, and others—have concerned your-selves with counterculture values and Oriental philosophy and religion. Do you ever think of yourself as a regional writer?

TR: Not really. You know the painter Jacques Louis David had a room, a studio, that overlooked the square where the major guillotine was located in Paris before the Revolution. And he would sit up there all day and watch heads being lopped off, blood flooding the cobble-stones. Then he would turn to his easel and paint those very sweet portraits of members of the court. Now there was a man who was rejecting his environment. Most artists have a more direct dialogue with their environment than David, and so do I. But while there is a sense of place in my work, and that place is the Northwest, I see myself not as regional but American.

SG: Wouldn't you agree, though, that people living out here on the West Coast are more likely to be influenced by Oriental ways of thinking and living?

TR: Well, the Northwest is, after all, perched on the Pacific rim facing the Orient rather than Europe, and that's bound to affect people in all sorts of ways. A lot of my orientations are Asian rather than European—but they were leaning that way before I moved here. Maybe that's one of the reasons *why* I moved here. Somebody suggested that my penchant for writing episodically came from the influence of Kurt Vonnegut, but I never read Vonnegut until after I wrote my first novel. In fact, that abbreviated, episodic style of writing came to me, in part, from the Zen koan, through John Cage. Back in Virginia, I read *Silence*, in which Cage made use of the Zen koan form, and that influenced me in that direction early on. Later, out here, the Tibetan concept of Crazy Wisdom became fairly central to my way of thinking, and so did aspects of Taoism and Tantra. I'd say that anyone who lives out here who *isn't* influenced by the Far East is behaving a bit like David.

SG: You grew up in the rural South. What was that experience like?

TR: I grew up in small Southern towns. I was born in Blowing Rock, North Carolina, a very interesting place because nine months of the year it was like Dogpatch. Literally. It was Appalachia all the way, impoverished, ignorant, populated by men who beat their wives and drank too much—a rather *mean* place, abounding with natural beauty and colorful characters, but violent, snake-pit and sorrowful, over all. In summer, it became transformed into a wealthy resort, and from June through Labor Day there was nothing on the street but Cadillacs and Rolls-Royces and Mercedes and Lincoln Continentals. There were high-fashion boutiques there, whose owners were from Paris and Palm Beach. Glamorous men and women who wore diamonds and played tennis and golf. There was a movie theater that for three months showed first-run films as soon as they opened in New York and Los Angeles; the other nine months, it was closed. So every June there would be this dramatic transformation, and the dichotomy between the rich, sophisticated scene and the hillbilly scene affected me very much. It showed me how the ordinary suddenly could be changed into the extraordinary. And back again. It toughened me to harsh realities while instilling in me the romantic idea of another life. And it left me with an affinity for both sides of the tracks.

SG: Did growing up in the South have any specific effect on your writing?

TR: From my perspective today I can see that the *juice* of my fiction comes out of the South, but I felt so repressed in the South that I'm not sure that if I had remained there I would ever have found a way to channel that juice. Virginia, where I spent a lot of time in my youth, is a fairly repressive place.

LM: You've said elsewhere that even as a kid you had the sense of being an outsider. Was that sense one of the things that helped lay the foundation for the "metaphysics of the outlaw" that you develop in your fiction? I gather that even as a young man you were already something of a rebel.

TR: I feel completely at home in the world, I like it here, but from the beginning I've insisted that my stay here be on my own terms and not society's. In that sense, I've been more allied with the outlaw than the outsider. I don't know if it helped shape the unbaked cookie dough of my talent, but one thing that was a *beacon* for me as a boy rebel was a roadhouse just outside Blowing Rock, a joint named The Bark because it was sided with cedar shakes that still had the bark on them. At The Bark, folks drank beer and danced. Can you appreciate the fact that among fundamentalist Southern Baptists drinking and dancing were major sins? My mother taught a Baptist Sunday school class for an age group of about sixteen to twenty-three, and once a week, Wednesday nights, this class would meet at our house. It was partly religious, partly social, but they did a lot of gossiping, and the hottest items of gossip always involved The Bark. "So-and-so was seen leaving The Bark Saturday night." "No! Well, I'll be!" Now, I was a little kid, seven, eight, nine, while this was going on, but they made The Bark sound so attractive, so fascinating! I just loved eavesdropping on those shocked conversations about the evils of that roadhouse. My little pals and I were all over those hills, and we frequently passed by The Bark, it was on a route between one of our hideouts and another, and we'd always stop and stare at it. We'd see men coming out the door with "floozies" on their arms, and they'd be smoking cigars and sporting tattoos, and they'd climb on a big Harley-Davidson and roar out of the red clay parking lot. I was so attracted that all I wanted to do was grow up to be old enough to go to The Bark, to drink beer, squeeze floozies, dance, get tattooed, smoke cigars, and ride a motorcycle. We moved to Virginia when I was ten and I never got back to The Bark, but I eventually *did* do all those other things. And they were every bit as good as I had imagined them.

LM: Was The Bark an early version of the roadside attraction in your first novel?

TR: No, The Bark was a zoo of a different order. But there were lots of roadside attractions in the South on the tourist highways that led to Florida.

SG: You were also an avid reader as a kid, weren't you?

TR: I read the stuff that most kids read—the kids who read at all— except for an atlas. One of my favorite playthings as a child was a world atlas that I read from cover to cover. I knew the capitals of all the countries until that frenzy of independence in the '60s, when all those new nations in Africa emerged; then I lost track. But I also devoured adventure and mystery stories—the Hardy Boys and all that—and comic books, too. I was always reading as a kid; I taught myself to read when I was five years old because I couldn't wait to get into books. In a way, books were more magical to me than The Bark, although The Bark was forbidden fruit and books were not— my mother always encouraged me to read and she read to me from the time when I was in the cradle.

LM: You ended up in a school of music, art, and drama—the Richmond Professional Institute. Were you interested in becoming a performing artist or a painter?

TR: No, I was interested in writing about art. I had earlier spent two years at Washington and Lee University and then I was out of school for four years. I was kicked out of my fraternity for lobbing biscuits at the housemother. Being expelled from a fraternity at Washington and Lee was tantamount to being expelled from the university itself, because it was the epitome of the preppie college and there was hardly a student there who wasn't in a fraternity. So I hitchhiked around the country for a year, landed in the air force for three years, and then I returned to school. While I was in the air force I met some painters, and that was quite a magical thing. Not only had I never seen a real painting, rather than a reproduction, but to actually go into a studio and smell turpentine, actually see people painting pictures for a living— well, this experience blew my mind and I became friends with these wild bohemian artists and grew very interested in art. At college I took mostly theory courses—I didn't learn how to play an instrument or anything, and although I did take a course in play direction and some courses in painting, I didn't really accumulate much in terms of practical technique. I wanted to write about art. I never thought I could create it.

LM: But you did some painting later on, didn't you?

TR: Yes, I have painted for years, when I've had the space. I used to write during the day and paint at night because they were such opposite disciplines that I found it very relaxing to paint after a long day at the typewriter. Lately I haven't had enough space to do any painting, so I've worked with rubber stamps. I design many of my own stamps, and recently I've made little rubber-stamp and watercolor collages.

LM: Just now, when you said that painting and writing were "such opposite disciplines," what did you mean?

TR: For one thing, they are physically opposite, at least in the way I practice them. I can get very tense at the typewriter—I end up with a sore neck at the end of the day. Writing is harder physical labor than digging ditches, at least for me, because I have rotten typing posture and don't deal well with machines. So to go then and paint and just move that brush around—well, it's a lyrical, fluid, liberating feeling; it's more like a dance, swinging and lifting and dipping your muse, rather than trying to knead some words out of her.

LM: Several of my favorite writers—Coover and Barthelme, for example—worked closely with painting while they were developing as writers. Did your experience with painting affect your views about writing?

TR: Probably. It may have heightened my visual sense, my passion for color and texture and shape in language. Language is alive for me, in my eyes as well as in my ears, and painting must have contributed to my good fortune in this regard. It probably also contributed to my appreciation of objecthood. I'm very interested in inanimate objects and in the mysterious network of connections—in terms of the poetic, psychological, and historical associations they inspire, as well as in terms of the energy fields—by which all objects are joined. I believe that every object leads a secret life of its own, although it isn't necessary to delve into those secrets to appreciate the object. Does this sound kooky? Is Claes Oldenburg kooky? Oldenburg understands the rich, complex life of the common object, and in a less profound way so does Andy Warhol. The pop artists deepened my relationship with objects, but so did the "old-fashioned" still-life painters such as Morandi and Cézanne.

SG: Were you interested in realistic painting or in nonrepresentational art?

TR: I consider the art I'm interested in realistic, but then I consider Jackson Pollock a realistic painter and Andrew Wyeth an abstract painter.

SG: Could you explain?

TR: Well, Wyeth's paintings are two-dimensional reductions of the three-dimensional world. Thus, they're abstracted from the external world. They are pictures *of* things. Pollock's paintings don't refer to things, they *are* things: independent, intrinsic, internal, holistic, *real*. Now, in a sense, books are abstractions in that they refer to countless things outside themselves. In my books, when I interrupt the narrative flow and call attention to the book itself, it's not cuteness or self-consciousness but an attempt to make the novel less abstract, more of a real thing.

LM: That's interesting, because I suspected that that strategy of reminding readers that they're reading a book, reminding them that the author is inventing what's going on, was designed, in part, to expose all forms of knowledge as subjective—that is, to remind the reader that mimetic fiction is another illusion, just as scientific and mathematical descriptions are metaphoric.

TR: I believe that reading is one of the most marvelous experiences a human being can enjoy. Being alone in a room with a book is so intimate, so individualistic, so kaleidoscopically imaginative; it's erotic to me, sacred. What I want to do with my fiction is to create an experience peculiar to reading alone, an experience that could not be duplicated in any other medium, something that can't be done in the movies, can't be done on television, on stage, record, or canvas. What this means, on the one hand, is devaluating plot to a certain extent, because if it's only a story you're after, how much easier it is to switch on TV or go to a film. Reading requires more from an audience than television or film; the audience has to participate more fully. Keeping plot secondary to "bookness" helps to make it a reading experience, a literary experience, an experience that could only be derived from words on a page. I also have wanted to avoid the escapism that frequently results from a mimetic approach. What I've wanted to do was to break into the narrative and say, "Look, this is a book—you're just reading a book. But it's nice, isn't it? It's still entertaining, isn't it? I still have your attention, don't I? Even though I'm popping through the page and pointing my finger at what I'm doing, even though you're not caught up in the belief that you're living on Tara plantation."

LM: What they're caught up in is reading words on the page.

TR: That's right—and it's still fun, and it's still serious, and it's still believeable, and you're going to keep on reading, aren't you? Because the art of reading is as valid and interesting and real as anything else.

SG: Did you do much fiction writing before you started on *Another Roadside Attraction*?

TR: No. I was waiting for the right moment to begin.

LM: You mean *Another Roadside Attraction* was actually the first piece of fiction you'd ever started? You had no apprentice pieces at all?

TR: Oh, I'd been writing stories off and on since I was five years old, but nothing I wanted to show anyone, and I'd never begun a novel or anything like that. I concentrated on nonfiction. I was waiting to find my voice. Once I found it, I was off and running. But I felt that I couldn't start writing fiction before my voice evolved. One of my art teachers was always encouraging me to go out and become another Faulkner, but that was the last thing in the world that appealed to me. By that I don't mean any disrespect toward Faulkner—I simply didn't aspire to *become anybody else*. So I really didn't want to write, and certainly not to publish, until I was certain my own voice had evolved.

LM: What was it that helped you find that voice? Was there a specific event that helped you crystallize your sense of voice?

TR: I think that the times—the '60s—had a lot to do with it. I was very much caught up in that whole psychedelic revolution, and I quickly realized that no one was going to write about it in an appropriate way. I could see that writers were going to *describe* it rather than *evoke* it. And as a matter of fact, that's exactly what happened—almost no good novels came out of the '60s dealing with the kinds of things we were experiencing then, because most writers described them in a reportorial, journalistic manner that was inadequate to reproduce the essence of what was going on. But I realized that I could capture this experience from the inside out, partly due to my experience with LSD. I based my first novel, *Another Roadside Attraction*, on a psychedelic model. Some people complained that *ARA* had no structure, but that book was carefully structured, I spent two years structuring it, although it was not structured in any usual way. There had been plenty of previous books that were nonlinear, but not nonlinear in the way that *ARA* is nonlinear. I don't think there has ever been a book quite like *ARA*, either in content or in form. It may not be great, but it is definitely one of a kind.

LM: When you said that *ARA*'s form is based on a "psychedelic model," what did you mean?

TR: Simply that its structure *radiates* in many directions at once, rather than progressing gradually up an inclined plane, like most novels, from minor climax to minor climax to major climax. There are lots of little *flashes* of illumination strung together like beads. Some of these flashes illuminate the plot; others merely illuminate the reader.

LM: Could you talk a little more about the effects that drugs had on your aesthetic sensibility?

TR: Mainly, psychedelics left me less rigid, intellectually and emotionally. Certain barriers just melted away. Reality is not a fixed thing, and I learned to move about more freely from one plane of existence to another. The borderlines between so-called reality and so-called fantasy, between dream and wakefulness, animate and inanimate were no longer as distinct, and I made some use of this newfound mobility in my writing. Also, there's a fairly narrow boundary between the silly and the profound, between the clear light and the joke, and it seems to me that on that frontier is the most risky and significant place an artist or philosopher can station himself. Maybe my psychedelic experiences prepared me to straddle that boundary more comfortably than most. Or maybe you'd say that, as a writer, I'm a borderline case.

SG: Larry and I find that most of our favorite artists share an ability to be serious and funny at the same time.

TR: Like the universe, you mean?

LM: What?

TR: Quantum physics has taught us that the universe is a balance between irrevocable laws and random playfulness. We've learned that part of the evolutionary process is purposeful and part of it is merely an adventure, a game. I don't know why I said "merely." Games are serious, too. And playfulness, when the player's consciousness is fully operative, can be profound. We could define life as the beautiful joke that is always happening—and find support for that definition in advanced science.

LM: The literary community is usually suspicious of playfulness.

TR: Isn't it a pity? The greatest weakness of the intelligentsia in this culture has been its inability to take comedy seriously. That's changing in science, at the higher levels. Maybe it'll change in literature as well.

LM: But a lot of comedy, or playfulness, if you prefer, *is* merely frivolous, isn't it? I assume you feel there are different ways of laughing at things, of playing with them, some of which *would* be frivolous.

TR: Yes, I do—although we must remember that, to the unenlightened, the god-laugh always seems frivolous. There is, however, a distinction between important humor and unimportant humor. Important humor is liberating and maybe even transformative. Important humor is also always inappropriate. If you go to a funny movie and you know it's going to be funny, you can enjoy yourself and laugh and have a fine evening, but nothing *liberating* happens to you. But a joke in the *wrong* place at the *wrong* time can cause a leap in the consciousness that is liberating to the human spirit. So it is this inappropriate area of humor in which I work, or at least aspire to work. But I should emphasize that I'm not praising the cynical, cruel, nihilistic humor too often typical of "Saturday Night Live." There's nothing liberating about that, either. We need to be able to make fun of things, anything, even the reputation of Christ, as I did in *ARA*, but there has to be in the mocking some sense of respect for life, in all of its crazy and necessary manifestations.

SG: How did you happen to choose the particular subject matter for *ARA*—the demythologizing of Christianity?

TR: The idea of the discovery of the mummified body of Christ had been kicking around in my head for six or seven years. I was fascinated by the fact that Western civilization is based upon the divinity of Christ in a lot of crucial ways. So what would happen if we were to learn conclusively that Christ was *not* divine? What would this say about the future of Western civilization? Could we continue to lead moral and ethical lives if Christ proved to have died and stayed dead? I had that idea in mind for a long time, and I did a lot of research into the life of Jesus and the history of religion. Actually, however, I didn't demythologize Christianity, I remythologized it. As Joseph Campbell has pointed out, a major problem with Christianity is that it interprets its myths historically rather than symbolically.

SG: Obviously *ARA* takes a pretty dim view of organized religion in general and Christianity in particular. Was there a special incident that had made you react against your religious upbringing?

TR: Yep, it was seeing Johnny Weissmuller for the first time. For years I had attended Sunday school. I also was subjected to a lot of Southern Baptist training at home. So I knew that Jesus was supposed to be "the big man," my hero. But then I saw my first Tarzan movie, and after that Jesus just didn't cut the mustard. I continued to like Jesus, and I still admire the myth—he's still a sort of hero of mine. In *ARA* I have a dialogue between Tarzan and Jesus which was an attempt to resolve, I suppose, all those conflicts in my early years when Jesus and Tarzan were competing—Jesus quite unsuccessfully, as it turned out—for being my main man. You know, religion is organized spirituality. But there's an inherent contradiction there, because the moment you try to organize spirituality, you destroy its essence. So religion is spirituality in which the spiritual has been killed. Or at least diminished. Spirituality doesn't lend itself to organization. The whole process is rather like Heisenberg's uncertainty principle. That was one of the messages of *ARA*.

SG: Your second novel, *Even Cowgirls Get the Blues*, also had its spiritual side—the spiritual side of feminism, modern woman's connection to the goddess, and so forth. And in *Still Life with Woodpecker*, where you were dealing with romantic love and outlawism . . .

TR: And objecthood.

SG: Yes, and objecthood. You managed to find a spiritual side to those things as well. Does *Jitterbug Perfume* have a spiritual theme?

TR: From one perspective, the perspective of subatomic physics, where matter and energy merge and become one, *everything* is spiritual. Including poodles with rhinestone collars. But, yes, *Jitterbug Perfume* concerns itself with immortality, which is the basis of most spirituality and all religion.

LM: Do you develop a theory of the afterlife?

TR: Not exactly. Whether there is an afterlife or not, beyond the pure energy level, is something that can't be known unless you die. Meanwhile, a rigid belief in an afterlife can be very harmful. A belief in Heaven can cause Hell. As long as a population can be induced to believe in a Heaven or a Nirvana, it can be controlled and oppressed. People will put up with all sorts of tyranny and poverty and ill treatment if they're convinced they'll eventually escape to a stress-free dude ranch for eternity. And then they're much more willing to risk their lives for their governments. Also, these old men who run our governments, as long as they believe that life is just a trial for eternal life after death, they will be less hesitant about leading us into a nuclear conflict. I'm convinced that, if we want to end war, then we've got to put all thoughts of an afterlife out of our minds. To emphasize the afterlife is to deny life. And denial of life is the only unpardonable sin. Amen.

SG: I'd like to take you back to something you said a minute ago about objecthood. Could I ask you about the Camel cigarette pack in *Still Life*? Did that idea occur to you in the midst of your work, or did you know from the beginning that you wanted to bring it in?

TR: This is a case where I had something specific in mind early on. At the beginning of that novel my ambition was to write about objects in a way in which they had never been written about in a work of fiction. People had previously used objects symbolically, of course, and had done so very beautifully and very effectively. But I wanted to write about objects *for their own sake*, to write about the object as if it had a life of its own—which I think inanimate objects do have. In order to get this out of the whole broad social context, I decided I wanted to find some way to put one person alone in an empty room with three objects. Well, that didn't quite work out, for reasons that are still pretty unclear to me; so I decided to concentrate on a single object. And it occurred to me that better than some natural object—like a snail's shell, or a pine cone, or a seashell, something that lends itself to poetic interpretations—would be a popular object, because I have an affinity with popular objects. So I decided to take something out of the su-permarket and use it, hopefully in a profound way. I began mulling over our common objects, and by far the richest was the Camel pack. There is a whole mythology and lore about the Camel pack that has gradually evolved in this century. Jokes and riddles have been invented by prisoners, by sailors, by men bored and alone. There are far more of these stories than I mention in the book; I just used a fraction of them.

SG: You must have gone out and researched this area once you figured out you were going to use the Camel pack.

TR: I did some research, although I knew some of the lore already. When I first thought of the Camel pack, I figured, This has got to be my object, because there is no other package design, no other common object, no other supermarket artifact that has that amount of richness and resonance.

LM: So you chose the Camel pack and the basic situation and then worked the plot of *Still Life* around these things?

TR: Right. I wanted to use the Camel pack, and I wanted to use the idea of one person locked in a room with the Camel pack, having to relate in a way in which we don't usually relate to inanimate objects.

LM: *ARA* seemed like a strikingly original novel when it appeared; but there were a number of other experimental works appearing during that same period with which your book shared certain affinities. Were there any writers you were reading during that period who did have some impact on you while you were working on *ARA*?

TR: Not any fiction writers. During that period I was mostly reading Alan Watts, Gary Snyder, Timothy Leary, Yogananda, people like that. The only fiction writer who spoke to me then was Hermann Hesse, and he certainly didn't influence my style.

LM: When I saw that reference to Bokonon in *ARA*, I assumed it was a kind of playful homage to Vonnegut.

TR: That was a curious incident. People who read my manuscript in progress kept mentioning Vonnegut to me, but I had never read him. A friend of mine stacked up her whole collection of Vonnegut novels and said, "Now I know you don't want to read these now, but when you're finished with your book, here they are." Well, I was reading an issue of *The Realist*—Paul Krassner's newspaper—and there was an article in there by Wavy Gravy in which he used as an epigraph the quote, "Certain travel suggestions are dancing lessons from God," and attributed the quote to Bokonon. Of course, that was from Vonnegut's *Cat's Cradle*, but I didn't know that. I liked the quote so much that I worked it into *ARA*, attributing it, again, to Bokonon. I actually looked up Bokonon in a religious encyclopedia, thinking he might have been some Persian cult figure or something. But I never found him. And this is even more interesting: One day I stopped off to see that friend who was the Vonnegut fan, and while she was getting ready to go to lunch with me, I picked up *Cat's Cradle*, which was on the top of the stack of Vonnegut books that she had waiting for me. And I very absentmindedly leafed through it and found that she had underlined one sentence—one and only one—and it was that very same sentence that I had already used in *ARA*.

SG: Brautigan's work is also frequently linked to your own. Did his fiction offer you any specific inspiration?

TR: When I finally got around to reading *Trout Fishing in America*, it encouraged me greatly. It was the first modern novel to successfully do away with plot. By "successfully" I mean it remained accessible and compelling. It's a landmark book. But I was well along with *ARA* before I ever read a word of it. People are always comparing me to Brautigan and Vonnegut and I can't understand it. The only thing I have in common with Brautigan is the use of imaginative, fanciful, outrageous metaphors and similes, but I was using them before he was and I can prove it. I'm not suggesting that he was influenced by me, either, because he wasn't. And Vonnegut, well, we've both employed an episodic structure, and once in a while our ideas dovetail, but I'm obsessed with the poetics of prose and he clearly is not, I'm optimistic and he's pessimistic, I'm complex and he's simple: His sensibility is much more middle aged and middle class. Vonnegut and Brautigan are far more interesting and important than most of those safe and sane ivory-carvers who get all the awards and "serious" acclaim, but anybody who's concerned with my influences had better look elsewhere.

LM: To where?

TR: To James Joyce, for openers. Next, to Alfred Jarry and Günter Grass. Then to Blaise Cendrars, Henry Miller, Claes Oldenburg, George Herriman, and the Coconut Monk.

LM: George Herriman?

TR: The creator of *Krazy Kat*.

SG: Who's the Coconut Monk?

TR: He was some outrageous Buddhist monk who buzzed around Saigon on a motorbike during the war and was forever presenting ripe coconuts to foreign diplomats and military leaders as an emblem of peace. He had a habit of saying something eccentric and beautiful and then vanishing into the jungle. His laugh could be heard all over the Mekong Delta.

LM: OK, speaking of laughter, let's talk some more about comic writing. As I'm sure you know, there are some critics and readers out there who don't take your work seriously because you are so playful and comic; and because, despite your frequent poignancy and the often savage satiric thrust of your books, you seem fundamentally optimistic. How do you respond to this kind of charge?

TR: I don't feel any need to respond to it at all. I suppose I *ought* to be discouraged. Comic writing is not only more profound than tragedy, it's a hell of a lot more difficult to write. There seems to be almost a conspiracy against exploring joy in this culture; to explore pain is considered not only worthy but heroic, while exploring joy is considered slight. This kind of attitude strikes me as nearly insane. Why is there more value in pain than there is in joy? This is not to say that pain, anger, alienation, and frustration can't inform us or shouldn't be explored, but only to ask why these emotions should be explored while joy is excluded. Part of this is due to a prevailing sensibility, particularly rampant in academic and journalistic circles, that it is simply not hip to be life-affirming or positive. Some critics prefer books that reflect their own neuroses, their own miserable lives. The buzzword in New York reviews these days is "gritty." A gritty book is a book to admire. How do you explain this hunger for the sabulous? Where I come from, only chickens and turkeys deliberately consume grit.

LM: Does this neurosis, as you call it, show up both in criticism and in fiction? And is it a matter of content alone, or does it affect style?

TR: All of the above. When Jim Harrison strayed from the dark side into the light side with his novel *Warlock*, the critics who had been washing his feet (and rightly so) now began to dice them with razor blades. He was punished for going AWOL from Camp Desperation. Yet *Warlock* is just as tough and true, in its own way, as Harrison's earlier work. *The World According to Garp* started out fine, the first twenty pages were absolutely marvelous, but the neurosis of the content gradually overtook John Irving's style, infected it, made *it* neurotic, so that sixty pages into the book the style had been reduced to morbid manipulation, to obscene hack writing. Scott Spencer's *Endless Love* suffered an identical fate. After a riveting, lyrical beginning it became so permeated by neurosis that toward its end Spencer was totally out of control. Not out of control in the exhilarating, hallucinogenic way of Hunter S. Thompson, but out of control emotionally. Hysterical, in the worse sense of the word. A vile, wimpy, whining, scab-picking display.

LM: There must be other contemporary writers you admire or feel affinities with.

TR: Lots of them. Too many to list. There is a tremendous amount of literary talent on the planet right now. For that matter, anybody who sits down daily and faces the terror of the blank page has my respect, and that includes Irving and Spencer. Bless them.

LM: How about younger, promising writers?

TR: There's a ripe crop of them, too. Ted Mooney, John Calvin Batchelor, and Eve Babitz. Todd McEwen wrote a sweetheart of a first novel called *Fisher's Hornpipe*, although his outrageous protagonist was whining at the end. (A sop to the reviewers, maybe?) David Payne is a born writer. And Francisco Goldman may be the best of the bunch, if he doesn't go Hollywood on us.

LM: Do you have any advice for younger writers?

TR: Maintain a pitch next to madness, but never take yourself too seriously. There are a few things in life that are more important than literature, but your career is *not* one of them.

SG: Could I ask you something about women? In all of your books you have a main admirable heroine who winds up meeting what is essentially a male mentor. This seems to suggest that men and women have crucial differences that need to be shared with each other, and runs against the idea that men and women are basically the same.

TR: They *are* different, and *vive la différence*! Men and women are not alike, and blacks and whites are not alike, and French and Germans are not alike, and gays and straights are not alike. One thing I really hate is the tendency today toward homogeneity. These differences among people are important and we're all enriched by them. The fact that a man is different from a woman enriches the life of both the man and the woman in ways that would be lost were we to become truly unisexual. This doesn't mean that either the man or the woman is limited by sexual definition. But to keep the gene pool from dwindling, to keep options open, to keep life bright and free and interesting, it's imperative that we have variety and maintain differences. It's important that the gypsies not be assimilated into the mainstream, and that certain aspects of black culture remain black. This idea of all of us becoming the same is a greater threat to our survival than nuclear warfare—it's a threat to our psychic existence. Every man has a woman in him, just as every woman has a man in her. Every black has many things in common with every white, just as every white has many things in common with every Oriental. These similarities are good, they're connections, they can help us live peacefully with one another. But the differences are more important than the similarities because the differences give life its fizz, its brew. Everything that makes life really challenging and interesting emerges out of these differences. The similarities form a good foundation, create a structure, a glue to hold us all together. But the really important things in life are a result of the tensions that arise from a balance of opposites.

SG: Once you actually sit down at your Remington, do you have a clear idea about where your novel is going to go? That is, do you work from an outline, have extensive notes about the characters and what's going to happen, that sort of thing?

TR: Not this pig. I begin with a general sense of the plexus of effects I wish to produce, but I try not to let the concept solidify too quickly or to let the picture fix. I want it to marinate in my imagination, I want to connect the dots a few at a time. When I can surprise myself every day, it makes it easier to go to my desk. If I'm going to sit at a desk six hours a day, five days a week, it's necessary for me to surround the act of writing with an atmosphere of drama and discovery.

LM: Your books are filled with an incredible amount of esoteric information, a bit like Pynchon's novels. How does this information find its way into your works? Do you write along and find something interesting and *then* decide to research it? Or is most of it available to you beforehand?

TR: I do research my subjects. For *ARA* I read seventeen books on the life of the historic Christ. For *Jitterbug Perfume* I haunted perfume shops and read everything available on perfuming. For *Still Life with Woodpecker* I actually meditated on a Camel package for days, alone in an empty room. But much of the esoteric information just bubbles up when required. I have a ravenous curiosity and a pretty fair memory, especially for cosmic details such as the rectal temperature of a hummingbird.

SG: Which is . . . ?

TR: A hundred and four, point six. Under normal conditions.

LM: Do you have any predictions for the future?

TR: Of literature or of life?

LM: Both.

TR: Well, I predict a period of accelerated growth in the evolution of human consciousness. But if there is a new Messiah, he won't walk down from some Asian mountaintop, he—or she—will climb out of a hot tub in California. And I predict that I'm gonna regret opening my big mouth in this interview. Let's unplug this machine and take a voyage up the Amazon.

Ted Gabbay

An Interview with
Ron Silliman

Since the early 1970s Ron Silliman has been developing various forms of plotless, creative prose that explore the relationship between public, private, and literary discourses. Working without fiction's usual structural constraints (character and plot), Silliman's works intend to focus the reader's attention on the sentence and the word. His early works— such as *Nox* (1974), a collection of sixty poems in fifteen pages, and *Mohawk* (1973), a work composed of twenty-six words spatially arranged according to a formula involving playing cards—are recognizably "poems" (whereas his later works should probably be labeled "prose poems"). They also exhibit Silliman's interest in how formal structures can recontextualize words, phrases, and sentences so they can be viewed from fresher perspectives. His two best-known works, *Ketjak* (1978) and *Tjanting* (1981), employ arbitrary structuring devices. In *Ketjak*, which was partially inspired by the repetitious structures employed by Steve Reich's music, each paragraph contains twice as many sentences as the previous one, repeating some sentences intact and elaborating on others. *Tjanting* is structured around the Fibonacci number series so that the number of sentences in each paragraph equals the sum of those in the preceding paragraphs. In *Tjanting* the sentences are not merely repeated; rather, their constituent elements (words, phrases) more actively engage each other so that they are recast, transmuted into new variations.

Since Silliman's texts are devoid of the usual sources of readerly interest—character analysis, plot development—what sustains our attention is the amazing variety of language, the play of Silliman's imagination as he snatches phrases out of, say, a poem or a work on linguistics and allows these to jostle with fragments of a conversation overheard on a bus or at the ballpark. Since the structures of his works are often predetermined, Silliman is freed to include a wide range of content without sacrificing cohesion. His readers gradually get a "feel" for the circumstances that result in these sentences. *Ketjak*'s language produces a vivid verbal grid system of the daily life in San Francisco— a portrait that is as telling, in its own way, as any novelistic treatment. Words, like people, are often disfranchised in our society; this disfranchisement is subtly encouraged by literary structures (and by our notions of "literature" itself), which insure that certain discourses appear more often than others. But in Silliman's works, "found language" from street slang can wrestle into contact with bureaucratic nonspeak or with lines from Wittgenstein or Gertrude Stein or W. V. O. Quine. The result is akin to a musical composition whose "content" is the flow of sounds, images, and words.

The startling and often amusing interaction of sentences in Silliman's prose pieces very much suggests the quality of the man. Although he is by inclination an intellectual, Ron Silliman has eschewed academic life, preferring instead to throw his lot among people for whom the manipulation of language is not an abstraction but a principal means of their victimization. Since dropping out of San Francisco State and the University of California at Berkeley during the 1960s, disillusioned by the prospects of institutional creative writing, he has worked mainly in grass-roots political organizations, such as prison reform groups and neighborhood outreach programs, in San Francisco.

The following conversation took place on a warm afternoon in May 1982 at our home in San Diego. We had already gotten to know Ron during his tenure as a visiting lecturer at UCSD that spring. The business of literary talk was often interrupted by exchanges about our many mutual interests: performance art, the music of Philip Glass, the Talking Heads, Brian Eno, Laurie Anderson, California politics, and (most passionately) baseball. But, as the texture of the following interview probably indicates, there is a charged intensity in a conversation with Ron Silliman that results from his intellectual curiosity, his openness to a wide variety of art forms, his relentless investigation into the governing structures that control life and art, and his willingness (even delight) in discussing contemporary fiction and poetry from both very abstract and highly personalized standpoints. After several hours of taping, we were ready to turn our attention to more serious matters—a visit to the ballpark, where the Padres would soundly thrash Silliman's beloved Giants. The names change (Chili Davis and Juan Eichelberger replaced

Gertrude Stein and Louis Zukofsky), and a few of the topics (more emphasis on the suicide squeeze than on the Projectivists' aesthetics), but the talk went on, between us and all around us.

Sinda Gregory: I suspect some readers have a difficult time placing your work within a tradition, fiction or poetry or journalism or prose poetry or whatever. What do you consider your work to be?

Ron Silliman: I consider what I write to be prose poems but not fiction, partly for formal reasons and partly because I'm not interested in "making things up." And although most readers aren't familiar with it, there is a tradition of the prose poem, extending back 160 years to the work of Aloysius Bertrand, which is seldom incorporated into the teaching of creative writing in the academy. Creative prose is subsumed under the term *fiction*, with the result that works that don't fit the category are ignored. But subsuming prose under the term *fiction* is like subsuming all of what can occur in a text under the rubric of *character*, or *narrative*. For example, the work of Baudelaire in prose is extraordinarily interesting. He was the first person capable of using prose as a closed, stanzaic form. Traditional modes of defining *literary* categories don't account for the way in which even expository prose is marked by the devices of literature. I often use Theodor Adorno's *Minima Moralia* to demonstrate how his essays, which may be only six or seven sentences long, use sentence length and prosody as elements clearly integral to his argumentation. Wittgenstein is another writer whose prose can be viewed from the same perspective. It's not an accident that a person who is an interesting stylist, like Derrida, can have a far greater impact than perhaps the weight of his ideas would suggest he should have, while equally useful thinkers who are not such compelling writers may be perceived as less important—Jurgen Habermas would be an example. By organizing our academic institutions around fiction rather than around prose, by subsuming all forms of prose into fiction instead of the other way around, a great deal of confusion has set in. At Berkeley, linguistics and rhetoric are departments apart from literature—compartmental aphasia.

SG: Can prose poems have as much popular appeal as the novel? Or is this a relevant issue for you?

RS: It's definitely a relevant concern, but this question is often posed incorrectly. Literature needs audiences, but not a "public." A homogeneous audience (or mass market) is one that effaces the individual characteristics of the reader, to arrive at a reader-as-cipher, much as television begets its viewer. There are *many* legitimate audiences, but not a single "super-market" that one should try to occupy. This diversity is recent, the result of the expansion both of literacy and of technology. Up until perhaps 1950, the increase in the number of possible readers meant larger audiences only for an essentially centralized small body of white, male, patriarchal writing. Women, people of color, lesbians and gay men were excluded or marginalized. The Jewishness of the Objectivists, for example, kept their work from being recognized as important for thirty years. As the elaboration of offset printing during the '50s gave rise to the small press revolution, poetry in America was cleaved in half by a debate between the so-called academics, writers who valued the preservation of convention, particularly the closed forms that originated in Europe, and the so-called New Americans, who countered with a speech-based poetics and a nationalism of open form. If you read much of the literature of the '50s and '60s you get the feeling that a great contest was being waged, and that one side or another would somehow eventually win. Presumably the losing side was simply going to wither and disappear. Not only has that not happened, but the amoebalike cleaving process has continued, both within this original two-party framework and outside it. Most notably, the rise of feminist culture has meant the rise of a women's literature that does not need to rely on the legitimation of male-dominated institutions for its sense of value.

SG: And each of these subcultures naturally produces a literary audience.

RS: Exactly. Each subgenre of poetry today reflects a different audience, a different community. Disputes as to the "excellence" of one kind of writing or another are in fact *sub rosa* arguments as to which social group will dominate the other. What we need to understand is how a subgenre of poetry both creates and is created by that social construct we call an audience. A very useful example is the work of Judy Grahn, which has done so much to make possible a kind of literature that was not even conceived of in the academic versus New American poetry debate—that is, lesbian writing. Works such as "The Psychoanalysis of Edward the Dyke" and "A Woman Is Talking to Death" are as complex, subtle, and efficient as any literary productions of the last thirty years. Yet, unlike my audience, the readers she seeks are not going to identify with her texts *as readers first*, but as women, and often as lesbian women. Such an audience may not have a thorough sense of literary history as an important characteristic; in fact, it may have a sense of literature as exclusive and patriarchal. Thus it's necessary for Grahn's pieces to appear artless, an effect she achieves through such devices as enjambment and variable capitalization. The only formal technique she ever foregrounds is parallel construction, yet the linguistic play in the texts seems limitless. Grahn's poetry is experiencing some fashion because it's directly related to a conscious social movement, and because many people, men as well as women, are just now coming to terms with what the existence of a lesbian community really means in our lives. But does it make sense to ask if it can have "popular appeal"? The important thing is that it does have value for its community, extraordinary value. The writing that has been associated with such magazines as *This*, *Hills*, *Roof*, *L=A=N=G=U=A=G=E*, *Tottel's Poetics Journal*, *A Hundred Posters*, *QU*, *Tuumba Press*, and *The Figures Press*, much of which has been in prose forms, is no less a community.

Larry McCaffery: How does this writer/audience relationship affect your own situation?

RS: The community that I'm a part of and interested in is an audience with very distinct social characteristics: overeducated, underemployed people in major urban areas. To some degree the New American poetries are the literature of major urban areas, whereas academic poetry is much more the writing of the interior in this country, the college towns, away from the coasts. As political scientists, such as Erik Olin Wright or Nicos Poulantzas, have noted, a major characteristic of these new classes arising in urban environments has been an inability to acknowledge its own collective existence, to know its own name. Thus even a political movement initiated by this group which has a clear demographic base, such as tenant's rights, tends to be posed in issue-centered terms: rent control. Likewise, many "neo-petit bourgeois" renters will vote against such issues, because they do not identify with this collectivity. So it's not surprising that more than one type of poetry is related to the middle strata, reflecting real differences that exist within it. My own totally partisan sense of this is that just this critique of the Subject—the recognition of the "I" as a discontinuous and overdetermined ideological construct, a social entity, and the *investigation of the individual* that such a recognition makes necessary— is the most direct path of that "absent name."

SG: Aren't you ever tempted, though, to create the kinds of works that would cut across these audience barriers, allow you to appear on "The Johnny Carson Show" and make a fortune?

RS: If I were interested in writing for the mass audience I would write for television or the cinema. This whole issue is a very tricky area: there is a great desire on the part of many writers to speak plainly to everybody. But "speaking plainly" is just one code of stylistic density among many others. There is no such thing as "natural language"; there are only *learned languages*. And there is no such thing as naturalism in literature. It, too, is simply an affected style. At the same time, there is no such thing as "simple individuals."

SG: Legend has it that you once stood on a streetcorner in San Francisco reading *Ketjak* to passersby. But *Ketjak* is an awfully difficult, complex work, and I suspect that most of your audience must have thought you were as crazy as most of the other street readers I've seen in San Francisco. I also know that you've been very active, both professionally and informally, in Bay Area community action. Don't you see a paradox at work here between your aesthetics—your work as an "experimental" poet—and your political desire to reach out to and communicate with the working class?

RS: My politics and my aesthetics are essentially different faces of the same argument. When I was editing *The Tenderloin Times* I would not use articles with the same textual characteristics as *Ketjak* or *Tjanting*, because they would not reach the audience I was trying to address. My poetic forms are addressed to very specific people who are *more easily addressed* in those forms. In terms of the situation surrounding that streetcorner reading of *Ketjak*: the book is so thoroughly involved with street language and found language, and that corner is where all the street preachers come to harangue in San Francisco, that my reading was a way of returning that language to its source. Part of the semiotics of that street corner is the question of the sanity of a given person reading aloud from a book—a question that is ostensibly taken care of by putting that person into a coffee house in a neighborhood near a college. I got some very interesting and positive responses from people passing by who not only don't usually listen to literature but who, listening to me, had no idea they *were* listening to literature. I'm glad I did it, even though I lost my voice and wound up spitting blood on the last few pages since it took four and a half hours to read the whole thing.

SG: Do you see your work and that of the other new prose poets as being an effort to reinvent the novel, to put it out of its misery after all its death agonies?

RS: The work of Barrett Watten, Charles Bernstein, Lyn Hejinian, Bob Perelman, Carla Harryman, myself and others is not so much reinventing the novel as taking the lessons of literature learned in the realm of poetry and, from these, developing a form that won't so much replace fiction as be capable of occupying the *space* of the novel, both in terms of size and in the concerns it can approach, explore, and represent. The great advantage of the novel, especially in the nineteenth century and in the first part of the twentieth, was that it was a genre *without conventions*. This put on the individual all of the responsibility to develop the work in whatever way it was going to be, whether *Tristram Shandy* or *Moby-Dick*. Total freedom means total responsibility. But at a certain point—the rise of genre fiction, or gothic fiction, or whatever—the question of convention in the novel became an important consideration. As the novel has become more and more related to the rise of publishing companies within the framework of corporate capital (at least it used to be this way—I think this is breaking down in our time), the conventionality of the novel has made it a restrictive form, limiting in the same way as the sonnet. And that problematizes it as a useful form. Of course, modernist novelists recognized this and have attempted to solve the problem of conventionality and how to represent the real world. But this problem is extraordinarily difficult, as everyone who has tackled it has repeatedly demonstrated.

SG: Doesn't this problem with conventionality arise in poetry as well?

RS: I'd say that what can be done now in terms of poetry is similarly problematic. Donald Wesling likes to argue that, since the rise of modernism, poetry that has undergone this revolution has adopted three forms: the dramatic monologue, the prose poem, and free verse. These are not necessarily three distinct genres, nor are they necessarily experienced in the same order in the same country. In these terms, you can talk about Japanese poetry or American poetry or French poetry. The question is, having done *that*, what is there left to do? Especially if, for example, it seems as if the whole question of free verse has come to its logical conclusion in the range of work between Olson and Creeley and Ed Dorn, on the one hand, and Ted Berrigan and Frank O'Hara on the other. Personally, I'd also argue that the dramatic monologue reaches its apotheosis with Browning and has not been useful since.

SG: Obviously, that leaves the prose poem as the one vehicle that has not been fully exhausted, especially the *long* prose poem.

RS: Yes, at least within the framework Wesling proposes, which doesn't seem to account for performance work, collaborations, sound texts, and concrete or visual poetry. Historically, the prose poem, except for Lautréamont and a very few others, has been a short form. But there is no inherent reason for this! The individual sections of Bertrand's *Gaspard de la Nuit* may be brief, yet the volume as a whole is a single work, almost a novel composed of verbal still lifes. Naming the form, Baudelaire exploited it merely to urbanize the short lyric. The prose poem has not been exhausted by any means—far from it—and has the potential to occupy the territory of the novel without the limitations of the novel: its conventions of character, plot, and dialogue. Virtually any undergraduate literature major in America can churn out passably mediocre fiction because it is so anchored in these conventions. But to attempt a poem is to confront language and reality, and the interventions each makes on the other. Often the prose poem has been misused, not explored in terms of its own possible dynamics but simply appropriated as a means of perpetuating a dying genre. In the hands of Robert Bly, prose poems are dramatic monologues, nothing more.

LM: Length here seems to be an important prerequisite if the prose poets want to be ambitious in the ways that novelists traditionally have been.

RS: Yes, it's almost the relationship of quantity: you can do something in 300 pages that you simply can't do in 30 lines. This question of scale is more than a matter of "bigness"; in terms of what can go on in a work, the number of elements that can be brought into play, the complexity of the relationships between elements, all these things are infinitely more possible in the longer forms.

LM: Do you recall what prompted you to begin *Ketjak?* Your other early works are clearly poems, even if not traditional in format, but *Ketjak* . . .

RS: Right, those early texts were pieces that other poets would have no difficulty identifying as poetry. *Ketjak* and *Tjanting* have prompted people to come up and say, "Why do you call these things poems?" But for me there was never a sense of breaking away from poetry. *Ketjak*, which in many respects marks my adulthood as a writer, was the next step in my work *as a poet*, not a step away. The concept for *Ketjak* had been in my mind for at least a year, but I didn't know how to proceed with it. I was setting down in my notebooks various ideas that might be worked out subsequently. One of these lines of thought was about structure in terms of ways that I had extrapolated from listening to various types of music. "Ketjak" itself is a musical form— it's the Balinese version of the Ramayana myth, with as many as two hundred singers. It's essentially a choral form, and I was interested in the concept of cumulative effort. There was also the music of Steve Reich, who had just performed *Drumming* in San Francisco at the Asian Art Museum. Reich's work is based on repetition. *Drumming* utilizes large, austere, repetitious structures—"phase structures," he calls them— that are based on the repetition of simple elements. These structures cause the work to have a mechanism of proceeding, going from beginning to end. If you're not writing narratively or argumentatively, the whole question of beginning and ending and how to proceed in a work are by no means trivial questions. Reich's work was a model that proposed an approach to this issue that was different from any I was familiar with.

LM: Could you explain how the structural basis of Reich's music relate to *Ketjak?*

RS: Reich separates the interior content of the work from an exterior form. His whole approach is very different from a notion that all romantic poets have tended to possess. From Wordsworth to Olson, they asserted that "form is never more than an extension of content." While this idea liberated the poem from demonstrating a purely convention-seeking and closed conception of structure (the high-bourgeois ideology that Pope satirically exposed and yet remained trapped within) and made possible a speech-based poetics that it has taken a century and a half to exhaust, it nevertheless subsumed one axis of meaning (form) to another (content). This is not an accurate account of the function of language within experience. Language intervenes and edits the real in our daily lives. Reich's work, particularly the early tape pieces of the 1960s, exposes this distortion by artificially (in the best sense of that word) separating the two dimensions. In *Come Out*, Reich took the tape of a sentence spoken by a nineteen-year-old charged with homicide during the 1964 Harlem riots from a description of this person's beating at the precinct station, focusing on the words "come out to show them." The syntax of the host sentence is quite interesting: "I had to, like, open the bruise up and let some of the bruised blood come out to show them." But the procedures to which Reich subjects the phrase have nothing to do with that structure. The phrase is recorded in two channels and then played so that one gradually moves ahead of the other, until eight "voices" are attained. The result has the texture of a million birds beating their wings and, to my ear, is very similar to the effect of the Balinese ketjak. *Ketjak* is structured so that every paragraph has twice as many sentences as the previous paragraph, with every other sentence being a repetition of the sentences (in exactly the same order) from the previous paragraph. One way to think of *Ketjak* is to imagine putting one sentence on one square of a checkerboard, two on the next, four on the next, and so forth. The fact that repetitions occur creates a sense of cohesion and continuity— you are continually returned to a specific place, and you begin to expect this. This repetition is generic rhyme, a system for setting up readerly quantifications throughout the text. I also found that I could focus attention on the sentences themselves, rather than only on larger structures. This was something that I did not anticipate; it happened in the process of writing. But I had been looking for something like this as early as 1968—focusing attention on the *present*, rather than on larger structures.

SG: By "larger structures" I assume you mean things like character and plot in the traditional sense.

RS: Exactly. A work built around those structures ensures that the reader's attention is always going to be defused by having to pay attention to what was going on three pages earlier and having to wonder what will be occurring four pages from now. This tends to decenter the consciousness and focus of the reader so that she is not experiencing the "presentness" in the work. This diffusion violates my experience of the world. Even though I am often thinking about a whole series of things and people, those thoughts occur continuously *in the present*. There is no such thing as a continuous past, such as the aorist tense of fiction, which *is* a fiction—that tense is precisely what *is* fictive about fiction. The repetition factor of *Ketjak* breaks up the context of those "old" sentences and also puts the new sentences into contexts other than those in which they were originally conceived. I was fairly careful *not* to have too many sentences that followed from those immediately preceding. This was relatively simple, since very often as I was creating *Ketjak*—which took five months—there would be a month or two between the writing of one sentence and the next. It is very difficult, though, to write continuously from that perspective, so this whole process forced me to direct my attention *inward*, to focus on the *sentence*. And it seemed to work.

LM: We've been discussing *Ketjak's* form, your attention to the sentences, the attempt to keep the reader focused on the present. What about the so-called content of the book? In some respects *Ketjak* seems a kind of interiorized novel, presenting a portrait of life and language in the mid-1970s. What were your intentions in this regard? Or were you not much concerned with content?

RS: *Ketjak* is very content centered. It has been pointed out to me by various other people that there is a great deal of "dailiness," a real taste for the humble, in *Ketjak*. That sense was very important to me, and still is; it was something I had not been able to approach using a speech-based metaphor for the text. I was recently reading a Viktor Shklovsky essay on Vasilii Rozanov called "Plotless Literature" in which he talks about Rozanov's use of "plotlessness" in Russia eighty years ago. Shklovsky says this approach was totally consistent with an interest in what he calls "objects in the kitchen." I, too, have some sense of the importance of objects in the kitchen. I don't want to subscribe to the theory of epiphanies in literature here, but I do feel that what has taken on many of the most important characteristics, emotionally, for people in our time are the objects for which we have no names, or those for which we have no particular symbolic importance. A shoelace would be an example of such an object; so would closets, and certain musical instruments. The dobro was a very consciously chosen figure in *Ketjak* simply because I know of no other writing that mentions it. The sentence in which the dobro appears has to do with communal living on a houseboat on the bay in Marin County; this is a form of American life not much acknowledged by the language of public institutions, which includes creative writing. Presenting these "ignored" areas of experience was and is of definite concern to me, and, in that sense *Ketjak* is extremely content oriented.

LM: Why is it that certain "contents" become ignored? Is it mainly a matter of convention, or do certain objects have a reason for being talked about over and over again?

RS: The question of what is appropriate content is mainly conventional. People tend to have things in the world that they are taught to view as meaningful. All the rest, of course, continue to exist in the world; they acquire meanings that often become the repositories of emotional responses, responses that at first glance may seem irrational but that are actually the consequence of societal input. We don't articulate our responses to these objects because we have not been preconditioned to recognize their contents. Exploring that territory seems to me to be far more important than producing another campus novel or a book about another failed love affair.

LM: Do you intend, then, to use these "kitchen objects" as objective correlatives, in Eliot's sense of objectifying inner emotional states?

RS: Not in the sense of objectifying inner emotional states. These items are indexes of contemporary American life in ways that serve as indexes for such responses in other people's lives.

SG: This raises an interesting issue: the nature and function of the articulating voice in your fiction and its relationship to you as Ron Silliman. Would you say that you appear in your works as a kind of character?

RS: No, I'd say that the voice in my works is the product of the language that appears there. The subject in *Ketjak* and *Tjanting* and the three poems that will eventually be published in *The Age of Huts* is a consequence of the types of language that appear in each work. Peter Yates, a composer and music theorist, argues that the "content" in music is actually a function of aesthetic consistency—that in any given work there is a "statistical average" of all the different things that are going on, which in contemporary music can be an awful lot. Even someone as discontinuous as John Cage, for example, nevertheless creates an identifiable tone in his works, a tone that is present even in a piece as decentered as "Empty Words." That sense of consistency, that summing up of all the kinds of layers that appear in each work, definitely has the sort of balance that I don't find far from what I would recognize as my own "voice." But I'm not attempting to give that voice a psychology in any traditional sense, an "address" in the sense of a Zip code. This voice is constituted through a lot of exterior information. One way these voices find their way into my work is through my use of found language. There are, for instance, some significant chunks of Willard Van Orman Quine, a person whom I disagree with almost entirely but whose mind I find fascinating. In *Ketjak* there's also a lot of advertising and street slang, none of which is exactly "me." As every advertising writer knows, whatever you have read you have thought. In that sense those exterior voices do participate in creating that larger voice. "The words are my life," says Louis Zukofsky, and to that extent my works are indeed autobiographical.

LM: What interests you, from a formal standpoint, in found language? Is this the same impulse that made Braque and Picasso place objects from the world into their collages?

RS: I don't think so. I've heard my work described by David Antin and others as "collage technique," but I've always felt uncomfortable with that designation. In the traditional work of the collage there has never been much interest in examining and then *returning the interest in those objects back into the world in which they occur.* Usually there's not a political or critical usage of these objects, whereas I am very much concerned to bring out those aspects.

SG: Could you give an example of what you mean by the "political and critical uses" of these found objects—these objects being the words themselves, I assume?

RS: Sure. A good example would be technical jargons. The law is a classical example of a jargon, suggesting that all words can be purged of connotations—and it illustrates the fallacy of this suggestion. The different interpretations of the Supreme Court from one generation to the next, which are significantly based on different political pressures at any given period of time, have a lot to do with the fact that in 1980, say, certain words have very different connotations than they did in 1954 or 1832. The entire history of the so-called immutable laws of our nation is based on precisely that denotative fallacy. Professional jargons are often both euphemistic and open about their authoritarianism when looked at closely for the values in the language. The California Department of Corrections had over 8,000 forms in its bureaucracy in the mid-'70s, only one of which—the San Quentin execution document—actually used the word *prisoner.* That's one end of the scale. The other might be the subtext of the personnel interviewer's closing line, "We will be happy to keep you in mind." Both usages display one-sided power relationships and the social capacity of the language user to manipulate and encode reality. In my work I try to choose sentences that unveil these values. I'm also very interested in the way street language creates neologisms. Ghetto slang represents a dispute over who gets to create meanings in the society. When the counterculture of the '60s was decisively beaten, its elaborate anti-institutional vocabulary very quickly appeared dated, even quaint. The advantage of the forms I've used is that no types of language are ostensibly prohibited because the constraints of character, plot, and setting do not apply.

LM: At what point did the titles "Ketjak" and "Tjanting" suggest themselves?

RS: In the case of *Ketjak,* I knew the musical form several years before writing that book, and my interest in the form had a great deal of intensity at various points. But the title did not immediately attach itself to the text. With *Tjanting* I was already working with the text when I came across the instrument tjanting, which is a writing implement in batik, despite what it sounds like aurally. Roughly six weeks into what would be the three years of writing that work, I came across this instrument; the absolute minute I saw it and learned its name, I knew exactly what the title of my work would be and was ecstatic all afternoon. I have problems with my titles, as all authors do, because titles are remarkably ambiguous in terms of their relationships to the text as a whole. I agree with Walter Benjamin's distinction between captions and titles—captions *penetrate* a text and highlight certain elements, while titles *name the whole.* But the issue is very ambiguous. Think of the radically different implications of using "He Do the Police in Different Voices" and "The Waste Land" as the title of Eliot's poem.

SG: Could you discuss the minute-by-minute processes that occur when you're creating a highly formalized work like *Ketjak* or *Tjanting?*

RS: The specifics differ substantially from piece to piece. At the moment, I'm working on two sections of *The Alphabet,* for which I'm not only using different procedures and notebooks, but even different pens. In the case of *Tjanting,* which was not begun until after the conclusion of *The Age of Huts,* the initial impulse centered on a few very simple ideas. In *Ketjak,* three years earlier, I had developed a paragraph form that both repeated and expanded, giving me a great deal of freedom and still allowing a strong sense of cohesiveness. I felt sure that the simple doubling of sentences from paragraph to paragraph was not the limit of that idea, since, in the most literary sense, it was nothing less than rhyme. I also had a desire to see if I could come up with bipolar structure, something that would pull the poem back and forth, a formal analogy for both struggle and dialectics. One possibility was to begin with two parallel paragraphs, so that the first paragraph would be repeated and expanded in all ensuing even-numbered ones. I was aware of the Fibonacci series, in which each item in the sequence is the sum of the two previous numbers. I was also quite conscious of, and attracted to, the fact that this system is the numerical pattern most often found in nature. It also has the advantage of having the number one for the first two items in the series: 1, 1, 2, 3, 5, 8, 13, 21, 34, 55, 89, 144, etc. Using each figure to determine the number of

sentences in a paragraph gave me the beginning parallel structure (1, 1)
I was seeking plus a progressional asymmetric form that would none-
theless be sensed as coherent by a reader. Unlike *Ketjak*, where development from one occurrence of a sentence to the next is minimal,
I took a device from "2197," one of the works in *The Age of Huts*, in
which a recurring sentence is radically rewritten so as to appear distorted, broken, artificial. In both works I sought a means of revealing
how even the clearest of sentences, the most "inevitable" of logics,
was no less a Frankensteinian construction. In "2197" this was accom-
plished by superimposing the vocabulary of one sentence onto the
syntax of another, while in *Tjanting* the recurrent sentences devour
themselves. For *Tjanting* I had a lined accounting notebook in which
I intended to put together the final "correct" copy, but I felt that it
was too large to carry around with me and write wherever I went, as
has always been my practice. I decided to use a tiny pocket journal
that Lyn Hejinian had given me for the initial collection of sentences,
which were to be transferred, *not* in their original order, to the larger
book. Once I made these decisions, all of which preceded the writing
and which took ten months to figure out, I was able to begin.

SG: Do you find such highly formalized structure inhibiting? Or did
it liberate you by opening a predetermined "space" that you are free
to fill?

RS: Once I had made those initial decisions, I ceased to be concerned
with form except insofar as it might exist at the level of syntax or
prosody within the individual sentences, so I hardly felt constricted. I
am *not* a formalist. For twenty-one months, the process of *Tjanting*
consisted of writing individual sentences, as they occurred to me or as
I found them, in a series of pocket notebooks, at work, on the bus,
before breakfast, at political meetings or readings or concerts, whenever,
and once every couple of days or week I would sit down for a more
extended period, up to five or six hours, and integrate these sentences
into the text, while rewriting or deconstructing the recurrent sentences
as they came up. Often when I was working in the larger journal new
material would be generated in response to everything I was working
with. In fact, one of the advantages of this method is that the writer
is dealing with so many things simultaneously that the opportunities
to see and exploit possible connections, and to develop the writing in
any number of areas, are vast. But at any given moment, the process
is one of writing by pen in a notebook, looking very hard at an individual sentence or phrase or word, examining what it might be saying,
how it might be saying it, considering its social implications, its place
in the text, the prosody, what other sentences and phrases might lead
into it, even the physical shape and color of the individual letters, or

how the ink dries into the grain of the paper. For me, the pleasure of writing is absolutely fixed within the localness of this context. I want the reader to share that aspect of this experience, which is why the focus is so heavily placed on the individual sentence. If the sentences don't "follow" or build abstractions, such as character or plot, to carry the attention away from what is in front of the reader, there is no place to go but into the present, the real.

SG: Despite the absence of narrative structures, the relationship between one sentence and the next in your text is obviously not accidental. But the importance of this relationship, even the *nature* of the relationship, seems to vary.

RS: Yes, and that's an important point. In *Ketjak* I was learning how to separate sentences out for the first time, so there was very little sense of anaphoric referral between one sentence and the next, minimal conscious plays from one to the next. In *Tjanting* there is an awful lot of that kind of in-structuring going on. For example, I might have one sentence referring to a sexual experience and the next will have to do with turning on a pilot light. In determining what sentence to place where, these sorts of relationships figured heavily. The whole procedure is very multilayered. I've heard my writing described as based on chance techniques, but I don't work that way. It's not that I want to disparage the ability of chance techniques as a method of disrupting the habits of the ego on the text, but on the other hand this approach has a tendency, if used over a long period of time, to lead to works without shape. And I'm extremely interested in developing the sense of shape. It's not an accident that both *Tjanting* and *Ketjak* begin with short paragraphs and end with long ones.

LM: Earlier you mentioned your lack of interest in character and plot. Your work seems to question the basic assumptions on which these notions are based, but you seem to be coming at this issue from a different perspective than metafictionists such as Coover, Barth, and Federman.

RS: Yes, we share some assumptions, but I also see metafiction as being ultimately a compromise in this regard. While it tries to solve many of the same problems that today's poets are confronting, it still does so from the perspective of character and narrative. This is why Kathy Acker's works are so radically different from metafiction as such. Metafiction hardly ever addresses the question, "Is the character a construct?" or "To what degree is a character a construct?" Even in fragmenting things, metafictionists still have to rely on that final appeal back to the level that is ultimately a compromise, ignoring, among other things, the fact that people experience their lives discontinuously. This is something that, to my mind, forever compromises the work of

Samuel Beckett—his sentences are wonderful, but his works are not. To have a character at all is very seldom to critique the idea of "What is a person?" If the words are my life, and if all of the meanings of the words and the ways I receive them are social and derive from social sources—from family, friends, jobs, education, the welfare office, all those inputs—exactly at what point do I get to be the autonomous, continuous person who can be the guilty and unreliable narrator of most fiction, including metafiction? Such individuals do not exist in life and, accordingly, become a problematic basis for fiction.

SG: You mentioned Reich as proposing a kind of structural model for *Ketjak*. Are any other artists working in this area?

RS: Several. Beyond the "pattern-music" composers, such as Phil Glass or Terry Riley, is William Duckworth. "The Time Curved Preludes" is totally based on the Fibonacci number series. A sculptor named Mario Merz also does works based on it. There's even a newsletter of artists, mostly painters and musicians, published by the Fibonacci Association of San Jose. Duckworth's use of these ideas, in particular, seems close to what I am doing, in that he often uses the series to signify or generate quantity.

LM: Several writers I know also use various forms of arbitrary structural devices—people like Abish, Federman, Steve Katz, Ron Sukenick. What sorts of things cause you to be attracted to this approach—and why did you choose the specific approaches on which you rely?

RS: I was attracted to the Fibonacci series because it's one that occurs in nature. The relationships within the curve of a mollusk shell and the placement of leaves around a branch are both Fibonacci structures. These are forms that look extremely simple, elegant, and almost accidental in their grace. The Fibonacci series proposes a relationship to mathematics as pure abstraction and to the idea that nature and mathematics are not separate. It also has the ability to generate spatial relationships, quantitative relationships that are shapely and perceptible from one paragraph to the next. I was looking recently at the number of prime numbers under 10,000; there are 1229—itself a prime number, which is not an accident. Yet the relationship between the prime numbers is such that there is very little difference between one prime number and the next, particularly when you get up into the middle thousands. There is no way to develop a good-looking work out of these prime-number relationships, no way I could create a pleasing work out of *that* arbitrary structure—and neither could Walter Abish or Steve Katz—without submitting it to some other kind of operation that would knock out a lot of the prime numbers so that you could develop some sense of appropriate shape. Without some other operation, a sense of scale is lost. And scale, at least in my work, is essential in creating an impression of progress, movement, development. Scale motivates the reader. A paragraph that has 9907 sentences and another that would have 9923 will not be perceived as being smaller and larger. This is an important consideration, especially when using non-narrative structures. I should admit that I almost flunked math in high school, so I don't propose myself as a mathematician. I tend to appropriate things as I need them.

LM: Obviously, in a fundamental sense, the structural conventions on which you based *Ketjak* and *Tjanting* are no more artificial than the conventions of realistic fiction. The shapes that emerge are different, and may serve different functions, but they're all conventional.

RS: Right. In terms of arbitrariness, *all* works begin, end, and proceed in terms of conventions. Of course, there's nothing *wrong* with conventions per se, whether or not we're talking about those of the first-person novel, the organic forms of Charles Olson or Wordworth's *Prelude,* or Whitman's free verse or purely closed forms. The real question is whether the writer is proposing value or simply operating from the thoughtlessness of lazy habit. If there is historical antecedent to the kinds of works that I write, it would have to be something like the sonnet, a closed form on a much smaller scale.

SG: Are there any other contemporary writers you especially admire or feel you have something in common with?

RS: A lot. Charles Bernstein, Lyn Hejinian, Barrett Watten, Bob Perelman, Kit Robinson, and Rae Armantrout immediately come to mind as people who for many years have had something important to teach me. Others I might mention in this regard are Robert Grenier, Bruce Andrews, Carla Harryman, Allen Bernheimer, and Kathy Acker. If there is one book that made me feel as I was reading it that all the effort everybody had been exerting for over a decade was totally worth it, Hejinian's *My Life* is that book. But there are so many others. I've been editing an anthology of "my kind of writing," entitled *In the American Tree,* for Ross Erikson's New Wilderness Poetics Series. That book will contain prose, poetry, and criticism of thirty-nine writers. It could easily have been twice as many. This is a fine time for writing in America. *A decentralized literature has a million important tasks.* Everyone seems to be hard at work.

Anne de Brunhoff

An Interview with

Edmund White

Edmund White's first novel, *Forgetting Elena* (1973), had the sort of critical reception a writer might dream of (among numerous accolades was one from Vladimir Nabokov, who called it the contemporary American novel he admired most). Written in an elusive, elliptical style, bare of metaphor, *Forgetting Elena* is a hallucinogenic novel, part science fiction, part detective story, part comedy of manners. The work exudes mystery—the mystery of human desires and motives, the mystery of the signs and symbols we use to communicate those desires. This sense of mystery also permeates White's second novel, *Nocturnes for the King of Naples* (1978), but there it is developed through a prose style that is altogether different. Lush, baroque, and marked by elaborate and complex metaphor, *Nocturnes* is as richly textured and otherworldly as a medieval allegory. *A Boy's Own Story* (1982) shows still another transformation of White's style. In this book, loosely based on White's own adolescent experiences during the 1950s, the prose has a less ornamental quality and the narrative proceeds in a more straightforward, realistic fashion—characteristics that may help explain its popularity with a wider audience than White had previously enjoyed.

These transformations, as the following interview indicates, are self-consciously sought by White. Such dramatic alterations of style, narrative structure, and use of language result partly from his conviction that a writer must always begin anew, that in order for language to function it must be freshly conceived. Certainly there is also the element of play in White's stylistic changes—a willingness to experiment with the variety of forms that human expression can take, an appreciation for our restless, curious need to try on different masks, different personae. These changes of voice have been affected as well by White's evolving ideas about politics and about social and sexual contracts. As White well knows, to be an openly gay writer in today's society is to be thrust into a political arena—no less than personal liberty is at stake, as organizations across the country continue to campaign against homosexuality. White's first nonfiction book, *The Joy of Gay Sex* (1979, co-authored with Dr. Charles Silverstein), aimed both to demystify the experience for heterosexuals and to provide practical information for members of the gay community. To practice certain forms of intercourse in our society is not only a sexual act but a political one as well, and in this sense *The Joy of Gay Sex* has had an influence far beyond the usual sex manual. White's next nonfiction book, *States of Desire: Travels in Gay America* (1980), is more overtly political in its intent. As White traveled across the United States—meeting and interviewing men from a variety of backgrounds, experiencing what gay life is like in conservative cities as well as in its traditional enclaves such as New York and San Francisco—he came to deeper awarenesses about political and social disfranchisement and about how definitions of sexuality enter into civic as well as social contracts. Written in a journalistic style as a travelogue of his experiences, *States of Desire* forced White to develop a means of capturing people in brief character sketches and to present himself in the first person—techniques, as well as a kind of psychological exercise, that were to influence *A Boy's Own Story*.

These ongoing changes of style and voice made us feel a bit uncertain about the sort of man we would meet when, in May 1984, we huffed up the five flights of stairs to his Parisian apartment on the Ile St. Louis. As we waited on the ancient landing to catch our breath, we could hear opera music inside, and we could imagine White sitting in a smoking jacket and raising a jaded, ironic eyebrow—something out of *Nocturnes*. The man who opened the door was no Proustian neurasthenic aesthete but a warm, animated man who put us instantly at ease with his wit (which he frequently turned on himself) and his charm. While we got acquainted over lunch at a busy, family-style brasserie, White expressed his delight at being in Paris, freed temporarily from his teaching duties (he had won a Guggenheim Fellowship, which allowed him to finish his most recent novel, *Caracole* [1985]), and he sketched in some of the details about the Paris literary scene and about his personal background. White is a writer whose brilliance and articulateness are obvious even in casual conversation, but he was even more impressive when we returned to his apartment and the focus of our conversation became more literary and abstract. Not only does White have a wide-ranging view of all the arts, but he is able to discuss them with the passion and excitement of someone still making fresh discoveries.

Larry McCaffery: One hears a lot these days about "the gay sensibility." Is there such a thing?

Edmund White: I think there are *several* gay sensibilities, for gay people do not comprise a suprahistorical entity outside of history or politics. They are influenced by the culture around them, the way everybody else is. So, for example, to posit a "feminine sensibility" or a "French sensibility" or a "black sensibility" is irrational because it imagines that people exist outside of the historical conditions in which they live. It does seem to me there was and is a particular evolving gay sensibility in certain countries, within certain classes. But it's interesting that the most characteristic representatives of the gay sensibility of the *fin de siècle* culture of Europe were not gay—Huysmans in France and Aubrey Beardsley in England, for instance, neither of whom happened to be gay. In the same way, you could say that in the '30s and '40s there was a camp sensibility. But, again, not every major camp figure from that period was gay.

Sinda Gregory: Is there anything so clearcut that can be identified today in America? You indicate in *States of Desire* that you thought there was a change going on in the gay community, perhaps in response to gay lib . . .

EW: I don't know what it is now. Perhaps we're witnessing a reaction against "indirection." A writer like Genet is a classic case of gay indirection because he was always trying to attack a value system that had condemned him to the lowest rank by suggesting that such a system could be reversed. It's basically the Christian notion that the last shall come first. Genet develops the reversibility of values to the level of a metaphysical system that is incredibly beautiful. Now the sociological, historical, and political impulses behind that vision are changing, so probably the need to be that indirect is vanishing.

LM: Why aren't there more serious gay books being published today?

EW: In the mid-'70s there was a kind of enthusiasm for publishing lots of gay titles, but a lot of junk was brought out that didn't do very well, so now the number of gay books has fallen off for commercial reasons. Interestingly enough, gays represent a large part of the reading market for serious fiction. In America most readers are middle-aged Jewish heterosexual women who are college educated. After that, I suspect that gay men in their thirties or forties, also college educated, are the second-biggest market for fiction and literature. Maybe college students are a distant third. But gay readers aren't obliged to read only gay books. Like everybody else, they want to read the best books they can.

SG: The same sort of thing seemed to happen with women's fiction during the '70s—we had that glut of "feminine novels," usually victimization stories that publishers thought would go over well in the marketplace. But the "woman's novel" became a formula (probably much the same thing happened with gay fiction). It's time to move on to other dimensions of the woman's situation, explore things in different ways, deal with areas that have been overlooked.

EW: Exactly, and that's why Colette is so eternally fashionable: she was a woman who had a real life and a real *joie de vivre* and who was independent and who had a phase as a lesbian and a period as a performer, a mime artist, and she had these complicated love relationships with younger men, and so on. She had a lot of experiences that she writes about and she's perennially interesting. Much more interesting than the Marilyn Frenches of the world. With most gay fiction there remains a tremendous gap between actual gay experience and the gay fiction that's written about it. Most gay novels are still novels about coming out, including my own book *A Boy's Own Story*, but that situation has now been pretty thoroughly explored by gay writers. What gay people would *really* like, I suspect, is to read a rather sophisticated story about actual gay relationships. There are any number of very familiar, very real relationships between gay people that every gay person would instantly recognize, but these are rarely explored by gay writers.

SG: Your first novel, *Forgetting Elena*, was published in 1973, before the flood of gay fiction. Was one of the reasons it was accepted because it wasn't gay?

EW: Probably. All during the '60s I had been writing novels but *Forgetting Elena* was the first book I had written that wasn't gay. And it had a cold, icy, disciplined feeling about it that was very suited to the aesthetic spirit of New York City at that time, although it was repeatedly turned down (it went around to publishing houses for three years, from 1969 until 1972). Actually it was only finally published because Richard Howard intervened for it. He was the first writer I ever met. He guided my career for several years and is still a wonderful friend and mentor.

SG: When your narrator rejects Elena near the end of the book— was that a kind of symbolic rejection of heterosexuality?

EW: I never thought of it that way, but I'll also admit that I just wrote that novel not knowing what it meant exactly. I remember that Peggy Guggenheim was upset by his rejection of Elena and her death, and kept saying, "Why did you make her die?" I was confused and embarrassed by that question because I had never really thought about it. I felt very much in a trance when I wrote *Forgetting Elena*, so I never felt very responsible for the action, certainly not on any political or psychological level.

LM: *Forgetting Elena* has such a strange, charged atmosphere ("Kafka meets Henry James," Sinda has said)—were there any influences, literary or nonliterary, that affected the way that book was conceived?

EW: One interesting thing was that, then as now, I was reading a lot of Japanese literature. One of the books that had a big impact on me was a tenth-century court diary called *The Pillow Book of Sei Shonagon* written by a woman who was a Heian courtier. She was the ultimate aesthete in a society dedicated to judging everything from an aesthetic point of view—in other words, morality had been replaced by aesthetics. That aesthetic overlay to everything became central to *Forgetting Elena*. It was odd but there seemed to me a funny kind of interaction between my reading about this remote period and my experiences on Fire Island at the time. I was also very influenced by Susan Sontag's aesthetics when I was creating that book. In the introduction to *Against Interpretation* I seem to remember that she called a work of art a machine for creating sensation. That phrase haunted me. I was aware of manipulating readers without being aware of how I was doing it. There are a couple of other things worth mentioning about that book. The first artists I knew as an adolescent were abstract expressionists. I've always wondered, Why hasn't the idea of abstract expressionism been more fully embodied in literature? In a way, *Forgetting Elena* had a lot of the contentless push and pull of abstract expressionism. This was a lot more evident in its earlier versions. When the book came to Ann Freedgood at Random House it was nothing but these mysterious, floating incidents without any plot. It was she who insisted that I give it the form of a mystery story because she wanted a payoff. I made the changes she suggested, but in a sense I was violating my aesthetic notion for the book, the idea of creating these free-floating states full of dynamism. Imagine a painting by de Kooning in which you feel there is a tremendous amount of activity and surface flourish and interest in brushwork—that is, in "language" on the local level—and a feeling of a strange conception, but a conception *of what*? Of nothing, or only of art itself. That kind of verbal abstract expression is what I was interested in. I felt that Gertrude Stein had already explored the idea of creating nonsense in interesting and abstract forms, and I felt that approach seemed to be ultimately tiring to the reader because the reader, after all, will inevitably lose patience with such small compositional units. Better than juxtaposing words against words so that they would cancel each other out would be to juxtapose *scene against scene*, with the promise of a plot that didn't pay off. In other words, I would play upon the traditional novelistic expectations of the reader and would ultimately frustrate those expectations, thereby creating a machine for creating sensation, an abstract configuration that was dynamic, not static, but that was made up of the traditional building blocks of the novel (that is, scene, dialogue, character exchange, suspense, and so on) rather than, as Gertrude Stein had done, by having words cancelling out words.

LM: Other than Stein, were there any writers who were having an impact on your sensibility when you were starting out as a writer?

EW: Ronald Firbank, oddly enough, was and continues to be a writer I admire a lot and who has probably affected my own notions of fiction. There are two kinds of Ronald Firbanks: there's the one who seems to be a later expression of the *fin de siècle* spirit of Oscar Wilde—the campy, humorous, superficial, ornate writer he is usually taken to be. But there is a much more profound and deep, artistic side to Firbank in which he is comparable to Gertrude Stein, as he is a deep explorer of these same questions I've just been talking about. Americans are probably much more likely to see this side of Firbank than are the English, who are so complacent socially that they feel they can dismiss him (just as the French think of Colette as this writer their mother was always reading under the hairdryer, whereas Americans have no preoccupations about her place in society).

LM: Were you aware of the experimental fervor going on around you in the late '60s and '70s, the kind of aesthetic sensibility that was creating postmodernism and that seems relevant to the kinds of unusual structures your fiction favors?

EW: Sure, it was obvious that there was a spirit of experimentalism in the '60s that revolved around figures such as Coover, Barthelme, Gass, Wurlitzer. I was reading all those people and thinking about what they were doing. I even proposed a book to Farrar, Straus and Giroux during that period that would have been a study of them. It was an exciting period. Particularly Barthelme had a lot of flair and humor and dash. One of the things I felt, too, was that until then abstraction had always been rather *grey*. For instance, analytic cubism is grey. There's a totally arbitrary notion that what is abstract is cerebral, and what is cerebral should be grey (maybe because of the phrase *grey matter*). But at that period I was thinking, why can't abstractions be presented colorfully? In *Forgetting Elena* I could play with scarlets and hot pinks. Grimness is usually seen as an automatic bid for seriousness—people always take you *au sérieux* if you have a grim view of things.

LM: Could you talk a bit about the evolution of your style? Despite certain stylistic similarities (the use of the first-person narrator, an emphasis on lyricism in your prose, an eye for the surprising detail) all three of your novels are also very different. Have you been consciously writing in different styles?

EW: I read a remark once by Gide in which he said that he hoped that with each book he would lose the fans he had acquired with the previous one. This is certainly a foolhardy approach, since most critics want a writer to create a product that is easily recognizable. But to me it's more fun to keep exploring. I also remember once reading someone saying that in the twentieth century every serious writer with each book has invented not only a new novel but a new theory of the novel.

SG: Did writing your nonfiction study of gay life in America, *States of Desire*, influence the writing of *A Boy's Own Story*?

EW: Most definitely. In *States of Desire* I was creating *myself* as a first-person narrator for the first time, and that was something that had a direct bearing on what I was to do in *A Boy's Own Story*. *Forgetting Elena* and *Nocturnes for the King of Naples* had first-person narrators, but I thought of those narrators as being definite "characters" who in no way really resembled me. Obviously you're always using some part of yourself to fashion forth these narrators, but they both struck me as either exotic or funny. The first one, in *Elena*, is meant to be funny and the second exotic. Whereas I think of myself as a fairly straightforward and active person who tends to pursue others and make things happen (I have a deep anxiety that if *I* don't make something happen, then no one else will), the boy in *Nocturnes* is exactly the opposite: he is entirely passive, he's small, blond, pretty, and the world takes care of him. I remember once reading something by Rilke in his *Letters to a Young Poet* in which he says: Don't worry, the world is holding its hands beneath you, you won't fall. At the time, I thought, How absurd! The world isn't holding its hands underneath anybody— you must take care of yourself or disaster will be upon you. So in a way, *Nocturnes for the King of Naples* was an experiment in being somebody else, somebody who *does* trust the world, who is passive but seems to attract help and who always seems to land on his feet, somebody who seemed very foreign to my own experience. It was a kind of ventriloquism or acting, an impersonation of someone else. But with *States of Desire* I felt I had finally invented a first-person narrator who was closely related to me, who *was* me or some version.

The other effect that *States of Desire* had on my fiction writing was a smaller, more technical matter: it taught me how to do quick portraits of people. So I had learned how to characterize people quickly and I had learned how to be me in my work. With *A Boy's Own Story* a sufficient time had gone by since my adolescence that I could write about it from a new, different point of view. Some sort of relationship of attraction, even affection, existed between the I (the middle-aged narrator looking back at this adolescent self) and the boy himself—a relationship I call "the pederasty of autobiography."

LM: There's a passage in *Nocturnes* where your narrator says that to label our childhood as adults is probably always a falsification. Wasn't this distrust of using adult words to reconstruct childhood difficult to overcome in writing *A Boy's Own Story*?

EW: Yes, it was, and as a matter of fact I allude to that same notion in *A Boy's Own Story* when I mention that there is always a falsification of early experience by writing about it. On the one hand, you want to tell a story that has some coherence, some style, and some sense of well roundedness, and on the other you want to present some semblance of what the actuality was. Those impulses pull in different directions.

SG: That sounds like the old truth-beauty relationship. . . .

EW: Exactly. Truth and beauty are two opposed claims upon a writer at any moment. Beauty is all in favor of making a story that entertains, that's well formed, that's lively, in which there are recognizable causes and effects, in which there are decisive experiences, turning points, crucial scenes—a sequence of events that cohere to the Aristotelian notions of drama. That's what we call beauty. Then there's this other thing that we call truth which is completely elusive: there are no turning points in life, there are very few causes you can ever pinpoint, there are enormous gaps in one's memory, you are not a unitary character nor is your experience unity (in fact, you are an extremely fragmented person who becomes different in almost every situation). Some of these are issues or questions that I tried to expose and dramatize in *Forgetting Elena*. I chose what I thought was an extreme metaphor for this condition: amnesia. But my narrator is an embarrassed amnesiac who doesn't want to admit to anyone that he can't remember who he is, much less who they are; he is constantly molding himself on other people's expectations. He's a skillful faker. An extreme version of any kind of social interaction.

SG: You seem to have a deeply felt ambivalence about the process of molding and self-invention. That is, whereas in *Forgetting Elena* you seem to present this situation ironically and enjoy poking fun at it, in your other books you present the necessity (especially in gay life) of constant self-invention more sympathetically. I sense both derision and sympathy in your attitude, and I'm reminded of the passage in *States of Desire* where you say of gay life that "there is an obligatory existentialism forced on people who must constantly invent themselves."

EW: Writers usually write best about things they feel deeply about but also deeply *ambivalent* about. For instance, in her essay on camp Susan Sontag said that the only reason she was able to isolate it as a phenomenon was that she felt so deeply ambivalent about it. On the one hand, she, too, liked camp, but on the other she felt repelled by the whole aesthetic. Because she was of two minds about it, she was able to write about it with great feeling. In my case, particularly in my late twenties, I became obsessed with the question of sincerity, and this obsession is reflected in *Forgetting Elena*. Piaget talks about the different stages that children go through that get resolved on some higher level; it's not as though they find an answer to a particular question, they just stop asking that question, it's no longer relevant to them. Probably there are different Piaget stages that go on throughout people's lives; between the ages of twenty-five and thirty people often become obsessed with questions of sincerity and authenticity which later seem juvenile or uninteresting. *Forgetting Elena* was ultimately born out of that obsession, which I no longer feel or which I think needs to be examined on different levels.

LM: You seem to have largely abandoned the use of a heavily ironic tone in your work since *Forgetting Elena,* a tone I take it that gays have often employed as a mean of protection, of distancing themselves from painful situations. Has this move away from irony anything to do with the sense you mention in *States of Desire* that "my friends were so ironic that they never knew whether they were serious or not"?

EW: F. R. Leavis said that when he was at school there was a group of young men who were ceaselessly ironic, but that they used irony in order to disguise from themselves whether they were truly serious or not about anything. That sort of attitude can be harmful, both personally and artistically. Irony seems to be a very juvenile dodge, and it's one of those modes or themes in modernism that I find utterly tiresome. Another tiresome, perennially avant-garde question dithers over the border between life and art. After all, Pirandello explored that issue to everyone's satisfaction seventy years ago. When is it to end? Is it really interesting? To me the Japanese, who very early on realized this was a dull question, have a much more mature understanding that art *is* artifice and life is life and a confusion of the two is puerile.

SG: Why did you decide to tell your story as an autobiographical *novel* in *A Boy's Own Story* rather than as a straight autobiography?

EW: Perhaps an *autobiographie romancée* is more modest? One only wants to read the "real" autobiography of somebody who is interesting or famous, or who is old and has done something with his life. Second, by calling the book a novel and thinking about it as a novel, I felt obliged to render fully experiences that one only alludes to in an autobiography. Somebody who is really famous can say, "So in that year I discovered the double helix" or something like that, and everybody knows what that is and he's said enough. Calling a work a novel places one under the obligation to paint the scene more vividly.

LM: Could you talk a bit about the kinds of changes you made in developing the *novel* of your life, the nature of the aesthetic choices you made?

EW: The most basic change I made for aesthetic reasons was to make the book *more representative*, more normal, less crazy and eccentric than my own life really was. My family is certainly much more bizarre than the family presented in *A Boy's Own Story*. For instance, the boy there is much dimmer, less perceptive and precocious than I think I was at his age, and less sexually aggressive as well. And certainly the character based on my mother is a lot less interesting and complicated than my real mother, who did have that lucid, neurotic side I describe, but she is also an expert on mongolism and ran a clinic for the retarded at Cook County Hospital in Chicago; she published extensively on this subject and to this day she is writing monographs in the field. So she was a much more complicated, interesting person than in the novel. Of all the characters, I would say that the father is closest to reality.

LM: The figure of the father is important in all your books, but especially in *Nocturnes* and *A Boy's Own Story*, so much so that we assumed your own relationship to your father has been something you have been coming to grips with in your fiction. Has it been difficult to write about your father?

EW: Sometimes very much so. But especially in *A Boy's Own Story* my father was very present for me because he had just died. Really, it was his death that triggered my writing that book. Like the character in the book, he smoked cigars, and I remember being in a taxi maybe six months after his death, and the taxi driver was smoking a cigar, and I found myself bursting into tears. I thought to myself, My father frightened everybody and was a big, important, well-known man; but within another twenty years there will be no one alive who even knew him. It struck me very powerfully that he, who was so present and bristling—so that people always felt he was sucking all the air out of the room—now was no more present than his smell of tobacco. So, yes, it *was* difficult to write about him, difficult not to romanticize, glorify him, make him richer or more powerful, bigger or worse than he was. In *A Boy's Own Story* I wanted to be very honest, to keep him exactly as he was so that he would survive, not to mythologize him.

SG: Whereas in *Nocturnes* the father figure seems a very mythic figure indeed.

EW: He was very much so in *Nocturnes*, but he was only based on certain sides of my real father. There was a kind of Don Juan, playboy side to my father that I obviously built up and made a big thing out of in that book, but there were other models as well.

SG: Any thoughts on why you developed the mythological version before the realistic one?

EW: Sometimes people have to get the mythological aspects of their experiences out of the way before they can deal with the reality of them. Many gay men have a fantasy about having an affair with their fathers; it seems to be a persistent but seldom mentioned theme. But if you become intimate with gay men you find that many of us have had this fantasy (sometimes it gets transferred to an uncle or an older brother, but it tends to stay within the family). In *Nocturnes* the boy gets to play out his fantasy, not with the father but with someone who saves him from his father. The boy in *A Boy's Own Story* has this persistent fantasy that there will be a wonderful, snowy-haired English lord who will come and save him from his father; something like that actually happens in *Nocturnes*. In a way you could say that *Nocturnes* is a gay fantasy, while *A Boy's Own Story* is a gay reality.

SG: I was struck by the fact that although *A Boy's Own Story* is about growing up *gay*, the kinds of events that occur are the same sorts of things that all adolescents (including girls) go through; that sense of powerlessness, the compensating fantasies, the painful and exhilarating adolescent eroticism.

EW: This sharing of experience is always a great surprise for a writer; he feels he's writing this very peculiar stuff, and he's invented the most *crazy* thing he can imagine to put down on the page, so that his heart is pounding when he writes it—and that's precisely the passage that people identify with.

SG: The last scene, where the boy betrays that musician, was very powerful, and I especially admired it since it seemed so clear eyed in its depiction of an ugly, mean-spirited act. Since you obviously identified with the boy and since your presentation of him throughout is basically sympathetic, wasn't that a difficult scene for you to write?

EW: I felt both frightened and gleeful when I was writing that scene because I kept asking myself whether or not I was going to do it. I was very aware that the boy was sympathetic, and I knew I would be alienating so many readers by ending the novel that way—especially gay readers, who sometimes still have an apologist's attitude toward gay fiction. There's been a kind of neo-Stalinist aesthetic at work in gay literary circles demanding a "positive role model," whatever that is. To have my boy turn out so creepy seemed to be a way of alienating some gay commissars. Nevertheless, I felt that the ending made sense, even from a political point of view. You can't show somebody in a deforming period, like the 1950s in America, and then show him as happy, healthy, the perfect role model. Doesn't it make more sense to show that a deforming period deforms people? I felt that, once I had written the end of the book, I had succeeded in presenting a truth about that deformation that would have been missing if I had left it out. There is a kind of power-madness in the victim. If you are victimized, you want revenge, and you have these feelings of persecution *and* grandeur. Technically, that last scene was also important because I wanted a way to end the book, which was something of a problem. I still feel that the book is not well formed, that it's too episodic, not satisfying on the level of structure. Having gotten as far as I did, and knowing that the materials I had were more or less what I was stuck with—these shards, these chapters that didn't really flow together or add up to a whole—I very much wanted to give the book a sense of an ending. It occurred to me that, having been up until then reflective and seldom reporting direct action or dialogue, if I suddenly reversed myself and went into a straightforward description of action and used *lots* of dialogue, it would give a quickening feeling, a sense of shifting into a new key. I also could see that it would be a neat, nasty trick to play on the reader to make him identify with a character who becomes a monster, so that the reader must experience the monster within himself. Because we all do have one.

LM: When you say that you're not satisfied with the structure of *A Boy's Own Story*, doesn't that sense derive from trying to force unshapely reality into a structure it resists?

EW: It's that pull and tug of truth and beauty again. I do know that, since *Nocturnes* was almost completely imagined, it seems to have a better form because I wasn't distracted by trying to render real experiences, as in *A Boy's Own Story*. I do feel, though, that what *A Boy's Own Story* loses in formal coherence, it gains in vibrancy from the pleasure of describing things that really happened. It's more direct, simple communication, which seemed appropriate to the subject.

LM: People have described your books in musical terms. Do you think that way?

EW: I love music, it's my favorite art, and I like to think that I have a musical sense of composition. Now when I encounter somebody like Kundera, who really does have a musical sense of composition, I realize I don't have one at all. He has a precise and formal sense of structure which has obvious musical analogues: tone row, using certain words that he repeats through the book, repetitions of larger structures, and so on. It's all very organized in that way. I was very impressed with a description of Schönberg's music (not the later twelve-tone music, which was very systematic, but the earlier music of *Pierrot Lunaire*), of which somebody said, "Nobody could go on writing music this way for very long because it required *total* invention from moment to moment." That notion of always being "on," of being a performer who is always pulling this stuff up out of himself, is a very romantic notion of the artist that appeals to me. I never rewrote much when I was working on *Nocturnes* and I only wrote when I felt inspired; there was no regular process, and I would be terrified of writing each chapter. When I read writers' interviews, I'm always struck by the fact that they seem to have these regular hours and they are professional and they've built up this kind of craft. I've never had any of that feeling. With me I always have the sense that I'm winging it.

SG: But wait a minute: take a scene like the one that opens *Nocturnes*, the one at the strange warehouse. That episode seemed to set up *everything* that followed, including those images of fire and water, light and shadow, what is actual, substantial versus what is illusion, spiritual. When I reread the book, it seemed to me that scene was incredibly *crafted*, deliberate in its intentions. Were you winging it there?

EW: That actually was the first thing I wrote for that book, even though I knew in some way what the book was going to be, where it was headed. The idea of a rather static opening—an opening scene which is nonfunctioning in terms of plot but which acts as an overture or preview of things to come—is something that appeals to me. In fact, I've done it in all three of my novels. Of course, with *Nocturnes* one of the themes is the idea, Is this a book about God or is it a book about a lover? In considering the nature of this "You" that the narrator is addressing, the reader is supposed to ask, Is this a religious devotional work or is it a book about contemporary sexual devotion? The baroque era specialized in this confusion (which is one reason I tried to make the book have such a baroque feel to it). If you look at Bernini's statues, they seem to be extremely sensuous objects (everybody giggles about St. Teresa being stabbed in the side by St. Michael) but they're also serene and lofty expressions of religious sentiment. I was always impressed by this doubling of spiritual and carnal love, and I wanted to allude to that throughout the book, starting with the opening scene. The scene takes place in a famous abandoned pier in New York where people could go and have sex, everyone who was gay and lived in New York recognized the pier because all the glass from the roof was broken and it was all over the ground like diamonds, and everyone would go there every night; there were various levels, it was all dilapidated and dangerous, partly because there were always pickpockets there. But it was always spooky and beautiful. Anyway, this sex pier, which I describe as a church, seemed to me a good expression of this double message that I was trying to suggest throughout the book about sexual and divine love. In the book are buried lots of references to Sufi beliefs (I even took one poem by a Sufi poet that I translated into English and buried it into the last chapter). In the first chapter there's a sestina, and in the middle of the book there's an imitation of a baroque French sonnet, an anonymous poem called "Aux Yeux de Mme Beaufort."

LM: Obviously most readers won't recognize those references . . .

EW: No, they're developed only for those who care to follow such things. I admire Nabokov's method in this regard: when you read his books you're never *stopped* by a literary reference unless you're specifically aware of it; you never even know that he's made one. I *don't* like the other kind of game playing, where you're awed and puzzled by the author's erudition, constantly stopped by it. I don't want to intimidate my readers in that way.

LM: When you said just now that you knew where *Nocturnes* was heading, is that usually the case? Do you, for example, ever work from an outline or specific notes?

EW: No, although I do at least vaguely know where I want to head (or at least somewhere about a third of the way through the book I know). As I said, I try to write from inspiration a lot of the time, which can be a wasteful and frightening experience. But I usually know what the main issue of a book will be, or the kind of music I want to present.

SG: One of the things I respond to in your fiction (and this is difficult to formulate clearly) is the *texture* of your books, the richness of your prose, the surprise of your details. I assume that this texture is one of the things you're consciously aiming for.

EW: Yes, creating and sharing those details with my readers is one of the things I most enjoy about writing. I see it almost as an energy exchange—the writer works and stores up this honey in a cell, and then the reader taps it and the honey flows. A metaphor is a way of recapturing or reimagining experience. Nabokov is the real master of this. But Nabokov had something that nobody else has had—a gift for metaphor and detail *plus* a sense of pace, of speed. You can't stop reading him, there's that wonderful forward motion to his works that's exhilarating, which I also find in Stendhal at times. The absence of this is what is most distressing in a lot of American fiction now.

LM: In *States of Desire*, after you've told your psychiatrist some of your inner desires, he says to you, "Your desires are banal." Your reply is, "Of course, desire is *always* banal." And yet every one of your books is about desire in a basic sense. Is this banality one of the challenges for you as an artist—finding ways to overcome it, to turn it into something interesting, even beautiful?

EW: Nabokov usually writes about fairly banal, melodramatic subjects. Henry James's plots make good movies because they really *are* movies, cheap movies, too; they're usually about sex and money and power. So both Nabokov and James take this very familiar, cheap material and then do all their wonderful things with it. That's a nice trick. Readers will have patience with formal innovation when they are reading about something they care about, like sex or money. That's why the Bloom sections of *Ulysses* are more successful than the Dedalus sections—because most of us know what it would be like to be Bloom, with all his banalities, but very few of us know what it would be like to be Stephen. And so there are complex explorations of Bloom's consciousness involving formal experimentation, but the experimentalism doesn't put us off because we know what it would be like to have bought kidneys at the butcher's while your wife is still sleeping. Successful artists can always find ways to interest us in the familiar.

SG: The familiarity of sex would seem to be one of the biggest challenges . . .

EW: Sex scenes are very difficult indeed. For instance, with that little sex scene between Kevin and the narrator in *A Boy's Own Story*, the twenty pages that precede it are written in a very melancholy, elegiac spirit, with a full range of adult vocabulary, very little reported dialogue, and complex syntax for rendering adolescent experience. I was trying to pull out all the stops. Then suddenly there's the sex scene, which is composed solely of those little dialogue exchanges. This is a case where I was very aware of the powerful effect that structuring a scene in a certain way can have. Dialogue can be very powerful; it has the effect of a close-up if it's used with restraint. Tolstoy recognized this in *The Death of Ivan Ilych*, where he doesn't use any dialogue at all until the first moment that Ivan Ilych admits that he might be dying and he says to his manservant, "Rub my legs."

SG: Since sex itself is basically a repetitive act, it would seem to be especially important to use language freshly, to start over again, since it's an area in which clichés seem to emerge naturally.

EW: I don't think it's so much that. Since the act is repetitive, the language tends to be too in pornography, but that's not true about all sexual writing. Rather, I'd say that sex and pornography are two separate things that are in no way related to each other. Some people need pornography in order to feel sexual, and so they will look at dirty movies when they are having sex with a partner, or say dirty words to a partner, or in their own mind they will play a dirty movie or a dirty record. I think men tend to be pornographic in this way more than women, while women tend to be more romantic—but romance itself is "pornographic" in that it too is a language of desire which is highly codified and highly stylized, which is brought *to* the experience rather than being extracted from it. When most writers write about sexuality, they want to excite the reader rather than to awaken in the reader a sense of recognition— so they use the pornographic language, whereas a description of sexual encounters *as they really happen* is always a description of a comic situation, and therefore not sexy in the sense that it awakens sexual desire in the reader.

SG: Do you get negative responses from people because your books *aren't* pornographic? When most readers hear that you write "gay novels," I suspect they expect certain things that your books don't deliver.

EW: It's interesting how many gay readers are frustrated by how little explicit sexuality there is in my writing because most gay books published in the '50s and '60s were published specifically because there was a pornographic market for them—there was a specific category of gay pornographic fiction, cheap paperbacks sold under the counters. I know a lot of readers, especially those gay readers from that generation, are disappointed when they find out my books aren't just a series of jerk-off scenes. Again, approaching this issue from a technical standpoint, I think that if you deal exclusively with sex in fiction, you inevitably end up only with an episodic structure.

LM: Sinda and I both really responded to your comment in *States of Desire* about gay life extending the possibilities of being an adolescent into one's 30's, 40's, 50's, and even beyond—where "adolescent" means not having a fixed viewpoint, continuing to open yourself to experience, refusing to settle into familiar realities.

EW: I'm intrigued by the idea of neotony—the view that animals, as they move up the evolutionary ladder, retain into adulthood certain physical characteristics of infancy. So that, for instance, adult human beings look more like baby human beings than adult chimps look like baby chimps. In other words, human adults have glabrous skin, large heads, and in other ways we have a childish look not present in other animals, which have profound physiological differences between the way they look as babies and as adults. I like to use that as a metaphor for human behavior in gay culture today. It's also known by anthropologists that the longer you can perpetuate childhood, the longer you can perpetuate one specific, wonderful quality of childhood, which is play, innocent learning, learning without consequences, the ability to experiment with various new behaviors.

SG: You mentioned Firbank and Stein, among others, as writers you admired and who had some influence on your own work. Who are the contemporary writers you admire or feel affinities with?

EW: There's Coleman Dowell, whom I admire very much and about whom I've written a long essay that appeared in *Christopher Street* and in the *Review of Contemporary Fiction*. I admire him because he has a power that I don't have at all, a compulsive readability, a real love of narration. He's one of those people who tells story after story, and when he starts telling a story you can't stop listening and he can't stop telling it. Whereas I can never tell a story; I have no interest in stories. But I admire that ability because it's the central gift in fiction. Since I don't have that gift, I've been forced to seek it out in other writers. I find that I often respond to writers who don't write like me in the least—I love Chekhov and Knut Hamsun, for example, and we don't have much in common as writers. Another contemporary writer I greatly admire is a Yugoslav writer named Danilo Kis. He's had several books published in English: *Garden, Ashes, A Tomb for Boris Davidovich*, and *The Hourglass*. William Gass is another writer I respond to and so is Harold Brodkey. Of course, the greatest American writer, now or ever, is Thomas Pynchon; he's amazing. But after Pynchon, for me the best American writer is James Merrill. He is very fluent, and his ability to combine a high-society, comic tone with a confessional, ardent tone or a magisterial epic voice or the lyric voice of the nature poet is very wonderful. There's another writer, W. M. Spackman, who wrote *An Armful of Warm Girl*. He's a very elegant writer who writes everything as though it were 1930's sculpture—picture a slender girl being pulled along by a borzoi on a leash. The whole thing windswept and deco: elegant social comedy, entirely charming and entirely sexist.

SG: You've taught creative writing—do you find yourself trying to get your students to write like you?

EW: There are two ways of looking at literature. One is to feel that there is one great Platonic novel in the sky that we're all striving toward. I find that view to be very deadening, finally, and certainly it's a terrible view for a teacher or a critic to hold. The other view is that each person has a chance to write his or her own book in his or her own voice; maturing as an artist occurs when you find your own voice, when you write something that *only you* could have written. That's the view I have.

LM: In *States of Desire* you make the statement that certain aspects of New York City life—drugs, for instance—had "freed us from the tyranny of beauty." But in *A Boy's Own Story* you make the remark that "Beauty is the highest good." Aren't those two notions incompatible?

EW: I don't see them as being incompatible, although I think we have a very ambiguous relationship toward physical beauty in our culture. Most people respond to it quite strongly and want to possess it, or destroy it if they can't have it. I found that in the gay community for a while everyone was so tuned in to physical beauty that they tended to worship it alone. But what happened with the clone culture of the '70s was that, since now anybody could have a beautiful body— all you had to do was go to the gym and work out—people no longer had to depend on physical beauty alone to make an impact on people, there were other forms of beauty to explore. But I also feel it's important for an artist to be honest about the tremendous glamour and impact of physical beauty. A beautiful person acknowledges in the flesh what the artist is struggling to represent in his work. As far as drugs are concerned, they were a way of allowing people to see beauty in what was not conventionally labeled beauty. LSD and other hallucinogens permitted people to discover a closeness on a human level. There had been something stale and snobbish about gay life in New York City that was seasoned and swept clean by drugs. I feel rather strange about sounding like an apologist for drugs because, by and large, they've probably caused more harm than good, but one cannot deny the good they did. That is, there are certain drugged states that, once you've experienced them and if they haven't completely fried your brains, you'll remember in the future—a sense of a pantheistic unity with other people, the realization that there's a brotherhood of man, something deep and lovable about other people, even if they're funny looking or whatever. That's a sense that artists also need to recognize, acknowledge.

Index

Of related interest

Anything Can Happen: Interviews with Contemporary American Novelists
Conducted and edited by Tom LeClair and Larry McCaffery

American Poetry Observed: Poets on Their Work
Edited by Joe David Bellamy

The New Fiction: Interviews with Innovative American Writers
Edited by Joe David Bellamy